Plant.

# LIVING IN LONDON
## A PRACTICAL GUIDE

### Sixth Edition

**Illustrated by Pamela Plant**

**Written and Published By
THE JUNIOR LEAGUE OF LONDON**

Registered Charity No. 288427

About the Illustrator:

Born and raised in London, Pamela Plant studied at Harrow Art School and spent many years as a stage and television actress before turning her talents to painting and illustrating. Her love of London has produced paintings of old pubs, alleyways and tucked away garden squares and restaurants that remind the viewer that London is, at its heart, made up of many villages.

Pamela's work has been exhibited in galleries throughout London and her water-colours of London hang in many homes and offices all over the world. She has four children and when she's not exploring the backstreets of London, she's visiting and painting her second love - the Greek Islands. She resides in northwest London.

First Edition, 1981
Second Edition, 1984
Third Edition, 1988
Fourth Edition, 1990
Fifth Edition, 1993
Sixth Edition, 1995

The contents of this book are believed to be correct at the time of printing. However, The Junior League of London can accept no responsibility for errors or omissions or changes in the information contained herein.

ISBN: 0-9525195-OX

# Acknowledgements

Purchasers of this book make an important contribution to The Junior League of London's efforts to promote voluntary service. Monies raised from the sale of *Living in London*, combined with the time and expertise of over 200 trained volunteers, enable The League to develop, fund and staff its community projects. Because The Junior League is primarily self-funding, it is dependent on the public's generous support of its fund-raising activities, which enable The League to maintain its independence and innovative edge.

The Junior League of London thank the following for their generous contributions toward this edition.

### Sponsor

Marakon Associates

### Fellow

The American School in London
Executive Relocation Services

### Friends

Elaine Allen-Kontes
Donald and Mary Armstrong
Candy Beery
Mr. and Mrs. J. D. Birney
Robert and Lori Burke
Susan E. Condon
Mr. and Mrs. Peter B. D'Amario
Judith and David Epstein
Bruce and Anne Harmon
Mr. and Mrs. Oscar Huettner
Mr. and Mrs. Peter J. Ilias
Laurel Kanitz Sukawaty

Joseph R. Katcha
Pamela Ward Katcha
Brian and Robin Leach
Mr. and Mrs. Colin Murray
People and Property
Cynthia and John Register
Rosemary Asprey Robertson
Lisa Salzman
Ed and Laura Steins
Barbara and Jon Taute
Christine N. Weatherhead
Leesa Wilson-Goldmuntz

Special acknowledgement is made to Pamela Plant who has generously provided the illustrations for this and all previous editions.

*Living in London* is the collective result of the suggestions and recommendations of countless Junior League members. Without them and those members who have worked on the previous five editions this book could not have been made possible.

Note:

In keeping with our belief that 'when in Rome...', we have used English spelling throughout the book. As it is frequently used in the United Kingdom, we have also given all times in 24-hour time; thus, 2.00 a.m. is written 02.00 and 2.00 p.m. as 14.00.

Regional dialling codes for all telephone numbers outside the 0171 and 0181 Central and Greater London districts have been listed parenthetically before the telephone numbers. Street addresses followed directly by a post code with no city mentioned imply that it is a London address.

# Contents

Contents
VI

Contents
VII

*At Your Fingertips.....*

Contents
IX

# Foreword

When I came to live in London twenty years ago, fresh from Edinburgh University, oh!, how much easier life would have been had *Living in London* existed!

This compendium of information, facts and tips gathered together by people living in London is as essential for newcomers as any historical or cultural guidebook. It can - and does - transform the nightmare of arrival into a carefree, happy and informed experience for you and your family.

Coming to London from Edinburgh was much the same as arriving from Chicago or California: London was exciting and wondrous yet vast and unnerving in every dimension. Physically, it is enormous. There are two full-blown cities, the City of Westminster and the City of London which is confusingly known as The City. Logistics are everything, from where you decide to live to what you decide to do on a day out to which bank you keep your account at. Like you, I needed help with everything from mastering the public transport system to finding a plumber!

London is an entrepot where, armed with the proper knowledge, you can find the best of every cuisine and cultural activity, as well as befriend people from all corners of the world. London has a richer social and cultural mix than any other city I know. *Living in London* is your passport to all this and more: from finding your children a good school and understanding the health system to buying a good brownie when you are homesick, or understanding how the Brits talk!

Whether it's the theatre, jazz, opera, china, museums, flowers or even cricket that grabs you, now is the moment to indulge. London has it all in profusion and quality. (Your only problem is the frustration of not being able to be in ten places simultaneously).

To get to grips with all this, to make the right choices, to make your money go further and to get under the skin of London, you need *Living in London* to override all the practical problems of moving in, settling down and becoming part of your London community, you need *Living in London*.

It is, quite simply, your essential tool if you want to have a good time in this amazing city. (After twenty years here, I still buy each edition!)


Louise Nicholson
**Fodor's London Companion**

---

# Introduction

*Living in London* is unique among the numerous books written about London. It is a how-to guide that encompasses all aspects of moving to and adjusting to life in this extraordinary city. The book, written by the members of The Junior League of London, is designed to enable a family or an individual to plan a move in an informed manner and to settle into life in London and its surrounding areas with a minimum of stress.

The information contained on the following pages reflects countless years of expatriate living experience. Contributors to the text of *Living in London* number in the hundreds and have themselves moved nationally, internationally, or are native to the area.

The Junior League of London is an international organization of women committed to promoting voluntary service and to making a difference in the community through the effective action and leadership of trained volunteers. Its purpose is exclusively educational and charitable. The organization has been operating in London since 1979. Through the League's affiliation with The Association of Junior Leagues International all members benefit from the expertise and resources of an organization with over 190,000 members and 285 leagues worldwide. The first Junior League was founded in New York City in 1901.

The League directs its work primarily through its Neighbourhood Family Initiative, which addresses the needs of disadvantaged families living in the Colville community of West London and through its collaborations with the Monroe Young Family Centre and The Royal Academy. Over the years the League has developed several programmes that continue to benefit the community. The League is administratively self funded and self governed which means that donations and profits from fund-raisers are not used to help defray staff or board salaries or operating expenses but are used to make an impact in the community.

The sixth edition of *Living in London* is dedicated to all members past and present, whose energies, resourcefulness and dedication to community service have allowed the League to create a publication that not only serves a useful purpose but also helps to fund its community programmes.

Enjoy the wonderful experience that is *Living in London!*


Leesa Wilson-Goldmuntz
President
**The Junior League of London**

---

# Chapter One: Moving

## WORK PERMITS AND ALIEN REGISTRATION

### Work Permits

To be employed in Great Britain as an alien you must have a work permit. The employing company must apply for the work permit on your behalf through the Department of Employment, Overseas Labour Section, prior to your arrival. Once the application has been approved, a work permit is issued and sent to you. It must then be presented to the immigration authorities upon entry into the country and your passport stamped accordingly.

The permit applies specifically both to the job and to the individual. If a spouse or dependants (over 16) of a work permit holder wish to work, they may do so only if (1) they have received a Letter of Consent from a British embassy or consulate before travelling to the U.K. and (2) their passports are stamped "Given Leave to Enter the U.K. Until (Date)". The Letter of Consent gives dependants entry clearance into the U.K. and proves that they are part of the family unit. However, if a child is over 18 or does not have entry clearance, he or she will probably need his/her own work permit. Check with the Department of Employment (see below) or the Home Office (0171-686-0688).

For further information contact: Employment Department, Overseas Labour Section, Level 5W, Moorfoot, Sheffield, S1 4PQ (01142) 593290.

### Alien Registration and Police Registration

As an alien, you and your spouse must register with the Aliens Registration Office (A.R.O.) within seven days of your arrival in the country. Children under the age of 16 do not need to register.

If living in the Greater London area, which includes Wimbledon, Richmond and Esher, report to the Aliens Registration Office, 10 Lamb's Conduit Street, WC1; 0171-230-1208: nearest tube stop Holborn. The A.R.O. hours are Monday to Friday from 09.00 to 16.45. It is advisable to go early to avoid a long wait. There is a registration fee, as of January 1995, of £30 per person (a cheque will be accepted if you present a bank cheque card), and you must have your work permit, passport, and two passport-size photographs either in black and white or colour. There is a photo machine on the premises.

You will be given a green booklet (certificate) which you must produce within 24 hours, if asked to do so by the police or immigration officials. It is best to always carry this certificate with you in Great Britain. Also, the certificate will make re-entry into Great Britain easier when you travel abroad on trips lasting less than two months. The certificate should be submitted to the Immigration Office if travelling abroad for more than two months.

If living outside the Greater London area, alien registration is handled at your local police station. You may have to surrender your passport during processing, but it will be returned by post along with the certificate.

Any change of address or name change must be given to the A.R.O. within seven days. Only if it is stamped in your passport must your child register with the A.R.O. when he/she turns 16.

If you have any further questions regarding where to register contact: Home Office Immigration and Nationality Department - Public Inquiry 0181-686-0688, or your local police station or the A.R.O.

**Extensions of Stay**

The Immigration Officer's stamp in your passport indicates how long you may remain in the United Kingdom. In order to stay longer, you should contact (within the period of your stay) the Department of Employment, Overseas Labour Section, Level 5W, Moorfoot, Sheffield S1 4PQ, (01142) 593290. The Labour Section will make a decision, pass it on to the Home Office for comments and approval and then forward a letter to the employer. At present, after four years of residence, the permit holder and his or her dependants may apply for permanent residence which may (if granted by the Home Office) lift the need for a work permit. However, be aware that lengthy delays are probable, and it is not at all unusual to wait longer than 2 months for the Home Office decision.

**CLIMATE AND WEATHER**

Weather in London is unpredictable; however, there are no extreme conditions. The average temperature varies from a low of 0C (about 32F) to a high of 24C (about 75F), although it does occasionally reach the mid 80's (28C). July is the warmest month and January is the coldest and rainiest month. One common climate condition is the very soft drizzle.

A typical weather forecast may be: 'Partially sunny with cloudy intervals and possible showers'. Consequently you will find it helpful to dress in layers, so that one layer can be removed as the weather changes. An umbrella is a must. Purchase one that is convenient to carry.

The following temperature conversion charts may be helpful as the temperature is usually reported in Celsius instead of Fahrenheit.

### Fahrenheit to Celsius (Centigrade)

| | | |
|---|---|---|
| 20F | = | -6.67C |
| 30 | = | -1.11 |
| 32 | = | 0.00 (Freezing Point) |
| 40 | = | 4.44 |
| 41 | = | 5.00 |
| 50 | = | 10.00 |
| 59 | = | 15.04 |
| 60 | = | 15.56 |
| 68 | = | 20.00 |
| 70 | = | 21.11 |
| 77 | = | 25.00 |
| 80 | = | 26.67 |
| 90 | = | 32.22 |
| 98.6 | = | 37.00 (ave. human body temperature) |
| 212 | = | 100.00 (Boiling Point) |

### Celsius (Centigrade) to Fahrenheit

| | | |
|---|---|---|
| -3C | = | 26.66F |
| -1 | = | 30.2 |
| 0 | = | 32.0 (Freezing Point) |
| 1 | = | 33.8 |
| 5 | = | 41.0 |
| 10 | = | 50.0 |
| 15 | = | 59.0 |
| 20 | = | 68.0 |
| 25 | = | 77.0 |
| 30 | = | 86.0 |
| 37 | = | 98.6 (ave. human body temperature) |
| 100 | = | 212 (Boiling Point) |

An approximate conversion from Celsius to Fahrenheit is to double the Celsius and add 30.

## WHAT TO BRING AND WHAT NOT TO BRING

What to bring when you move to London is an individual decision. Obviously, your decisions will be based on the anticipated length of time you will reside in the U.K., plus your company's policies regarding size and weight allowance. It will also depend upon your housing, whether furnished or unfurnished, house or flat.

## What to Bring

The following items are generally not readily available in the U.K. If they are available, they may be considerably more expensive than in the U.S.

### *Personal Items*

Eye glasses, contact lenses, and related products. Special cosmetics and beauty products, particularly dermatologist-recommended ones.

Medical prescriptions - wise to bring with you on the airplane. Children's/ adult over-the-counter medicine that you particularly like. (See Children's Chapter for list of medicines not available in the U.K.).

### *For the Home*

European and English beds and bedding vary greatly in size from the United States, as well as being much more expensive. If you bring your beds, bring the appropriate bedding.

### *Foods*

Consult Chapter Nine of this book for a list of substitutes and items not found in England. If you have room, particularly in your sea shipment, stock up on your favourite items. When you are settled, you can find out what your neighbourhood has to offer.

### *Miscellaneous*

Children's games, sports equipment (baseballs, softballs, bats, footballs and basketballs, and bicycles). Special decorations for holidays including

Halloween, Easter egg kits and a Christmas tree stand, decorations, and tree lights.

**What not to Bring**

Telephones
Light bulbs (except appliance bulbs - see following section for explanation of electrical differences)
Electric clocks (will not work even with a transformer)
Liquor/Spirits (excluding wine), except duty free allowance
Cigarettes, except duty free allowance
Perfumes, except duty free allowance
Paints, cleaning agents or other combustible or flammable items
Plants and bulbs
Meat, fruits and vegetables
Certain fish and eggs
Most animals and all birds (alive or dead)
Items made from protected species including reptile leather, ivory and fur skins

*Special Note:* If firearms are being brought into Great Britain for sports purposes it is necessary to have a permit, and they must be shipped in a dismantled condition or be plugged. A permit may also be needed for decorative sports equipment.

**ELECTRICAL DIFFERENCES**

Deciding which American electrical appliances and equipment to bring to England or leave home can be confusing. U.S. current is 110 volts and 60 Hz (frequency or cycles per second) while English current (and most of Europe) is 220/240 volts and 50 Hz (frequency or cycles per second). Understanding what voltage and frequency is compatible with your electrical devices will facilitate your decision making. Some devices, if made for several voltages, can be used directly in the U.K. Some can be used with a voltage transformer, and some cannot be used at all.

**Adaptors**

The U.S. and U.K. plugs are different, so all electrical devices that will plug directly into U.K. receptacles require an adaptor. Or, you can simply replace all of the U.S. plugs with U.K. plugs. The latter option is the cheapest.

**Transformers**

In general, most American appliances are incompatible with U.K. electrical supply because of the voltage difference, 220/240V for U.K. vs 110V for

U.S. This means that if you try to use them in the U.K. they will burn out. You can get them to work if you use a *transformer*. A transformer is a plug in device that will convert 220/240V to 110V. Transformers are available in London and the surrounding area. Transformers are sized from 30 watts to 1,500 watts and are priced from £15 to £75, depending on the size. A hair dryer or electric curler will require up to a 250 watt transformer. A blender or food processor will require up to a 500 watt transformer, while a refrigerator will require up to a 1,500 watt transformer.

Transformers, depending on the size, can be used to power several appliances so you don't necessarily need one transformer for each device. However, they are bulky and heavy so portability is not practical. In fact they are a nuisance to carry around, so leave your U.S. vacuum cleaner at home.

### Appliances requiring a Transformer

Baby heating dishes, blender or food processor, can opener, coffee maker, deep fryer, electric cutters and curling iron, electric knife, hair dryer, humidifier, mixer, popcorn maker, sewing machine, toaster, toaster oven, vaporiser.

### Dual Voltage Appliances

Some appliances, such as VCR's, TV's, Stereo's, can function on 120 or 240V merely by adjusting a switch on the appliance. Check your appliances for this feature because it will allow you to use it in the U.K. without a transformer.

### Appliances incompatible with the Frequency

All U.S. appliances are 60 Hz while the electrical supply in the U.K. is 50 Hz. This frequency difference comes into play in appliances with a motor where speed of the motor is important. There is no simple device that will convert 50 to 60 Hz, so any device with a motor will run at a bit more than 80% of its normal speed, even if it is run on a transformer. For hair dryers, fans, washers, blenders, refrigerators, and dryers that might not be a problem. For analog clocks, that will be a problem.

In using certain devices with motors, like VCR's, personal computers, tape decks and CD's, the frequency difference is not an issue because the electrical current is converted to Direct Current in the machine so the device will run at the right speed, independent of frequency. So if they are 110-120V machines, they can be run on a transformer. If they are 120 or 240V machines, with a switch, they can be run directly in the U.K. Also be aware that some devices, like battery chargers or power packs for camcorders will run on any voltage up to 240V, so can be run directly in the U.K.

---

## Specific Appliances

### Refrigerator

To convert to English voltage, a refrigerator can be run on an appropriate size transformer. You may purchase a new refrigerator in the U.S. for U.K. 220/240 volts, 50 cycle current. American refrigerators may be purchased in the U.K., but they are very expensive. If you are renting, make sure there is space in the kitchen for a large refrigerator; English refrigerators often are small.

### Washing Machine and Electric Dryer

To use in the U.K. the washer can be run on a transformer. The dryer will probably be 240V so may be able to be used without a transformer, but the dryer should only be installed by a qualified electrician. Again, American washers and dryers are larger than U.K. appliances and may not fit in your particular house or flat. Gas dryers can be used in the U.K., if your flat or house is serviced with gas, but will need a transformer for the motor and may need a different pressure regulator for the gas.

### TV's and VCR's

While American TV's and VCR's can be run in the U.K. with a transformer, they have limited use because of the differences in broadcasting standards. The TV will not pick up British stations, by antenna or cable, unless it is a "multi system" TV, equipped with a switch for PAL system, which is the U.K. standard. Similarly, the American VCR will not play British videos unless it is a "multi system" VCR equipped with a switch for PAL system.

Multi system TV's and VCR's allow you to receive broadcasting signals and play videos in many countries. Consider buying a multi system TV/VCR in the U.S. before moving here because appliances are generally more expensive in the U.K.

### Telephones

Do not bring your telephones. They are not compatible with the U.K. phone system.

### Computer

Your computer, monitor and printer will run on a transformer in the U.K. Bring your surge protector.

*Lamps*

All lamps can be used in the U.K., provided they are used with an adapter or are fitted with U.K. plugs. U.S. light bulbs will explode if used in the U.K., because of the voltage difference, so leave your light bulbs at home.

## MISCELLANEOUS ELECTRICAL INFORMATION

Some electrical appliances purchased in the U.K. do not come with socket outlet plugs. Attaching a plug is an easy procedure but keep a store of plugs with both 3 amp and 13 amp fuses. Different appliances require different size fuses. Be sure to have the correct fuse for each appliance. If your appliance fails to work, check the fuse and plug before calling the electrician. Obviously, all electrical appliances are potential fire hazards and should be used with caution. Always consult an electrician if you are not absolutely certain how an appliance should be correctly operated.

If you have American electrical appliances that require appliance bulbs, bring the bulbs with you, such as bulbs for sewing machines, refrigerators and freezers.

Wall outlets in a flat or house may not be of a uniform size. For this reason, when you shop for plug adaptors, appliances or electrical needs, check the outlets in the room where the appliance/adaptor will be used. While the 13 amp square, 3 prong (pin) plugs are becoming standard, you may also find 2 amp, 5 amp and 15 amp round pin plugs.

American appliances are available in the U.K. in some of the larger department stores (although very expensive) and some used appliances may be purchased through various American organisations, including The American School in London newsletter, the Kensington and Chelsea Women's Club newsletter, The American Women of Surrey newsletter or *The American* - a subscription, bi-monthly newspaper - obtainable from: *The American*, Subscription Department, 114-115 West Street, Farnham, Surrey GU9 7HL: (01252) 713366.

For installation, repair and purchase of American appliances try Waldebeck Services, Unit 18, Abenglen Industrial Estate, Betam Road, Hayes, Middlesex UB3 1SS; 0181-848-7520, mobile telephone (refrigerators and stoves) (0831) 154516, (washers and dryers) (0831) 154514.

For your electrical questions and needs, Ryness Electrical Supplies has nine branches throughout London.

Moving

**Conclusion**

When you move to the U.K., your choice is to bring some U.S. appliances and use transformers with them or store them in the U.S. and purchase new/used appliances when you arrive. Keep in mind U.K. electrical appliances are more expensive than their U.S. counterpart but if you rent, many houses/flats come furnished with some basic appliances. Most Americans end up bringing some appliances and more often than not, they are the smaller appliances.

## SHIPPING HOUSEHOLD EFFECTS

Shipping of household effects depends on the length of the expatriate assignment and the type of house to be maintained. If it is a total move, start making arrangements and organising the move at once. If it is only temporary or short term, remember to include some favourite personal possessions, so your home away from home has your personality. These might be photographs, a painting, a needlepoint pillow, or favourite art object. Do not forget to include some of the children's favourite items.

Start your plans by making lots of lists:

> What is going with you on the airplane
> What is needed soon after you arrive (if you are going into temporary housing, it may be necessary to bring these items with you via excess baggage or air shipment)
> What is being shipped in a container via sea/air
> What is going into storage
> Things to give away
> Things to sell
> Things to discard
> Decoration plans

Once you have finally made all of these decisions, check the lists one more time, and then have them duplicated. There is nothing more frustrating than misplacing your only copy of one of these important lists.

**Selecting a Moving Company**

When selecting a moving company choose a reputable one. Investigate the company's performance record, even check references. Go over all items in detail with the moving company's representative and have them in writing. Get more than one estimate. Do not choose the cheapest firm simply because it is the cheapest; it may turn out to be a 'penny wise, pound foolish' decision.

Decide when items for storage are to be packed and placed in storage. Decide when the shipment is to be packed and when the container is to be loaded at your home. Know which ship is going to carry your container and when it is scheduled to depart from the U.S. and to arrive in England. Plan the unloading in England so the moving company can make arrangements with British Customs and the British removal company. After your goods have arrived in Great Britain, it can take several months before you receive them.

Be knowledgeable about the company's loss and damage protection - read all the small print on any contract. Be sure to know the scope and coverage of the insurance for the shipment. It is essential to have insurance. It might be wise to check with one or more private insurance companies, rather than relying on the moving company's insurance programme.

For insurance purposes it is necessary to have an itemised inventory. This might be done by categories, such as furniture, silver, paintings, and accessories, or room by room. Pick the system that best suits your needs and have everything appraised. Remember to value all items at replacement value. One good idea is to record everything with photographs. Make several copies of the inventory. One copy has to go to the insuring company, whether it be the moving company or an insurance agent. Take more than one copy with you for use when the shipment arrives in England. This inventory makes it easy to record any possible damages which might require repairs and an insurance claim.

**Packing Your Household**

Make sure your specifications and instructions are being carried out to your satisfaction. Make sure each box is labelled with contents and destination (even the room).

If you are doing any of the packing or unpacking, check for insurance coverage. Usually breakables are covered only when packed and unpacked by the moving company. The shipping charges normally include all packing and unpacking.

If you have excess baggage or an air shipment, be sure to include extra clothing, favourite cookbooks, measuring cups and spoons, some children's games and toys. As it may take some time to find housing and receive your shipment, it would be advisable to bring clothing and personal goods to last for several months.

**Packing Your Luggage for the Plane**

Depending on your immediate lodging when you arrive in England, you might want and need to be prepared for anything... especially if you have not seen your temporary housing.

---

Some items that might go into your luggage are a sewing kit and a small first aid kit, umbrella, address book, extra pair of glasses, extra prescriptions, can opener, flashlight, cork screw, small tool kit, carrying bag for groceries or laundry, the baby's stroller, needlepoint, books you have wanted to read, deck of cards, plus some old clothes for cleaning or painting and comfortable shoes. Do not be surprised if much time in the first few weeks seems to be spent waiting for workmen or deliveries.

Do not ship good jewellery - carry it on the airplane with you. Others who have moved to London have also hand-carried their flat silver, fur coats and other valuable possessions.

It is always wise to take a copy of any important legal documents with you. These could be wills, insurance policies, rental contracts on properties, investments, and a list of current charge accounts with their account numbers. Make sure a trusted friend or attorney knows the whereabouts of the originals. You may also want to carry copies of family medical records with you.

## CUSTOMS AND VAT

The British Government allows importing of all household or personal effects duty free - providing they have been owned six months prior to the date of entry into the U.K. Proof of purchase must be available on items less than six months old. Certain other household items may be dutiable. Newly married couples should be aware that there are special regulations regarding their move. There are also special regulations regarding the importing of inherited goods and antiques into Great Britain. There are restrictions on liquor and cigarettes. You are allowed the duty free amount of one quart of liquor and one carton of cigarettes per adult, which must accompany you on the airplane. Liquor and cigarettes which are shipped will be charged with the normal British duty, which is very costly. No living plants, meat, fruit and vegetables are allowed into the U.K. Refer to the list of "What Not to Bring" on page 5.

If at all possible have a file with a copy of the bill of sale for every valuable item, such as cameras, watches, jewellery, furs, silver, major appliances, etc. If you do not have these bills of sale, an alternative is a copy of an old insurance policy which itemises these articles. Carry these documents with you, do not ship them. If you will be travelling with jewellery, cameras, or a fur coat we suggest you carry that portion of the insurance policy or the bill of sale. This will make your life much easier when clearing customs on your return to England after personal or business trips.

All items which are not at least six months old are subject to duty charges and VAT (Value Added Tax - currently 17.5%). VAT is similar to sales tax in the U.S. In Great Britain, however, it is charged on almost everything and is usually included in the purchase price. Check with your moving company or the closest British Consulate, who will be able to advise you on which items may be subject to duty and excise tax plus VAT, as the customs and duty charges can vary from three to 24 per cent depending on the item in question. Duty on tobacco products, however, is as high as 90%. For additional information contact *General Inquiries, H.M. Customs & Excise Department*, Dorset House, Stamford Street, London SE1 9PY; 0171-928-3344 (Excise Advice Centre).

You are only eligible to reclaim the VAT on items you buy in Great Britain if you have not been in the United Kingdom for more than 365 days in the two years before the date you purchase the items. You must also intend to leave the United Kingdom with the purchased items within three months of the purchase date.

If you have lived in the U.K. for more than 365 days, in the two years before the date you purchase items, you are considered a departing UK resident, and different VAT regulations apply.

To reclaim the VAT on items you buy in Great Britain, you must have the retailer fill out the export documentation, Form VAT 435.

Instead of taking your items through customs at the port or airport when you leave the U.K., the retailer ships your goods directly to the ship or the freight forwarder for export. For more details, contact the Customs and Excise Department, or your international carrier.

**SHIPPING YOUR PET AND QUARANTINE**

Domestic pets entering Great Britain require a six month quarantine. Penalties for smuggling animals are severe. Such an offence will result in a heavy fine, a prison sentence for yourself, or the destruction of the animal. It must be remembered that Great Britain is rabies-free. It is a legal requirement to obtain a British Import Licence for your pet prior to your animal's arrival.

Arrangements for boarding kennels must be made and confirmed by letter before you leave the U.S. Allow four to six weeks to complete all paperwork and keep in mind that the most accessible kennels may have waiting lists.

Whether you vaccinate your animal or not (as required by the airlines), vaccination must take place again upon arrival in Great Britain - the U.S. certificate is not accepted.

A list of boarding kennels can be obtained by calling or writing to *The Ministry of Agriculture, Fisheries and Food*, The Government Building,

Hook Rise South, Tolworth, Surbiton, Surrey KT6 7NF; 0181-330-4411 (Rabies Section). See Chapter Ten for several kennel suggestions.

Do consider the proximity of the kennel to your residence, if you wish to visit your animal regularly. If your animal has favourite toys and/or bed, you may wish to bring these items on the plane with you. Do not bring tinned or dried foods as they will require an export/import licence, as well as a veterinary certificate stating that the tinned food has been heat-treated in an hermetically sealed tin.

Check with the airlines for the carrier dimension requirements for your animal. Such carriers can be purchased directly from the airlines after you have booked your flight. The carrier will travel air freight, as animals are not allowed in the cabin on flights into Great Britain. The carrier must be tagged with the kennel destination and the animal's import licence number. Your pet is met upon landing by a representative from the boarding kennel. You are not allowed to see your pet for one week, so you might consider sending your pet early to avoid the trauma of moving day. Check also with your vet as to the possibility of medication to prevent trauma/air sickness to your pet while in transit.

## ARRIVAL AT THE AIRPORT

The majority of people moving to London arrive by airplane. There are two main airports for London: Heathrow, which is 18 miles west of London, serves most major airlines; Gatwick, which serves many major airlines and charter flights, is located 30 miles south of London.

It is quite a long walk from the gates to the Immigration and Customs Control. If you have a large amount of hand luggage or a small child, it is a good idea to have luggage wheels and a baby's pushchair. Larger pushcarts/trolleys are available near the gates at Heathrow. Arrange in advance with the airline if you will need a wheelchair, are travelling with a newborn infant or have medical problems.

At the Immigration Desk (Passport Control) you will submit the British Landing Card given to you on the flight. Your passport will be stamped by the Immigration Officer at this point. Remember that the Immigration's Officer's stamp in your passport indicates how long you may stay in Great Britain. The officer will ask to see your travel documents or work permit so that he can stamp your passport accordingly. He may ask you a few questions regarding the reasons for your entrance into the country.

After you are through Passport Control, check the electronic board to find out the area for your flight's baggage claim. Once you are downstairs in the correct baggage claim area, find a pushcart/trolley or porter. If your luggage or part of it does not arrive in a normal length of time, contact a representative of your airline. Lost luggage can usually be traced within 24 hours.

## Customs

If you have nothing to declare, proceed through the area marked with the *green* sign.

If you have items to declare, you must go to the area marked with the *red* sign. The customs inspector will probably ask you a few questions and may ask to see these items. You are required to pay any duty or tax at the time the belongings are brought into the country. Be sure to travel with English money. Foreign currency or travellers cheques can be cashed at the airport banks.

## Transport to London

*By Bus*:   London Transport's Route A1 Airbus runs from Heathrow (all terminals) to Victoria Station with intermediate stops on Cromwell Road and Hyde Park Corner, (Knightsbridge).   Route A2 runs from Heathrow, all terminals to Russell Square via Holland Park, Bayswater, Baker Street Station and Euston Station. Bus service is convenient and inexpensive.

*By Underground*: The Piccadilly Line runs from Heathrow to Central London. It is inexpensive and convenient, but not recommended if you have a large amount of luggage.

*By taxi*: The taxi rank is located just outside the terminals and signs will direct the way. The taxis are registered and authorised to be in these areas. The fare is usually based on the meter charge, plus extras for baggage, passengers, weekend travel, etc. If you are travelling beyond Central London and the meter charge will not apply, settle the fare before starting the journey. If in doubt, consult a policeman or traffic warden.

*By train from Gatwick*: British Rail has a regular service from Gatwick to Victoria Station. You will need to purchase a ticket at the ticket office in the terminal.

*By rented car*: Car hire services are available from firms such as Avis, Hertz, and Budget at both airports. We only recommend this form of transportation if you know exactly how to get to your destination. Reservations are needed.

*By chauffeur*: This must be arranged in advance, perhaps by your London office.

**IMPORTANT PERSONAL DATA**

The following lists pertain to personal matters and information. We recommend that you complete the necessary information and then make one or more copies to keep in a safe place. In the case of an accident, a fire, theft, or an emergency, these lists will be helpful in filing claims. Certain information will have to be added when you arrive in London.

It may be useful and convenient to list the information directly onto these pages.

**General Information**

Wife's Social Security Number:

Husband's Social Security Number:

Wife's Passport and Renewal Date:

Husband's Passport and Renewal Date:

Children's Passports and Renewal Dates:

Wife's Employee Identification:

Husband's Employee Identification:

Wife's Insurance Policies:

Husband's Insurance Policies:

Children's Insurance Policies:

Wife's Health Insurance Number:

Major Medical Policy Number:

National Health Insurance Number:

**Financial Information**

Wife's Current Account:

Husband's Current Account:

Joint Chequing Account:

Savings Account:

Other Bank Accounts:

Certificate of Deposit:

Safe-Deposit Box:

Address of Bank:

Location of Key:

Brokerage Account:

Mutual Fund Account:

Securities (serial numbers):

**Automobile Information**

Wife's Driver's Licence:

Husband's Driver's Licence:

Children's Driver's Licence:

Car Identification:

Car Registration:

Licence Plate Number:

Car Insurance and Renewal Date:

Car Tax Renewal Date:

AA/RAC Membership Number and Renewal Date:

MOT (Ministry of Transport) Test Certificate Renewal Date:

Area Parking Permit Renewal Date:

**House Information**

Title (Land) Deed:

Mortgage:

Buildings Insurance:

Contents Insurance:

Landlord:

Television Serial Number:

VCR Serial Number:

Television Licence Renewal Date:

Stereo Serial Number:

Radio Serial Number:

Tape Recorder Serial Number:

Camera/Camcorder Serial Number:

Musical Instrument Serial Numbers:

Sewing Machine Serial Number:

**U.S. Credit Cards**

List name, account number, and address to report loss.

Bank Cards:

Travel and Entertainment Cards:

Oil Company Cards:

Store Charge Account Cards:

**U.K. Credit Cards**

List name, account number, and address to report loss.

Bank Cards:

Bank Cheque Cards:

Store Charge Account Cards:

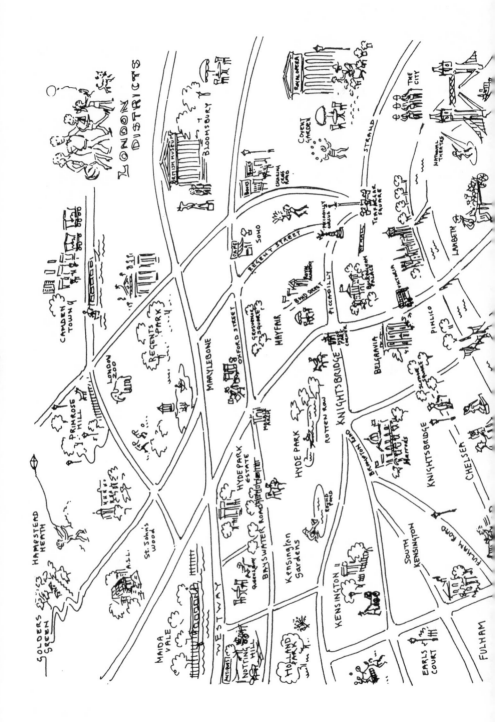

# Chapter Two:  Housing

What makes London such a wonderfully liveable city is that it is made up of many small 'villages', each with its own particular charm.  Deciding on the best location for you and your family is difficult only because the choices are so great.  You must consider a number of factors:  high cost of certain areas, proximity to work and schools (or easy transportation to them), convenience of shopping facilities, and atmosphere.  If it is at all possible, any house-hunting trip should begin with a morning spent driving around the city, taking in the flavour and overall feel of each area.  By the time your tour ends, your list of areas in which to search may be considerably shorter than it was at breakfast time.  Those few hours can save you days of wasted time and energy, not to mention frayed nerves.

Greater London is divided into 32 boroughs.  The first decision to make is to decide whether you want to live in Central London, in one of the smaller outer suburban communities of Greater London or in the country.

The following short descriptions of some of the London areas may be of assistance.  These are desirable communities in which you may want to begin your house hunting.

## LIVING IN LONDON

### Central London

The communities of Central London are expensive but convenient for shops, theatres, restaurants and clubs.  These areas have a high proportion of international residents.

Unfortunately, area codes do not follow a logical order and therefore, for example, some parts of Chelsea are SW3 and others SW10.

### *Mayfair (W1)*

Just to the east of Hyde Park is the area known as Mayfair.  This area has a large number of luxury hotels.  Many of the large elegant houses have been divided into short-lease lets (rentals).  The area is limited for large grocery shopping (the local custom of daily shopping still prevails).  It is extremely well situated for many of the finest clubs, restaurants, antique shops and designer boutiques, but it is primarily commercial rather than residential in character and thus lacks the neighbourhood 'feel' of many other areas.  The U.S. Embassy is located here.

### Belgravia (SW1)

Near Buckingham Palace and Hyde Park, this area consists of magnificent Regency squares, late Georgian terraces and charming mews houses. Some of the larger impressive houses are now used as embassies and consulates, others have been divided into flats. Belgravia is one of the more expensive and desirable areas of London, and similar to Mayfair, large grocery shopping is limited.

### Pimlico (SW1)

South of Victoria Station to the Thames, this area has lovely white stucco squares and terraces. Its quiet streets owe much to the complicated one-way traffic system. It is within walking distance of most of the great sights of London. Pimlico is a more affordable alternative to its neighbouring communities of Belgravia and Chelsea, but it also has many small hotels and B&Bs due to its proximity to Victoria Station.

### Knightsbridge (SW1, parts of SW3 and SW7)

South of Hyde Park and in the shadow of Harrods, this area features lovely Victorian squares, crescents and tall, brick Victorian mansion blocks (apartment buildings). These locations are convenient for shopping and transportation.

### South Kensington (SW7 and parts of SW5)

This area, centred around the Natural History Museum and the Victoria and Albert Museum, features many lovely communal gardens and large houses and flats. The Lycee is located in South Kensington so you will find a large French community.

### Chelsea (SW3 and SW10)

South of Knightsbridge, bordering the Thames, SW3 has many charming residential areas consisting of smaller terrace houses, squares and streets. Sloane Square and King's Road are convenient for shopping, although the latter's reputation as one of London's trendiest areas is now more tradition than fact. Chelsea also boasts many cosy local pubs and restaurants, as well as excellent antique shops and markets. Southwest of SW3, SW10 is composed of all types of period buildings from detached houses to pleasant terraces, some converted to flats. The neighbourhood around The Boltons is especially charming.

## Fulham (SW6)

Just beyond Chelsea, Fulham has some lovely, large parks and many young English families, as well as increasing numbers of Americans who are attracted by the larger gardens and better value for the money.

## Kensington (W8)

South and west of Kensington Gardens, Kensington has lovely tree-lined residential streets and squares. Kensington High Street offers convenient shopping.

## Notting Hill (W11)

Certain sections of this area, which is just north of Kensington, are becoming increasingly popular due to their large houses, often with good size private or communal gardens, and their easy access to the West End and the City. (It's worth checking when looking in this area if the particular property you are interested in is on the Carnival Route - the largest annual street party and carnival in Europe, held normally over the last weekend in August).

## Holland Park (W14)

Surrounding Holland Park, this area features some of the largest detached and semi-detached houses in London. It is also convenient to Kensington High Street.

## Marylebone (W1)

North of Oxford Street and south of Marylebone Road, this area has many 18th century streets and squares as well as charming mews. It offers convenient shopping and easy access to the City. While it is relatively near the American School, the overall atmosphere of the community is more commercial than residential, especially with its medical district, Harley Street, famous for all its doctors' offices. Regent's Park is also very convenient.

## Maida Vale (W9)

West of Marylebone, this area retains some of its mid-19th century villas and palatial mansion house flats in a wide variety of styles. Within this area is 'Little Venice', a secluded basin of the Grand Union Canal, popular with small pleasure craft.

### Hyde Park Estate (W2)

West of Marble Arch and to the north of Hyde Park, this area has modern blocks of flats (high-rise apartments), as well as some lovely squares mostly rebuilt after the war. It is convenient for Oxford Street shopping and Mayfair.

### Regent's Park (NW1)

The elegant residential area around Regent's Park is most famous for its glorious Nash Terraces overlooking the park. Its impressive homes include Winfield House, the residence of the American Ambassador. Modern blocks of flats, the London Zoo and the Open Air Theatre all add to its diversity.

### North London

### Islington (N1)

East of Regent's Park, Islington is a friendly, lively place with modern terraced houses, Victorian villas and smartly restored squares. It is close to Camden Passage, noted for its antique shops and market.

### St. John's Wood (NW8)

Northwest of Regent's Park and suburban in feeling, St. John's Wood has many low, detached and semi-detached houses as well as large blocks of flats with beautiful views over the park. The American School in London is located here.

### Swiss Cottage (NW3)

North of St. John's Wood, this area has large blocks of flats, low terraced houses and modern townhouses with a cosmopolitan flavour. The heart of Swiss Cottage is dominated by a large public leisure centre attached to the main library.

### Hampstead (NW3)

North of Swiss Cottage, this suburban village has a quaint international flavour. The high street is dominated by exclusive boutiques, cafes and restaurants. Its winding streets feature brick townhouses and large detached houses, many of which have been converted into flats. It is adjacent to Hampstead Heath with its many walking paths, golf club, art shows and outdoor concerts in summer.

---

## Hampstead Garden Suburb (NW11)

North of Hampstead this area is definitely a suburban enclave. It features cottages and beautiful four, five and six bedroom homes, many stately Georgian and ambassadorial types, with well manicured gardens. It has two small but varied shopping areas. Many homes back on to Hampstead Heath, and in some parts it is necessary to have a car.

## Highgate (N6)

Northeast of Hampstead Heath, Highgate Village is quietly residential with a definite country atmosphere. It has a golf club and many old and new homes with large gardens. Parking and driving are quite easy.

## A Note on Parking:

Parking within certain London boroughs, notably the City of Westminster and the Royal Borough of Kensington and Chelsea, is allowed only at meters (always scarce) unless a car displays a valid resident's parking permit issued by the borough. This is worth keeping in mind when choosing where to live.

## West London

Going westward from Knightsbridge are the residential areas of Brook Green, Chiswick, Hammersmith, West Kensington and Shepherds Bush. Tree lined streets of large houses, many of which have been converted into flats. This neighbourhood is well served by public transport with the Central, Piccadilly and District lines running through the vicinity. It is also on the right side of London for a quick journey on the M4 to Heathrow Airport. With riverside walks and pubs and excellent facilities for shopping, leisure and health this area is ideal for families planning to settle in London for a considerable amount of time.

## East London

To the east of Tower Hill, is a newly developed area known as Wapping and the Docklands; these are mainly warehouses, which have been converted in the last ten years to a very high standard, or new developments - most have a river view. All have off-street parking, 24 hour porter and some have indoor swimming pools and other fitness facilities. Transport is improving and the Docklands Light Railway runs a service between Tower Hill, Bank, Beckton, Stratford and Island Gardens. Canary Wharf is the new business area, which has made East London particularly appealing to professional young couples.

## South London

### *Battersea (SW8)*

Just across from Chelsea Harbour. Landmarked by the now derelict Battersea Power Station. Battersea is cheaper than living north of the river, with many brick Victorian mansion blocks and larger late Victorian family properties. Excellent facilities for shopping, parking, education, health and sports. Permits for parking are not necessary on most roads (except round Clapham Junction).

### *Clapham (SW11)*

As always popular with families, this area surrounds Clapham Common. Large Victorian family properties, on tree lined streets with on-street parking. Clapham's three tube stations are served by the Northern line, making this a recommended location for young city professionals who are looking to buy rather than rent. Permits for parking are not required.

### *Putney (SW15)*

Bordering the south bank of the Thames, Putney has a chain of attractive open spaces with extensive sporting grounds, especially rowing clubs. It contains the first high-rise flats in London as well as many two-storey homes with lovely gardens. There is a busy and convenient street for shopping as well as the Putney Exchange, an enclosed shopping mall. Putney has main line and bus links to Central London as well as a tube station, but this is not so close to the area's residential neighbourhoods.

## Greater London

More and more newcomers to London are moving to communities farther from the centre. These communities are often less expensive, have fewer foreigners and retain more of their historic character. Most have every type of housing: rows of charming brick terrace houses, tall stately Georgian terraces, and large detached houses in spacious gardens.

Perhaps the only disadvantages are the longer commute to the City and the necessity for a car in most locations.

### *Barnes (SW13)*

Located west of Putney, on the Thames, this area features low terraced houses from the late Victorian and Edwardian eras. It has a wonderful 'wilderness' Common, sporting grounds and swan pond. Barnes offers bus and train transportation, but not a tube station.

---

### Richmond (TW10)

Southwest of Barnes, Richmond is a lovely suburban village with large houses and beautiful gardens. Its many parks add a delightful 'country' atmosphere. Richmond Park comprises 2,000 acres of parkland, and Richmond Green is often the setting for cricket matches.

### Wimbledon (SW19)

Wimbledon, famous for the tennis tournament held here every summer, is located eight miles southwest of Central London. Wimbledon has a suburban atmosphere, with Wimbledon Common comprising 1,200 acres of land for riders, walkers and picnickers. The Village has a wide range of shopping and the train and tube station offers convenient transportation to London. Centre Court is a new shopping complex next to the station.

Other equally charming areas worth consideration are *Blackheath (SE3)*, *Dulwich (SE21)*, *Kew (TW9)* and *Greenwich (SE10)*.

## LIVING IN THE COUNTRY

Within commuting distance of London are some wonderful suburban communities with large houses and enormous gardens. There is no question that for what one has to pay for a house in London, one can find almost palatial splendour in the rural areas. But yet again, one must consider the commute into London.

Surrey, south of London, encompasses many charming villages - Cobham, Esher, Walton-on-Thames, Weybridge, West Byfleet and many others - all with good public transportation into London. The American Community Schools, the TASIS England American School, and Marymount International Schools are also located in Surrey.

Northwest of Central London are the communities of Wembley, Harrow, Pinner and Ruislip. These areas are popular for their suburban atmosphere and more garden-for-the-money value. They primarily contain semi-detached and small detached houses.

Further northwest are the communities of Northwood, Chorleywood, Moor Park and Watford with large houses and gardens. These areas are convenient to the London Orbital (M25) and the many suburban superstores.

## RELOCATION FIRMS

Inquire whether your company recommends a relocation firm in London. If this service is available to you, by all means look into it. These firms can introduce you to the local real estate market, explain the U.K. educational system, make appointments at schools, acquaint you with driving test requirements and provide information on leisure and sports facilities. Such firms are particularly useful in the absence of a multiple listing system as they will contact all estate agents in an area.

*Executive Relocation Services*, 7 Princedale Road, W11 4NW;
   0171-221-4867

*Interdean*, Relocation Management, 3/5 Cumberland Avenue, NW10 7DU;
   0181-961-4141

*Karen Phillips, Property Consultant*, 2 Leinster Mansions, Langland Gardens, NW3 6QB;   0171-794-2400.   Specialises in St. John's Wood, Hampstead and surrounding areas.

*Pricoa Relocation Management*, 136 New Bond Street, W1;
   0171-629-8222.

*People and Property*, 18 Coulson Street, SW3;
   0171-225-1313.

*Relocation Resources International*, Premier House, 70 Greycoat Place, SW1;
   0171-799-1444.


**ESTATE AGENTS**

These are similar to American real estate agents, although it should be noted that estate agents are not required to have a licence or undergo training.

Estate agents only have a listing of homes in their immediate area although many firms now have offices scattered throughout London.  There is no established multiple listing system in London, although many agents have good working relationships with certain agents in other areas and can set up a network of agents for you.  However, you may have to pay additional commissions.  Most estate agents work Monday through Friday, but weekend hours are becoming more common.  Do not be surprised if the estate agent books an appointment for you to see a flat or house, and then gives you the keys to view the property on your own.

The following is a list of some of the estate agencies we have found to be helpful.  In case of agencies with several locations, we have listed the full address and telephone number of the main office, and their branch locations; ring the number shown for additional details.

**Central London**

*Allsop & Co.*, 100 Knightsbridge, SW1 (Knightsbridge tube);
0171-584-6106.

*AMA International*, 20 Seymour Street, W1 (Marble Arch tube);
0171-724-4844.

*Aylesford & Co.*, 440 King's Road, SW10 (Sloane Square tube);
0171-351-2383: Also in Kensington and Wimbledon.

*Chestertons Residential*, 2 Cale Street, SW3 (Sloane Square, South
Kensington tube); 0171-589-5211: Battersea, Chiswick, Docklands,
Fulham, Hampstead, Kensington, Little Venice, Mayfair, Notting Hill,
Pimlico, Putney, Tower Bridge, Wimbledon.

*Douglas & Gordon*, 21 Milner Street, SW3 (Sloane Square tube);
0171-730-0666 (lets) and 0171-225-1225 (sales): Also in Battersea,
Clapham, Fulham, Putney, Sloane Avenue and Wandsworth.

*W. A. Ellis*, 174 Brompton Road, SW3 (South Kensington tube);
0171-581-7654: Handles properties primarily in Knightsbridge,
Chelsea, Belgravia, Kensington and South Kensington.

*Farrar Stead & Glyn*, 152 Fulham Road, SW10 (South Kensington tube);
0171-373-8425: Covers SW3, SW7 and SW10 areas.

*Friend & Falcke*, 293 Brompton Road, SW3 (South Kensington tube);
0171-225-0814: Also in Belgravia, Clapham, Fulham, Wandsworth,
Brook Green and Barnes.

*Gerald Kay*, 3 Chester Mews, Belgravia, SW1 (Victoria tube);
0171-245-9117: Central London.

*Hamptons*, 6 Arlington Street, SW1 (Green Park tube);
0171-493-8222: Also in Chelsea, Wimbledon, Hampstead and
Kensington.

*Knight, Frank & Rutley*, 20 Hanover Square, W1 (Oxford Circus);
0171-629-8171: Also in Chelsea, City, Docklands, Knightsbridge and
Wapping.

*Marsh & Parsons*, 9 Kensington Church Street, W8 (Kensington High Street);
0171-937-6091: Also in Bayswater, Holland Park, Notting Hill and
Shepherd's Bush.

*McGlashans Property Services*, 34 Gloucester Place Mews, W1 (Marble Arch/Baker Street tube); 0171-486-6711: Primarily in West End, Hampstead, Swiss Cottage, Amersham, Ruislip, Finchley and Chalfont.

*Jean Oddy & Co.*; 0171-625-7733: Jean is an American who finds well-equipped properties throughout Central London and as a professional service she also provides orientations to help make all moves happy and hassle-free.

*Susan Rafi-Shah*; 0171-602-8579 (telephone and fax): Individual property consultant who specialises in finding, vetting and selecting rented houses and apartments mainly in Central London.

*Savills*, 20 Grosvenor Hill, W1 (Bond Street, Green Park tube); 0171-499-8644: Also in City, Docklands, Hampstead, Kensington and Sloane Street and throughout England.

*Winkworth & Co.*, 123A Gloucester Road, SW7 4TE (Gloucester Road tube); 0171-373-5052: 30 branches across London.

*John D. Wood & Co.*, 26 Curzon Street, W1 (Green Park tube); 0171-408-0055: Also in Battersea, Chelsea, Fulham, St. John's Wood, Wandsworth, Wimbledon and Kensington.

**Greater London and the Home Counties**

*Surrey*

*General Accident Property Services*, Walton-on-Thames; (01932) 220548.

*Hamptons*, Esher; (01372) 468411.

*Mann & Co.*, Esher; (01372) 462211.

*Nationwide Residential Lettings*, Esher; (01372) 466614.

*Buckinghamshire*

*Hamptons*, Beaconsfield; (014946) 77744.

*Woolwich Property Services*, High Wycombe; (014944) 65585.

---

*Rafferty Buckland*, Beaconsfield;
(014946) 75432.

**Berkshire**

*Barton & Wyatt*, Wentworth;
(01344 842857).

*Chancellors Residential*, Ascot;
(01344) 872909.

*JSC Services*, Ascot;
(01344) 882746.


Once you have narrowed your list of areas, consider the type of housing you desire - a flat, townhouse or detached house. Refer to the list of English terminology at the end of this chapter for further descriptions of housing types.

As you are shown various properties, keep in mind some of the following:

> On street/off street parking
> Storage space
> Shower pressure
> Separate washing machine and dryer (often they are all-in-one)
> Outdoor space
> Refrigerator/freezer size
> Number of floors/stairs
> Elevator access
> Height and width of corridors and stairwells (especially in conversions)
> Proximity to school/work/shopping/transportation
> Proximity to parks and playgrounds


## SPECIAL CONSIDERATIONS

### Rent/Let

If you are planning to rent rather than buy, you should be aware of the Housing Act 1988 which regulates your right to extend your tenancy and the Landlord's right to re-possess the property or increase the rent. Your solicitor (lawyer) can explain this in detail. You should not sign a tenancy agreement or lease without first having it approved by a solicitor familiar with such documents. Your company may have an in-house lawyer who can do this for you, or you can contact the Law Society, 113 Chancery Lane, WC2 (0171-242-1222) for names of firms specialising in such work.

Recommendations from friends are useful. Also recommended: *Haslam and Payne*, 31 Queen Anne's Gate, SW1; 0171-976-0776; or fax 0171-976-0699.

There are two important aspects of the housing market you may encounter:

A.    Many rentals are fully furnished which can make your move very uncomplicated. You only need to bring your clothes, the children's toys and other personal items. But often the furnishings are not of a very good quality. It is possible to negotiate with the owner to remove the furnishings and move in your own. If you find you need additional storage for furniture that won't fit into your house/flat, see Chapter Ten for self-storage locations.

B.    Some rentals are only available as a 'company let', which means that the lease is made out to your corporation and must be signed by the Managing Director or his/her appointee. The company therefore guarantees the tenancy.

**Temporary Accommodations and Service Flats**

Service flats are fully furnished apartments which can be rented by the week or by the month. This accommodation provides maid and porter service. If you have not been able to come to London on a house-hunting trip and arrive with the whole family, service flats can be much more pleasant than staying in a large commercial hotel. Many companies deal with these on a regular basis, so enquire at your London office or check with an estate agent or relocation firm. Recommendation for serviced apartments: Draycott House, 10 Draycott Avenue, Chelsea, SW3 3AA (Sloane Square tube); 0171-584-4659.

**Insurance**

If your London office cannot recommend an insurance broker, you might telephone the *British Insurance Broker's Association*, 14 Bevis Marks, EC3A 7NT; 0171-623-9043, for a recommendation.

**Mortgages**

Check with your bank or building society for current details. Be aware that it may be difficult to obtain a mortgage when purchasing a leasehold with fewer than 50 years left on the lease.

**Surveys**

Your bank will arrange for a surveyor to inspect the property before the exchange of contracts. If a defect is found later, you should be aware that you have no recourse against either the bank or the surveyor. Therefore, many people find it wise to hire their own surveyor to advise them on the state of the property.

## Utilities

Do not forget to arrange to have the electricity, gas, water and telephone services transferred to your name. It can take months to have telephones installed so see that the previous owners leave their telephone equipment in the house. It is generally best to have this provision written into the contract. (Often cellular phones are available during a waiting period and a landlord may pay for this).

## ENGLISH TERMINOLOGY

The following list of real estate "jargon" will hopefully eliminate any confusion in communication.

*Airing Cupboard:*     Cupboard housing the hot water tank, with extra space suitable for drying damp clothes.

*Bathroom:*     A room used for bathing; always contains tub and sink, very often has a toilet, sometimes has a bidet.

*Block of Flats:*     Apartment building/house, whether modern high rise or converted mansion.

*Boiler:*     Furnace usually combined with hot water heater.

*Building Society:*     A savings and loan bank.

*Bungalow:*     One storey ground floor house.

*CH:*     Central heating.

*CHW:*     Constant hot water.

*The City:*     One square mile along the River Thames. It is self governing and the heart of the financial community.

*Cloakroom:*     Toilet and wash basin.

*Communal Gardens:*     Grassy area in most "squares" that provides outdoor space for residents of the square. Access is by key only and an annual fee is charged for maintenance and landscaping. All have rules regarding access for dogs and permitted children's activities.

| | |
|---|---|
| *Conversion:* | A flat in a house that was originally for single family occupation. |
| *Detached House:* | A house that stands apart from any others; generally surrounded by its own garden. |
| *Fireplace:* | Will not be wood-burning, as the burning of wood is banned in London by the air pollution laws. 'Smokeless fuel' may be purchased for use instead of wood or the fireplace may be fitted with gas jets. |
| *Fixtures and Fittings:* | Contents of house or flat. This term may include anything from major appliances to the linens, carpets, curtains, and lighting fixtures. Some of these may be included in the asking price, but do not make assumptions about anything, including the kitchen cabinets and appliances. |
| *Flat:* | Apartment. |
| *Freehold:* | Refers to the outright purchase of building and land 'in perpetuity'. |
| *Garden:* | Grassed or paved area usually to the front or back of the property. May or may not include landscaping. |
| *GFCH or GCH:* | Gas-fired central heating. |
| *Gazumping:* | One of the least attractive local customs. During the period between agreeing to a sale or rental and the exchange of contracts, the present owner may accept another offer. This most often occurs if he/she subsequently received a higher bid than you and he agreed on. In a rising market, this may occur distressingly frequently. |
| *Government Stamp Duty:* | Tax on a percentage of the purchase price of a house. |
| *Ground Rent:* | Sum paid to the owner of the freehold for the use of the land when you have purchased a leasehold. |
| *Housing Estate:* | Sub-division or apartment complex. |
| *Key Deposit:* | A deposit for keys required by some estate agents when they do not accompany you to view a property. |

| | |
|---|---|
| *Leasehold:* | Refers to the purchase of the right to occupy a house or flat for a specific number of years, sometimes as many as 999. The land underlying the property remains in the hands of the owner of the freehold, who will charge a small amount for the rental of the land. At the end of the lease, the property reverts back to the owner of the freehold. The leaseholder is responsible for maintaining the property in accordance with the conditions established by the freehold owner. Also, many leaseholds have restrictions on major external and internal renovations. The shorter leases tend to be less valuable properties, although new leases are generally negotiated at realistic prices. |
| *Let:* | Rent, lease. |
| *Loo:* | Toilet, with or without wash basin. |
| *Maisonette:* | Apartment on two or more floors. |
| *Mansion Flat:* | Large, old-fashioned apartment, usually in a good area. Usually possessing good storage space and large rooms but often lacking modern conveniences. |
| *Mews House:* | Converted carriage house, with small rooms and lots of 'character'. |
| *O.S.P.:* | Off-street parking. |
| *Reception Rooms:* | General term for living room, drawing room, sitting room, dining room or study. |
| *Terraced House:* | Townhouse. Attached or row of houses; two to five floors high. |
| *Self-contained:* | Has a separate entrance. |
| *Semi-detached:* | A house that is joined to another house on one side only. |
| *Shower:* | Small hose with shower head; may be attached to the tub's tap and affording minimal pressure. Although expensive, pressure pumps may be installed to provide an American-style shower. |
| *Unfurnished:* | May mean no carpets, light fixtures, appliances. |

*Water Closet (WC):*      Room with toilet.

*Yard:*      Open area with dirt or concrete base.  No grass.

Housing

# Notes

# Chapter Three:
# Money, Banking and Taxation

## BRITISH CURRENCY

British currency, normally referred to as sterling, comprises two monetary units: the penny (called the 'p') and the pound. One hundred pennies equal one pound. Coins include the penny, two pence, five pence, ten pence, twenty pence, fifty pence and the one pound coin. The notes are called pounds (£) and come in five pound, ten pound, twenty pound and fifty pound notes. You may hear a two pence coin referred to as 'tuppence', a five pence as a 'shilling' or 'bob' or a pound called a 'quid'. The term 'quid' comes from the Latin expression 'quid pro quo' meaning one thing in return for another, no doubt dating back to the Roman occupation of Britain.

## BANKS IN LONDON

Although most of the major U.S. banks have branches in London, many of them do not offer 'retail' or personal banking services to expatriates. Contact your London Branch to see if they will provide chequing and savings account services and importantly 'plastic' that is compatible with the U.K. network of ATM's and accepted in most shops.

It is generally a good idea to open an account with a U.K. bank. The four largest U.K. banks (the 'clearing banks') are Barclays Bank, Lloyds Bank, Midland Bank and National Westminster Bank. They have numerous branches throughout London and the rest of England. Since the major banks offer essentially the same services you will probably choose the bank with which your firm has a business relationship, or the bank located nearest to your home or office. Although personal references may be required, your passport will be the main requirement for identity purposes. A letter of introduction from your firm helps and if you require immediate 'credit' facilities, copies of your U.S. bank statements will also speed the process.

## BANKING SERVICES

Since the removal of exchange controls in October 1979, there are no longer any restrictions on the amount of sterling that expatriates may deposit and withdraw from their bank accounts in the U.K. The U.K. banks offer two basic types of accounts: 'current accounts' (chequing accounts) and 'deposit accounts' (savings accounts) although there are variations of each type of account. Building Societies (similar to the U.S. savings and loans associations) also offer current accounts. Most British banks now offer interest on current accounts, or if you are persistent, most banks will provide *'sweep accounts'*. This means the bank will automatically transfer excess funds from your current account to your deposit account. In reverse, the bank will move funds from your deposit account to your current account to maintain the agreed credit balance. You should obtain a 'direct debit/cheque guarantee card' for your current account (see below). At the request of the customer, statements are sent quarterly or monthly. Cancelled cheques are returned only if requested and a fee is charged. Free banking is currently offered by most banks as long as you maintain a credit balance.

Monthly or quarterly bills, (telephone, electricity, gas, water, council tax) may be paid at your bank by two methods. One method is to use the *giro slips* attached to most bills. The slips can be grouped together and all paid with a single cheque. The bank stamps your bill providing a record of payment, proving beneficial as cheques are not normally returned by the bank. The second method of payment, and perhaps the easiest, is the use of a *standing order* or *direct debit payment*. In both cases, you instruct the bank to pay a fixed or varying amount to a specified payee either upon request or at regular intervals (i.e. £1,000 rent every month to estate office on the 15th or whatever your electricity bill may be to the electricity company on the 30th, etc.).

**Bank Hours**

Although many branches now stay open as late as 17.30, regular banking hours are from 09.30 to 15.30, Monday through Friday (09.30 to 15.00 in the City of London). Many banks will close at 12.00 on Christmas Eve. All major banks have cash machines which operate approximately 24 hours a day at most of their branches and increasingly, elsewhere. You must apply to your bank for a suitable cash card. Saturday hours (09.30 to 12.00) are currently being offered by some of the U.K. clearing banks mainly in their London and suburban branches.

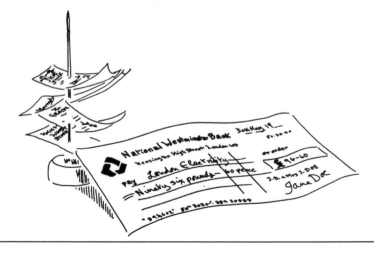

Money, Banking and Taxation

## Cheques and Cards

Sterling cheques are usually 'crossed', meaning that they have two vertical lines running down the middle. A crossed cheque is for deposit only and cannot be cashed by a third party. Hence, the endorsing of cheques for cash is not done in the U.K.

Writing a sterling cheque differs slightly from writing a U.S. dollar cheque. When writing a cheque there are two important points to remember.

1.    The date is written with the day, the month and then the year. For example, 5 March 1995 or 5-3-95. Do remember to either put the day first or spell out the month.

2.    To write the amount, you must write 'pounds' and 'p' or 'pence'. For example, £10.62 is written 'Ten pounds and 62p' or 'Ten pounds and sixty-two pence'.

All U.K. clearing banks are now on a 3 day cheque clearing cycle. Cash deposits, however, are credited immediately. Although you may cash a cheque for any amount at your own branch, cashing a cheque at either another branch of your bank, or at another bank requires your cheque card, and if over the value of your card (£50 or £100), it also requires prior arrangement with your own branch. With a cheque guarantee/direct debit card you can normally cash up to £100 daily at other branches and banks; sometimes a small fee is charged.

Most cheque guarantee cards now also incorporate a direct debit card facility, whereby you can use the card on its own, without writing out a cheque. 'Visa' card is the most famous one closely followed by 'Switch' (a black and white 'S' within a green square sign found on your cheque guarantee card). The advantage is that you have a clear audit trail on your statement of account (service provider or retailer's name appears on your bank statement).

## Bank Credit Cards

There are numerous bank credit cards in the U.K., Barclaycard (Visa) and the Access card (MasterCard) being the best known names. These cards can be used throughout the U.K. and in Europe where the appropriate sign is displayed. Similar U.S. cards are also accepted. Initially getting one of these cards can be difficult, if you don't already have a credit record in the U.K. A letter or phone call from your company can speed the process.

## Travellers Cheques

Travellers cheques and foreign currency can be purchased from all the major U.K. banks; however, it is usually necessary to give a few days notice.

Money, Banking and Taxation

Travellers cheques can also be obtained from Thomas Cook and American Express offices located throughout the U.K. Cashing dollar travellers cheques often incurs a large fee if the bank does not have a relationship with the travellers cheque company.

## Transferring Money

If you want to transfer money from your U.S. chequing account to your U.K. current account, you purchase sterling from your U.K. bank with a cheque in dollars drawn on your U.S. bank account. Normally the bank negotiates your small dollar cheques and credits your sterling account immediately. In the case of larger dollar amounts, the bank may collect your dollars before crediting your account or a facility for immediate credit may be agreed.

The process of transferring large amounts of money may take 10 to 14 days to complete by post. Transfer by telex may be completed in 48 hours.

If you wish to remit money to the U.S., ask your U.K. bank to draw a dollar cheque (draft) on your behalf against the sterling in your current account. The bank will either issue a cheque in dollars or, for a nominal charge, transfer amounts to your U.S. bank by mail, cable or telex.

## TAXATION

When you leave the U.S. to live in Great Britain, your tax status changes. Because you live in the United Kingdom the Inland Revenue has primary jurisdiction over your income; but you also have an obligation based on your American citizenship to report and pay U.S. income tax.

## United Kingdom Taxes

The system of taxation in the U.K. differs in many ways from the U.S. system. In particular:

1.  The U.K. tax year runs from 6 April to the following 5 April.

2.  The tax return includes no calculation of tax to be paid and therefore no payment is submitted with the return.

3.  Filing requirements in the U.K. are less strict, however there are some penalty and interest provisions and you would be well advised to ensure your return is received by the Inland Revenue by 31 October following the end of the tax year.

4.  Your tax inspector will issue a notice of assessment of tax if it is believed that tax has not been completely deducted at source. If the income assessed is not correct you must appeal against the assessment within thirty days of issue.

---

5. Tax may be payable at different dates, depending on the type of income.

6. Interest may be assessed on tax not paid by its due date.

Publication, IR20, *Residents and Non-residents: Liability to Tax in the United Kingdom*, which is published by the Inland Revenue, discusses the taxation of individuals in the United Kingdom.

U.K. taxes are administered through the Inland Revenue, and local offices are listed in the telephone directory. If you are employed by a company in the U.K., PAYE (Pay-As-You-Earn) will be deducted from your salary. If you are self-employed, your accountant will advise you, as you will assess your own tax, or you may report to your nearest Inland Revenue office which is listed in the local telephone directory. Single and married women are responsible for paying their own taxes and filing their own tax returns. Each person is entitled to a tax free personal allowance which at the time of this printing is £3,445.00. Each married couple is entitled to an additional allowance of £1,720.00 which is first allocated to the husband. However, this may be transferred to the wife where either the husband's income is insufficient or an election is made to transfer all or half of the allowance. From 6 April 1995 this allowance is restricted to relieving tax only at the 15% rate.

If you intend to reside in the U.K. for a temporary period only, (temporary can mean a number of years) you normally will not be considered to be domiciled here. In this situation, if the source of your investment income is in the U.K., or if such income from your investments outside the U.K. is remitted to you in the U.K., you will be taxed on it in the U.K.

Social security taxes (FICA in the U.S. and National Insurance in the U.K.) are payable in the U.K. just as they are in America - withheld from your pay cheque if you are an employee, and payable with your income tax if you are self-employed. Under the totalisation agreement between the US and the U.K., Americans working in the U.K. generally will be required to pay social security tax either in the U.K. or in the U.S. but not in both countries. Which country you pay to is determined by the length of your anticipated stay in the U.K.

*VAT* (Value Added Tax) is similar to a sales tax. 17.5 per cent VAT is included in all your purchases, except groceries, children's clothes and certain other items. It is not deductible against either U.S. or U.K. income taxes, but if you have your own business, you may pass the VAT you pay in connection with that business on to the ultimate consumer of your goods or services, provided your gross turnover is above a certain amount of your goods and services and your business is registered for VAT (i.e turnover of over £45,000 annually).

*Council Tax*. The council tax is a local tax set by local councils to help pay for local services. There will be one bill per dwelling to be paid by the resident or by the owner where the property has no residents. The amount paid will be based on the value of the dwelling.

*Capital gains tax, inheritance tax and other U.K. taxes* and duties on your property may significantly affect the way you wish to set up your estate. American lawyers in the U.K. are usually skilled in adapting your will to protect your estate.

## American Taxes

American citizens are taxed by the U.S. on their world-wide income with a tax credit, subject to credit limitations, for foreign income taxes paid.

*Filing requirements*: In general American citizens wherever they live in the world, must file a tax return if their income exceeds a certain amount. Men and women, single or married, are equally responsible. Filing dates are automatically extended for Americans abroad from 15 April to 15 June, but interest is applied from 15 April to any tax due.

Publication 54, *Tax Guide for U.S. Citizens and Resident Aliens Abroad*, is available at the IRS office of the U.S. Embassy, 24 Grosvenor Square, W1A 1AE (Marble Arch, Bond Street tube); 0171-408-8076, or you may write to Forms Distribution Center, P.O. Box 25866, Richmond, VA 23260, U.S.A.

Married taxpayers are each entitled to elect to use the $70,000 exclusion to reduce their foreign source earned (employment) income, if they meet one of two tests, the bona fide residence test or the physical presence test. A bona fide resident has lived in a foreign country for an uninterrupted period that includes an entire tax year. The physical presence test is met by being physically present in a foreign country for at least 330 full days in any 365 day period. In the first year of foreign residence, if a taxpayer wishes to elect the exclusions but does not yet qualify when the tax return is due, he may file an extension to a date after he meets the qualification.

1. *Foreign Earned Income Exclusion*: If your tax home is a foreign country and you qualify under either the bona fide residence test or the physical presence test, you can exclude the actual amount of foreign income earned during the year, up to a maximum of $70,000.

2. *Housing Cost Amount Exclusion*: A taxpayer may also choose to exclude from gross income certain housing costs that have been provided by the employer in excess of a specified base amount.

After these deductions, any remaining earned income and all unearned income is taxed as if it were the only income and, therefore, will generally be taxed at a much lower effective tax rate. If both husband and wife work separately, the foreign earned income exclusion is computed separately, even if they file jointly.

*Moving and Replacement of Personal Residence.* Various moving expense deductions are provided in the law. Additionally, any gain from the sale of a personal residence may be rolled over by buying a new property within four years if during that time you are living outside the U.S. Do note that this four year limit only applies while you are living abroad.

*Foreign Tax Credit.* As you are generally subject to tax both in the U.K. and the U.S., a foreign tax credit for foreign income taxes paid may be used, to some extent, to offset U.S. taxes due on foreign income.

*Social Security Taxes.* FICA continues to be payable by most Americans who are employed by a U.S. company in the U.K., or certain affiliates, and from the onset do not intend to stay for more than five years in the U.K. In most other situations U.K. National Insurance contributions are payable.

*State and Local Taxes.* You may not be liable for state or local income taxes if you live abroad, although this depends on the state from which you have come. However, you remain liable for any taxes on property (real estate or personal property) that generates income in the U.S.

*Canadian Taxes.* In general, if you can establish that you are no longer a resident of Canada you do not have to pay taxes in Canada on income earned outside Canada. Specific questions can be directed to the International Tax Office, 2540 Lancaster Road, Ottawa, Ontario K1A 1A8, Canada; (613) 952-3741.

## TAX ASSISTANCE

For further information on your U.K. or U.S. tax obligations, you may contact the Inland Revenue, your U.K. or U.S. accountant or lawyer, or your company's personnel or expatriate employee departments. For U.K. tax enquiries, there are various local enquiry offices in London listed under 'Inland Revenue' in the telephone directory. The IRS office in the U.S. Embassy can assist you, at no cost, in filing your U.S. returns and the Consular Office of the U.S. Embassy has lists of American Accountants and lawyers who can assist you for a fee.

## SAFETY DEPOSIT BOXES

Safety deposit boxes are privately run safety deposit centres. Local commercial banks do not have facilities for individual safety deposit boxes. The banks do provide 'strong rooms' for their customers' valuables to be stored in; they may be in a cash or 'deed' metal box.

# Chapter Four:
# Post Office, Telephone and Utilities

## THE POST OFFICE

The British Post Office is a government agency and provides a wider range of functions than its American counterpart. It provides numerous services which are described in its booklets, *Putting the Customer First*, and *Parcel Force*.

The Post Office is divided into 3 sections which each have their own Customer Service Centres. Their telephone numbers are as follows:

| | | |
|---|---|---|
| Letters | - | Refer to Royal Mail in telephone directory for the nearest office |
| Parcels | - | 0800-224466 |
| Counter Services | - | 01345-223344 |

Another useful telephone number is the London Postcode Centre - 01343-111222.

### Payments

Payments may be made at Counter Services in either cash or cheque. These include:

Household bills that are part of the National Giro Service

Accounts System (council tax, gas, electricity, etc.)

Savings bank deposits

Savings Certificates

Government securities

Postage and telegraph accounts

Postage forward parcels/Redirection of mail forms

Private box and bag rentals

Delivery fees (customs charges, insufficient postage)

TV licence

Most post office counters are open Monday to Friday from 09.00 to 17.30 and on Saturday from 09.00 to 12.00. Neighbourhood post office hours vary. The post office at 24/28 William IV Street, WC2N 4DL; 0171-930-9580 (near Trafalgar Square) is open from 08.00 to 20.00, Monday to Saturday.

## PUBLIC CALL BOXES

Call boxes (public telephones) are generally available in larger shops, pubs and along the street. Call boxes generally take 10 pence, 20 pence, 50 pence and £1 coins. When using the older phones, dial the number and wait for the bleeping sound before inserting coins. Newer phones operate with the insertion of the coin before dialling. If an additional coin will be required, ample warning is given by another bleeping sound. Do not ask someone to ring you at the pay phone unless you are certain that it will accept incoming calls.

Many new public telephones operate on British Telecom Phonecards available from most newsagents and post offices. In units of 10 to 200, Phonecards start at £1.00

## THE TELEPHONE COMPANIES

### British Telecom (BT)

To obtain a new telephone service you must contact the local Telecom sales office by dialling 150 for residential service and 152 for business service. It will take approximately one week to obtain new telephone equipment. You will have to pay a connection fee for each line requested as well as a deposit against future charges (£90 in 1995).

British Telecom will only install one phone line unless asked. Be sure to specify how many lines you want installed when contacting the Telecom office. Be sure to request phone books and a listing in the phone directory if so desired. If you would rather not be listed, you must request "Ex-directory". British Telecom does offer special services in most areas like call waiting, call forwarding and caller ID. BT also offer telephone charge cards.

As an alternative to renting telephone equipment from BT you can purchase new telephone equipment at a local BT shop or any High Street electronics retailer such as Dixons. *British Telecom, Mobile Communication*; (0800) 222655, is a telephone sales centre that will rent telephones for any length of time or sell and deliver new equipment to you. *First European Communications*; 0171-221-9555, rents short term cellular phones and will deliver and pick up the equipment.

Telephone charges are based on metered units. The unit charge varies according to the time the call is made for local, national and international calls. Time periods for calls made within the U.K. and internationally are:

*Daytime Rate*:   Monday to Friday   08.00 - 18.00

*Cheap Rate*:   Monday to Friday   18.00 - 08.00;   All weekend

The quarterly bills generally give a single total charge for metered units and charge for all directly dialled national and international calls, but you can request a fully itemised bill. Call your local British Telecom office for details. The customer service number is (0800) 332222. Operator assisted calls are listed separately and are more expensive. There is also a charge for directory enquiries. It is possible to have a meter installed on your phone for a significant fee, if you wish to monitor your use of metered units. If you believe that there is a discrepancy in your bill, you can appeal to British Telecom. Instructions for this process appear on the back of the Telecom statement.

Telephone charges can be reduced by using the 'Freephone' services when possible. Some companies and organisations maintain 'free of charge' numbers which are reached by calling the operator (100) and asking for a 'Freephone Call' to the specific 'Freephone Number'.

You will receive credit for charges incurred as a result of equipment malfunctions (e.g. crossed lines) by reporting it to the operator.

**Alternative Telephone Companies**

*Mercury Communications Limited*, P.O. Box 49, Birmingham, England, B1 1TE, is the only comprehensive alternative to British Telecom and is accessible to all customers without having to rewire. Mercury's service to individual customers covers only long distance calls within the U.K. and internationally and includes monthly itemised statements and, depending on the type of long distance phone calls made, cheaper rates compared to other companies. The Mercury network is now available in most parts of the U.K. Call Mercury Assistance (0500) 500194 for further information.

*Cable Companies*: Certain cable companies are offering a cheap telephone service to customers in their area. This service has been known to be less reliable than the major telephone companies. Contact your local cable company for more information.

*AT&T*: Offer two long distance services: The AT&T card, and *U.S.A. Direct Service*. Both offer operator assisted international rates. Call (0800) 890011 for more information regarding their services. A variety of custom calling cards exist (such as restricted cards, universal cards, and international cards).

*MCI*: Also offer long distance phone service. *MCI CALL U.S.A.* offers a toll-free call to an MCI operator who will complete your call anywhere in the U.S. An MCI card is also available to those living overseas. The number for general enquiries is (0800) 890222.

*Swift Call*: Offer low rates and access to 800 lines to the U.S.A. Call 0171-488-2001 for more information.

Telephone directories and Yellow Pages are published for London and the other cities and towns in Great Britain. The dialling codes for all other cities and towns outside of London are listed in the front of each directory.

**SOME IMPORTANT TELEPHONE NUMBERS**

| | |
|---|---|
| Fire, police ambulance | 999 |
| Operator assistance, U.K. | 100 |
| Operational assistance, International | 155 |
| Directory Enquiries | 192 |
| Directory Enquiries, International | 153 |
| Fax Directory Enquiries | 153 |
| Telephone repairs | 151 |
| Telemessages within U.K. | 100 |
| Time (From 0171/0181) | 123 |

| Direct Dial, U.S. | 001 | |
|---|---|---|
| Transport within London<br>(London Underground) | 0171-222-1234 | (tell them where and when you are going and they will suggest how to get there) |
| Transport outside London | 0181-744-2411 | |

## UTILITIES

### Electricity

If you, rather than a landlord, are responsible for electrical services, you must contact your local Electricity Board, listed in the telephone directory under 'Electricity'.

*London Electricity Board*, (LEB) services London. *Southern Electricity* covers Middlesex, north of the Thames. *Eastern Electricity* handles areas north of Camden and Chigwell, Essex. They all have regional sales showrooms that sell appliances.

Electricity meters are read quarterly and bills will be sent following the reading. The bill will include electricity units used and their unit price, plus a quarterly standing charge.

England has several types of electrical plugs; the most common is a square shaped, three pin plug. It requires a fuse and has a 'ground' wire. It is wise to know how to change the fuse in plugs. Using the correct amperage will avoid overloading the circuit or blowing the fuse. As a safety factor, all lamps and all appliances should always be turned off at the main point as well as the switch.

It would be wise to familiarise yourself with the type of fuse box in your house. This is easier before a problem than in the dark!

### Gas

The same conditions apply for gas service as described for electricity. Consult the telephone directory under 'Gas'.

*North Thames Gas* services the largest area, including Central London, plus areas to the east, west, and north of the Thames. *South Eastern Gas* covers the region south of the Thames. *Eastern Gas* handles the area north of Hornsey.

**Water**

*Thames Water* supplies water for Greater London. Detailed information and telephone numbers are found in the telephone directory.

Bills are sent semi-annually and include charges for water plus sewage services. Water is billed according to the 'rateable value' of the property, rather than water used. This charge sometimes is paid by the landlord.

In most houses, the only water coming directly from the main line (therefore considered drinking water) is the cold water tap in the kitchen. Water from other taps comes from storage tanks on the premises. The hot water goes through a water heating unit. Frequently the water pressure will be low, if it is not pumped.

**Television**

The users of television sets must possess an annual licence, obtainable from any post office. Renewals are sent automatically. One licence covers all the television sets in a household. Radios require no licence.

*Cable*: In addition to the four channels available for free (BBC 1, BBC 2, ITV 3 and Channel 4), Cable or Satellite television may be available in your area. Different cable companies service individual geographic regions with approximately 10 companies currently servicing the London area. Not all locations are cable ready at this time. *Cable Communications Association*; 0171-222-2900, will inform you which cable company services your area and how to go about contacting them.

*Satellite*: In order to receive satellite communication you may either purchase or rent an individual satellite dish to be installed at your residence. You must then subscribe to a subscription plan, payable on a monthly basis. Satellite dishes are available from many local high street electronic and appliance shops. Packages are available to rent from either *Radio Rentals* or *Granada*, both listed in the directory under local locations. To subscribe to the available channels such as CNN, MTV and SKY, contact *British Sky Broadcasting*; 0171-705-3000.

**NOTES**

# Chapter Five: Transportation and Travel

## PUBLIC TRANSPORTATION

The best way to get to know London is on foot. Buy a good street guide and off you go! Just remember, the traffic will be coming from the opposite direction and pedestrians do not have the right of way except at a zebra crossing. Zebra crossings are marked with black and white stripes across the road and a flashing yellow light. Always look both ways but particularly to the right.

For speedier travel, the bus and underground (commonly called the *tube*) systems can take you almost anywhere you want to go. Free maps of the underground and bus routes are available at all ticket offices of London Transport. The routes of both are clearly marked with a colour coding system. If you take the bus or underground regularly, check with London Transport for the most economical ticket scheme. The number for general enquiries is 0171-222-1234. Currently a 'travel card' can be purchased weekly, monthly, quarterly, biannually and annually at newsagents and underground ticket windows. In addition, a one-day travel card is available after 09.30 a.m. weekdays and all day Saturday and Sunday. All travel cards can be used on buses, trains and tubes in the London area. The underground, buses and trains do not operate on Christmas Day.

### Underground (Tube)

In order to purchase an underground ticket, you can go to the ticket window and ask for a ticket to your destination. You can avoid possible delays at the ticket booth by using the ticket machines that exist in many stations. Signs are posted over the machines, listing fares. Some older machines require exact change. You must keep the ticket and hand it in at your destination. Fares are based on the distance travelled, although children under five ride for free and children under 16 and adults over 60 are entitled to reduced fares. The underground operates from 05.15 until approximately midnight daily with reduced schedules on Sunday and holidays. Rush hours are 08.00 to 09.30 and 16.30 to 19.00. Smoking is not allowed on the underground trains or in the stations. Dogs are allowed to travel on the underground. There are often a few stations that are closed due to construction so it is wise to check with the station before you begin your journey. A pocket map of the entire tube network is available free from most underground ticket windows.

London is divided into six concentric zones for both bus and tube fares. The more zones you cross, the higher the fare. There is a wide variety of ticket categories; the London Transport Booklet 'Tickets', available at underground ticket windows, will help you determine your fare.

## Buses

Buses are less expensive than the underground but can be slower in heavy traffic. Buses have different timetables on Sunday and holidays but some run throughout the night. Most bus stops have notices indicating which buses stop there and their route. Some stops are 'request' stops and these are marked with red signs. For a 'request' stop, you must signal the driver to stop the bus. On the older 'two man buses' you take your seat and the bus conductor will come to you for your fare which is again determined by the distance travelled. Hold on to the ticket, so that you will not be asked to pay again. Many buses are now 'one man buses' where you pay the driver as you enter. 'Hoppa' buses are smaller minibuses which cover short hops throughout London. The view from the top of a double decker bus is a delightful way to see London. Bus maps are usually available at most underground ticket windows.

*The Red Arrow* buses offer a limited stop or express service between Victoria, Waterloo, London Bridge and Liverpool Street stations and major shopping and business areas. On Red Arrow buses the exact fare must be paid on entry as no change will be given.

*The London Country Buses*, the Green Line, are green in colour and serve communities within a 40 mile radius of Central London. There are stops within London, indicated by green bus stop signs. If a Green Line bus goes in your direction, you may take it. The fare is still based on the distance travelled. Call *London Country Bus Service Limited* for additional information:

| | |
|---|---|
| London Country South-West | 0181-668-7261 |
| London Country North-West | (01923) 673121 |
| London Country North-East | (01707) 376582 |
| Kentish Bus | (01474) 325533 |

*National Express Coaches* link London with other cities in England and Wales. Consult the *National Express Office*, 13 Regent Street, SW1 4NR; 0171-730-0202. *Scottish Citylink Coaches*, 298 Regent Street, W1R 6LE; 0171-730-0202, are part of the government owned Scottish Bus Group connecting London with cities in Scotland.

## Trains

*British Rail* links the major cities in Britain with modern, high speed trains. It also maintains commuter lines between the cities and outlying areas. Tickets can be purchased at the ticket office of any train station or at most travel agencies. British Rail offers first and second class travel to most areas. It also offers various ticket schemes, such as cheap day return (round trip), excursion, season, family railcard, etc. You should ask about the most economical way to get to your destination before purchasing a ticket. As with the underground, train tickets are handed in at the destination.

British Rail also maintains a 24-hour 'dial and listen' timetable service from which you can obtain timetables and fare information for major destinations. It also has general enquiry numbers for all of the areas it serves. This information is located in the telephone directory, under British Rail. The passenger train service information numbers for British Rail stations in London are:

All numbers are prefixed by 0171 -

| | | | |
|---|---|---|---|
| Blackfriars: | 928-5100 | Liverpool Street: | 928-5100 |
| Cannon Street: | 928-5100 | London Bridge: | 928-5100 |
| Charing Cross: | 928-5100 | Marylebone: | 262-6767 |
| Clapham Junction: | 928-5100 | Paddington: | 262-6767 |
| Euston: | 387-7070 | St. Pancras: | 387-7070 |
| Fenchurch Street: | 928-5100 | Victoria: | 928-5100 |
| Holborn Viaduct: | 928-5100 | Waterloo: | 928-5100 |
| King's Cross: | 278-2477 | | |

Note:    The above numbers are usually engaged. Hint: Try phoning first thing in the morning.

Trains for various destinations depart from different stations as follows:

*The North*
Euston
King's Cross
Marylebone
St. Pancras

*The South*
Blackfriars
Cannon Street
Charing Cross
London Bridge
Victoria
Waterloo

*The East*
Fenchurch Street
Liverpool Street

*The West*
Paddington

*The Continent*
Liverpool Street
Victoria
Waterloo    (see page 65)

**Motorail**

British Rail provides motorail services for passengers to transport cars, motorcaravans, and trailers to parts of northern England and Scotland. Overnight motorail trains contain sleeping cars. It is advisable to book early, because this service is very popular. If you wish to book space for your car or a sleeper, ring (01345) 090700. British Rail stations that have motorail services are:

Euston (Edinburgh, Aberdeen, Carlisle,
    Inverness, Stirling):                           0171-922-6459
Bristol (Edinburgh):                              (01272) 2911001

Information regarding French Motorail Services can be obtained from: SNCF French Railways, 179 Piccadilly, W1V ABO; 0171-409-3518.

### Taxis

The familiar black London taxi, now occasionally in other colours, is the most expensive but often the most convenient form of transportation. Taxis are controlled strictly by law and all areas within Central London are regulated by meters. During periods of fare increases and before meters are adjusted, your fare may be higher than the meter indicates but new fares will be explained and posted inside the cab. It is customary to tip 10 to 15 per cent for short journeys.

Taxis are limited by law to carrying four adults (two children are counted as one adult). One can hail a taxi which has its 'for hire' sign lighted on the roof, queue at an appointed taxi stand or ring one of the taxi companies (listed in the Yellow Pages under 'taxis'). London also has 'mini-cabs' (also listed under 'taxis') that are unlicenced and cannot be hailed in the street.

It is important to negotiate a mini-cab price when you book and it is helpful to have a good idea of where you are going, as mini-cab drivers are not required to know London streets and directions. Standards and prices vary, so it is advisable to use a mini-cab service recommended by a friend.

If you use a reputable taxi company, and become comfortable with them, not only will they offer a courier service (pick up and delivery of goods, packages and food), but they will also take your children to and from school and home or wherever necessary. Personal and corporate accounts can be set up.

## DRIVING IN BRITAIN

Owning a car is not essential in Central London because of the excellent public transportation. If you prefer the convenience of a car, you can buy, lease or rent a vehicle easily. It is strongly recommended that you purchase and read *The Highway Code* (available in most bookshops) which outlines the British driving regulations before beginning to drive in Britain. The differences just begin with driving on the left-hand side of the road!

When deciding to have a car in Central London, you should consider the following. Traffic and congestion are problems, as in any other major city, and petrol is expensive. Parking is limited to car parks and meters for non-residents in certain areas. Street parking in those areas is only possible for residents with permits. Parking violations may result in fines, towing or the 'Denver clamp', all of which involve considerable expense and inconvenience. On the other hand, having a car makes picking up groceries and other bulky items easier and getting out of the city for a weekend more convenient.

In the unfortunate case of 'getting clamped', you can call *Clampbusters* at 0171-735-7253. For an annual fee plus a service charge they will unclamp your car, deliver it to your home and handle the paperwork.

### Car Parks

If you are not fortunate enough to locate a parking meter on the street, you may opt for a car park. Blue signs with a white 'P' direct you to public parking in unfamiliar surroundings. They can be expensive but are usually quite safe and reliable if you must travel by car. They are often rather far apart. Listed below are three of the most central.

| Drury Lane Car Park,<br>Parker Street<br>WC2B 5NX<br>0171-242-8611 | Selfridges Ltd.<br>Orchard Street<br>W1H OHB<br>0171-493-5181 | Barbican Centre Garage<br>Silk Street<br>EC2Y 8DS<br>0171-638-4141 |
|---|---|---|

Car park procedures can be confusing. Before leaving your car take a minute to investigate. A sticker procured from the machine must be attached to the windscreen in a 'Pay and Display' car park. Some car parks operate on a two-ticket system. Before returning to the car, one inserts the entry ticket (received at the entrance barrier) into the meter, pays the amount due, receiving an exit ticket to be inserted at the exit barrier. Many car parks are not attended, so have plenty of change on hand to operate the systems.

**Purchasing a Car**

Purchasing a car is expensive in Britain but there is a good market for second hand cars. The London evening papers, Sunday papers, specialized car magazines, *The American* and the American School in London monthly newsletter are all good sources. There is also a monthly magazine called *the Motorist's Guide to New and Used Car Prices*. Both the AA and the RAC will thoroughly inspect and value second hand cars for their members, for a fee.

If you plan to return to the U.S. within a year, there can be tax advantages and other savings in buying a car made to American safety and environmental specifications. If you plan to bring your American car to Britain, you must consider the safety and environmental specifications that may require you to make substantial alterations to your automobile here. For example, unleaded petrol is available, but not required, in Britain. If you are 'green minded', almost any car dealer or garage will convert your car from leaded to lead-free for a minimal charge. The exception to this is the car that is six or seven years old.

**Leasing a Car**

Leasing of cars by companies is a common practice in Britain and dealers can supply details of the various lengths of time and conditions. Car rental firms provide the usual services. Cars with manual transmission are common and less expensive to rent. Hertz, Avis, Godfrey Davis, Europcar, Kenning and Travelwise are well known rental agencies.

**Insurance**

Third party insurance is compulsory and it is advisable to have comprehensive insurance as well. 'No claim' reductions and other options are available. You might bring a letter from your previous insurance agency stating that you are entitled to 'no claim' insurance. It is recommended that you contact several insurance companies regarding types of coverage and cost. You should also have a clear understanding with your insurance company regarding claims and the kind of licence you possess.

**Driving Licences**

It is important to obtain a proper driver's licence, as driving without one is illegal and will affect your insurance. *The Department of Transport's Driver and Vehicle Licensing Centre*, Swansea SA6 7JL; (01792) 782341, has issued guidelines, *'Driving in Great Britain as a New Resident or Overseas Visitor'* (D385):

> If you hold a valid driving licence or International Driving Permit (and are not barred from driving in Great Britain) you may drive here for 12 months those vehicles covered by your licence. If you are here as a visitor the 12 months begins on the date that you last entered Great Britain. If you are a new resident, the 12 months begins on the date you took up residence.
>
> At the end of the 12 months you must hold a valid British driving licence if you wish to continue driving here. Application for a licence must be made on form D1. Copies can be obtained from most post offices. Our leaflet D100 explains at Section A whether you may apply for a full or provisional licence. You should allow at least three weeks for the licence to be issued.
>
> If you are entitled to apply for a full Great Britain licence you should send proof of your entitlement with the application form. Make sure that you apply within one year of coming to live here if you wish to exchange an EEC licence.
>
> You may take a driving test before or after the 12 month time limit has expired providing you hold a driving licence which entitles you to drive here. If you need to pass a driving test, it would be advisable to apply for one well before your time limit expires as there are sometimes delays in obtaining a test appointment.

There are many firms offering driving lessons. The best known is the *British School of Motoring* (BSM), which has many branches. Another firm is the *London School of Motoring*, 112 Brixton Hill, SW2 1AH; 0181-674-8211. The school can advise you as to the requirements, handle applications and instruct you in the different techniques. Examples of the different techniques include putting the gear into neutral and the handbrake on whenever the car is stopped, and feeding the steering wheel around rather than crossing one hand over the other when turning. *Your Driving Test* published by the Department of Transport is also a useful tool. It lists available driving instructors and test centres, and breaks down the driving test components.

The driving test itself consists of an eye test, an oral test on the *Highway Code* and a 20 to 30 minute driving test. There is no limit to the number of times that it can be taken. If you wish, the driving school instructor will accompany you to the test and acquaint you with the test route. It is important to remember that if you take the test on a car with automatic transmission, your licence will be restricted to automatic transmissions. If, however, you take the test on a manual transmission car, your licence will be valid for both manual and automatic automobiles. Once you have obtained a British driving licence it does not have to be renewed until you reach the age of 70.

If you wish to expedite the application process, you might state that you are willing to take the test at any time and at any location.

**Maps**

Even London taxi drivers and natives keep good maps of London in their automobiles. Some of the most useful are *London A to Z, Nicholson's London Street Guide, Geographer's* and *One Way London*.

**Automobile Associations**

You may consider joining the AA (Automobile Association) or the RAC (Royal Automobile Club) for emergency services, as there is no other way of ensuring service in an emergency. These organizations also offer breakdown insurance for trips to the Continent and can even provide legal service in court.

*The Automobile Association*, Fanum House, Basing View, Basingstoke, Hants. RG21 2EA; (01256) 20123.

*The Royal Automobile Club*, 130 St. Albans Road, Watford, Herts. WD2 4AH; (01923) 233543.

If you are a member of Triple A (AAA) in the U.S., your membership can be transferred to the AA here in the U.K.

**Road Tax**

A compulsory Road Tax must be paid each year for each car. Upon paying your Road Tax, you will receive a round sticker which is to be displayed inside your windscreen. If you are buying a car through a dealer, he will generally take care of this detail as part of the sales procedure. If you have brought a car with you to the U.K., forms are available at your local Post Office branch. Annual renewal forms will be sent to you.

**M.O.T.**

If your car is over three years old, you must have an M.O.T. test each year to prove its 'roadworthiness'. Garages are licensed by the Ministry of Transport to give this test and generally can do it in 24 hours, or while-you-wait. There is a fee for this service. You must present this certificate along with proof of insurance when paying your Road Tax.

## Garages

While all garages are different, do not be surprised if you have to book weeks in advance in order to get your car serviced or repaired.

## Petrol Stations

Petrol stations in Britain will <u>not</u> honour U.S. gasoline company credit cards. They will accept Visa, Access and sometimes Diners Club and American Express. Some stations offer personal accounts, payable monthly. Petroleum companies in the U.K. do not issue credit cards for individual users.

## Resident's Parking

In many boroughs you are entitled to purchase a Resident's Parking Permit (check with your town hall for eligibility). This means you can park in areas reserved for residents only. These areas are patrolled regularly by traffic wardens and fines are given if you are in a restricted area without the proper parking permit. Resident parking regulations are usually in effect Monday through Friday from 08.30 to 18.30, Saturday from 08.30 to 13.30. The times vary from borough to borough. To obtain a permit, check with your local town hall.

## Accidents

What to do if you have a car accident, as advised by *The Consumer's Association*. Keep a copy of these instructions in your glovebox should you, unfortunately, need them.

1.  <u>Stop</u>: The law requires you to stop and stay for a reasonable time. You must also give your name and address to anyone involved or affected by the accident.

2.  <u>Get the other driver's information</u>: Name, address, phone number, insurance company, make and registration number of car.

3.  <u>Write down</u>: The names and addresses of witnesses and their vehicle registration numbers.

4.  <u>DO NOT discuss what has happened</u>: If you admit liability, offer apologies or payment, or take the blame, your insurance company may refuse to settle.

5.   Call the Police:  If anyone has been injured, if you've damaged anyone's property (including animals), if you think the other driver has committed an offence, or if you are sure you are not to blame.

6.   Write down what has happened:  Injuries to persons, damage to vehicles, state of traffic, weather and road surface conditions, identification of other vehicles involved, what was said.

7.   Make a sketch map:  Which includes direction of travel, position of cars, any skid marks, road signs, or positions of witnesses.


## FOREIGN TRAVEL

The opportunity to travel throughout the United Kingdom and Europe is one of the great advantages of living in London.

There are guidebooks, brochures and package tours for every holiday imaginable.  A package tour can be arranged for inexpensive or luxurious holidays and includes air fare for either a scheduled or charter flight and hotel accommodation - B&B (bed and breakfast) or half board (breakfast and another meal). Package tours may include airport transportation, sightseeing trips, private accommodation in a villa, ski chalet, or apartment and car hire.

You can book package tours through any travel agency or tour operator. Some of the well-known tour operators are Thomas Cook, Thompson, Horizon, Global and Blue Sky.

*The British Travel Centre*, 12 Regent Street, SW1Y 4PQ; 0171-730-3400, is open between 9.00 and 18.30, Monday to Friday and 10.00 to 16.00 on Saturday and Sunday. (During the summer they often extend their hours, so you may want to call ahead).  The Centre provides travel information and booking services for tickets, accommodation, events and entertainment throughout the British Isles.

It is normally advisable to book package holidays, or make your own arrangements, well in advance, especially for peak holiday times. School and traditional holidays, such as Christmas and Easter, long weekends and the month of August are popular holiday times.  Most English, Europeans and Americans take their holidays in August; it may be wise to avoid this busy month, especially for trips to resort areas and major European cities. If you have the flexibility, you can opt for a late booking, making enquiries and booking just a few weeks or even days in advance. Prices drop considerably when airline seats, reserved hotels or ski chalets are not filled to capacity.

Check with your travel agent to determine the most economical way to travel as there are numerous categories of air fare available. Each category has various conditions and it is necessary to comply with all conditions in order to be eligible.

## Ticket Brokers

These companies offer charter flights at a discount. Charter flights are linked to package tours, but ticket brokers will sell tickets on a seat-only basis.

You will find ticket broker and tour operator advertisements in Sunday and daily newspapers.

## Bucket Shops

These sell unofficially discounted air tickets and offer great reductions on air fares to the Continent, Asia and elsewhere. Bucket shops deal in surplus seats which the airlines are unable to sell through retail offices and travel agencies. Found in unremarkable offices in side streets, bucket shops post discounted fares in the window. They also advertise in the classified sections of newspapers. A good bucket shop will only require a nominal deposit. You should check with the airline to make sure you are listed on the passenger list.

You can call *The Air Travel Advisory Bureau* 0171-636-5000 when wanting to know which travel agencies can give better rates to certain destinations.

Always check into the conditions of the discount fares, which may include a required length of stay and cancellation charges. You may want to purchase travel insurance to cover you in the event of cancellation. It is recommended to use only IATA or ABTA approved brokers as many holiday makers have been left stranded when some of the less reliable companies have suddenly folded.

## Travel Agents

The names of a few travel agents:

Abercrombie & Kent      0171-730-9600

Trailfinders            0171-938-3366 (long haul)
                        0171-938-3232 (European and Trans-Atlantic)

Supertravel             0171-962-9931

## AIRPORTS

There are five airports conveniently located close to London, the largest of which is Heathrow. Check the London telephone directory for additional information.

Heathrow Airport
Hounslow, Middlesex TW6 1JH
0181-759-4321 (flight enquiries)

The underground (Piccadilly Line) may be taken all the way to Heathrow. Trains run every four to eight minutes. Journey time is roughly 50 minutes.

For arrival and departure information you can call the specific terminals:

| | | |
|---|---|---|
| Terminal 1: | British and Irish airlines: | 0181-745-7702 |
| Terminal 2: | European airlines: | 0181-745-7115 |
| Terminal 3: | Inter-continental airlines: | 0181-745-7412 |
| | | 0181-745-7067 |
| Terminal 4: | British Airways inter-continental flights: | 0181-745-4540 |

You can also receive flight information from the specific air lines. These numbers are listed in the phone book under BAA (British Airport Authority).

Gatwick is located south of London and has regular services to over 40 destinations.

Gatwick Airport
Gatwick, West Sussex RH6 ONP
(01293) 535353

Fast non-stop trains (Gatwick Express) depart Victoria Station every 15 minutes, 05.30 to 22.00; five times an hour 22.00 to midnight; and hourly midnight to 05.00. Journey time is about 30-40 minutes.

There are two airports situated north of London:

Stansted Airport
Essex CM24 8QW
Bishop's Stortford
(01279) 680500

Luton Airport
Luton, Bedfordshire LU2 9LY
(01582) 405100

Transportation and Travel
64

Serving the City of London:

City of London Airport
Docklands E16 2QQ
0171-474-5555

**Parking/Car Valet**

*Fly Away*; 0181-759-1567 is a unique service at Heathrow Airport for the traveller who parks their car in the car park at Heathrow. Not only will they collect your vehicle from you at the terminal, but will have it waiting for you upon your return. For an additional fee they will wash, wax and service your car while you are away.

For a complete listing of Airlines consult the London Yellow Pages under "Airlines".

**CHANNEL TUNNEL**

There is now a high speed train link between the U.K. and the Continent which greatly reduces the time needed to travel from London to the Continent, with or without your car.

For more information contact:

*Eurostar* (passengers only). Leaves from Waterloo with destinations to: Paris (Gare du Nord), Brussels (Gare du Midi) and Lille (Europa). Telephone: 0181-784-1333 for information and reservations.

*Eurotunnel Shuttle* (passengers and cars). Folkestone to Calais. Telephone: (0990) 353535 or (0990) 700800.

# Chapter Six:  Healthcare

## BRITISH HEALTH SYSTEM

### The National Health Service

Great Britain has a government subsidised National Health Service (NHS) and as a resident of the U.K., by the deduction of National Insurance from your salary you are entitled to medical coverage at little or no additional cost. This service includes:

* Doctor care - with home visits if necessary
* Dentistry and orthodontia
* Specialist and hospital care
* Eye tests and glasses
* Child-care clinics for under fives
* Family planning services

This service is also available to foreign visitors on an emergency basis. British taxes paid by you or your employer go towards these services so eligibility should be checked. Advice about eligibility is available from the *Department of Health and Social Security (DHSS)*. The head office is located in Richmond House, 79 Whitehall, London SW1A 2NS. Health enquiries telephone 0171-210-4850. Social security enquiries telephone 0171-210-5983. In addition there are offices located in all London boroughs and telephone numbers are listed in the telephone directory under 'Health and Social Security, Department of'. *The Citizens' Advice Bureau* provides free information and advice about the NHS. Check the telephone directory for the nearest office location or ask at a local library.

The NHS produces several leaflets explaining its different services. They are available from social security offices, family doctors and through the *Health Publications Unit*, Storage and Distribution Centre, Manchester Road, Heywood, Lancashire OL10 2PZ;  (01706) 366287.

### NHS Registration

All permanent U.K. residents are eligible to register with the NHS. Eligibility for temporary residents depends on whether you or your spouse is paying British income tax and National Insurance. For an expatriate and his/her family, the individual's company will often obtain a NI (National Insurance) number which is needed in order to apply for NHS registration. If this is not the case, you may obtain a NI number by applying in person at one of the DHSS offices. Bring your passport to the office (and marriage certificate if name on passport differs from that of husband) and the necessary tax payer identification paperwork from your or your spouse's employer. The DHSS will in turn issue you a NI number.

To obtain a NHS number, you must register with a local doctor (known as a G.P.) who has vacancies for NHS patients. (Note: not all G.P.s handle NHS patients, some handle strictly private patients). It is up to the discretion of the G.P. to register temporary residents with the NHS. If the G.P. decides to accept you as a patient, he will take your personal details including your NI number and length of stay in the U.K., and then apply to the local Family Health Service Authority (FHSA) for your NHS number.

Call your borough's FHSA for the names, addresses, and telephone numbers of G.P.s in your area. Lists of doctors are available at local libraries, main post offices, Community Health Councils, and Citizens' Advice Bureau. Local chemists (drugstores) may have a list, but they are not permitted to make specific recommendations.

There are often waiting lists for many NHS doctors. As some doctors see their quota of NHS patients and then take on others on a private basis, the doctor may suggest you see him privately and go on his NHS waiting list. Within the NHS, for medical attention other than general family care, you must be referred by your G.P. to see a specialist. Known in the U.K. as a consultant, this doctor is anyone other than a G.P. Most specialists practice under the NHS and on a private basis.

A drawback of the NHS is that if your complaint is not an emergency, you may be required to wait before receiving attention (this includes non-emergency operations). In these instances, consulting a private doctor may be an advantage as there would be no waiting list. Under certain circumstances, both NHS and private doctors are willing to make house calls.

In the U.K., specialists and general practitioners are addressed as 'doctor'. Surgeons, however, including dental surgeons, obstetricians and gynaecologists, are referred to as 'Mister', 'Mrs.' or 'Miss'. The "surgery" or "operating room" in a hospital is called a "theatre", and the office of a medical professional is called a "surgery". In some instances the surgery is located in a home instead of a clinic or office building.

## PRIVATE MEDICAL CARE

An option to NHS medical care is private treatment. Although much more costly, it allows you to have control over when treatment should take place and who should perform it. Most doctors will agree to see patients privately. The Consular Section at the U.S. Embassy has a list of doctors available, and although the Embassy cannot make specific recommendations, it can be a starting point. The best references are personal recommendations from business colleagues, friends and neighbours.

---

Additionally, there are several privately staffed and run hospitals in the London area. These facilities are available to private care patients only. These hospitals are usually modern, offer private rooms, and overall good facilities. They may not be, however, as fully staffed or offer the wide spread emergency care of the NHS hospitals. Many large NHS hospitals, such as St. Mary's and Queen Charlotte's offer private wards, where limited semi-private and private rooms are available for private patients.

Employee sponsored group health plans issued in the U.S. may be extended to the U.K. with employer consent. Any questions regarding extent of coverage should be directed to the Personnel Office of your employer. You may wish to consider subscribing to an English form of medical insurance. BUPA, WPA and PPP are three of the most popular plans. The *Which Report*, a consumer magazine published by the Consumer Research Association, gives a factual comparison of each plan. This report is obtainable by contacting the Consumer Research Association at 0171-486-5544.

## NHS AND PRIVATE SERVICES

While the choice of private or NHS treatment for major operations is not to be taken lightly, for many minor concerns or maintenance type examinations, NHS clinics are reliable and close to home.

It is a very good idea to visit your local NHS health centre to become familiar with the facilities and services available to you. These will include ante-natal clinics and classes, baby clinics, under-5 clinics, health visitor programmes, family planning, marriage guidance counsellors, well-woman clinics, well-man clinics, travel vaccinations, physiotherapy, dietetic advice, chiropody, and social workers.

### Maternity Services

It is necessary to become a patient of an obstetrician promptly. Your G.P. can recommend an obstetrician.

If you decide to go with the NHS, you will have free care throughout your pregnancy and delivery. In the case of a normal delivery, the NHS provides a midwife to attend your birth along with an obstetrician and full medical support staff on call at the hospital in case of complications. You will have a private birthing room, but during recovery you will be on an NHS ward which usually has 4 to 8 beds. Do not expect a private or semi-private room unless you have made arrangements in advance to pay an extra fee for a private room if one is available at the time of your delivery.

A midwife is a specialist in normal pregnancy, birth, and the post-natal period. As well as doing the ante-natal checks, she can deliver your baby, perform ultrasound scans, and care for you once you have had your baby. She may work in the hospital or be based in the community. In some areas, you can book directly with a midwife instead of your G.P. Telephone the Director of Midwifery at your local hospital and ask if there is a midwives clinic or a G.P./midwives clinic in the community.

Traditionally, you are booked under a consultant at the hospital and receive your ante-natal care from members of his team, assisted by midwives. You visit the hospital for all your ante-natal care, and you are delivered by labour ward midwives and the obstetrician on duty at the time you arrive to deliver your baby. Although the consultant leads the team, unless your pregnancy is complicated, you may never actually see him.

However, there are now other options for delivery within the NHS. Call your local hospital or speak to your G.P. to see whether these options are available in your area:

*Shared Care* - You visit the hospital two or three times during your pregnancy and for any special tests. The rest of the time you are cared for by your G.P. and/or your community midwife. When you go into the hospital to have your baby, your baby will be delivered by hospital midwives.

*Midwives Clinic* - Most of your ante-natal care is done by a team of midwives at the hospital who may work in teams under a consultant. Your baby is then delivered by the same team of midwives, who take care of you on the post-natal ward too.

*G.P./Midwife Care* - Your ante-natal care is done by your G.P. or community midwife at the surgery or local health centre. When you go into labour, you are cared for by community midwives and your G.P. is informed. If complications arise, you will be transferred to consultant care.

*Domino Scheme/Midwife Care* - Your ante-natal care may be shared between the community midwife and your G.P., or done by the community midwife at the surgery or local health centre. The midwife may visit you at home for ante-natal checks, and you may go to the hospital for any special tests. When you go to the hospital to deliver your baby, your midwife or another on her team will attend the birth and provide your post-natal care once you have returned home.

*Home Birth* - Home births are becoming more common in the U.K. as they are gaining support from the medical community. Your ante-natal care may be undertaken entirely by your community or independent midwife with your own G.P. or another doctor acting as back-up. The midwife will deliver your baby at home and also provide your post-natal care.

If you choose private care, you are assured that your obstetrician and a midwife will assist your delivery. In the case of an unexpected emergency situation, there is always an obstetrician on call in both private and NHS hospitals. Private doctors may use both NHS and private hospital facilities. Please note that black cabs may refuse to transport you to hospital once in labour. If you are planning to deliver at a private hospital and need transportation contact the hospital to arrange for a private ambulance. If you call 999 for an ambulance, they must take you to the nearest hospital.

Whether you choose NHS or private care, your choice of hospitals for your delivery will be limited to the hospital or hospitals at which your obstetrician is registered. In the case of a private hospital, accommodation must be reserved much in advance and a deposit made at that time.

In London most large hospitals offer good maternity facilities. Hospitals with exceptional maternity facilities including neonatal intensive care units are:

*Humana Hospital Wellington,* Wellington Place, NW8 9LE; 
    0171-586-5959 (private)

*AMI Portland Hospital for Women and Children*, 209 Great Portland Street, 
    W1N 6AH; 0171-580-4400 (private)

*Queen Charlotte's Maternity Hospital*, 330 Goldhawk Road, W6 XG; 
    0181-748-4666 (NHS/private)

*St. Thomas' Hospital*, Lambeth Palace Road, SE1 7EH; 
    0171-928-9292 (NHS/private)

*St. Mary's Hospital*, Praed Street, W2 1NY; 
    0171-725-6666 (NHS/private)

*Hammersmith Hospital*, Du Cane Road, W12 OHS; 
    0181-743-2030 (NHS/private)

The NHS offers preparatory 'parent classes' at local hospitals and clinics. A listing of independent ante-natal courses and refresher courses for repeat mums is available through your obstetrician. An additional organisation involved in natural birth preparation classes nationwide, is *The National Childbirth Trust* (NCT), Alexandra House, Oldham Terrace, Acton, W3 6NH; 0181-992-8637. The NCT is a not-for-profit organisation formed expressly for the purpose of education for pregnancy, birth and parenthood. They have over 350 branches in the U.K. Contact them for information on what courses are offered in your area.

If you are delivering at a private hospital, ante-natal preparatory classes run by hospital midwives are also available. In addition, see Chapter Seven for a further listing of privately run ante-natal preparatory classes.

### Paediatrics

Your local health clinic or G.P. offers a full service of paediatrics, as well as *Child Health Clinics*, which specialize in children only. Check with your local DHSS for one close to you. The following services are available.

1.  Immunisations and boosters as necessary.

2.  Developmental checks (i.e. hearing, eye sight, weight, height) at 6 weeks, 8 months, 18 months, three years and 4 years (pre-school). The service then continues via the school system.

3.  Child psychotherapy, educational psychology for learning and behaviour problems, speech therapy and orthoptists.

4.  Health Visitors who pay house calls to answer any questions you may have, discuss problems, remind you of injection dates, and help orient you to local play groups, and registered childminders in the area.

All clinics have emergency numbers to be used after hours and many G.P.s will make house calls in emergency situations.

### Dentistry

Lists of NHS dentists are posted in the same fashion as NHS doctors. As an NHS dental patient you are expected to pay 80 per cent of the cost of the work done. The most you can be asked to pay for all that needs to be done during one course of treatment is £275.00. Expect to be asked to pay all or part of the charge in advance. Before each and every visit you must ascertain that the dentist will treat you as an NHS patient, otherwise you could be treated as a private patient and asked to pay the full cost of the treatment. You are automatically entitled to FREE dental health care if you:

1.  Are under 18 years of age, or a student under 19 years of age and still in full-time education.

2.  Are expecting a baby and were pregnant when the dentist accepted you for treatment.

3.  Have had a baby during the 12 months before your treatment began.

For further information, consult *NHS leaflet D.11.*

### Ophthalmics

Your sight can be tested only by a registered ophthalmic optician (optometrist) or an ophthalmic medical practitioner. If you want to find an optician, go to your local library for a list of registered opticians in your area, ask at your local Citizens' Advice Bureau or look in the Yellow Pages under "Opticians".

Free eye tests are available to people under 16 years of age or under 19 years of age and still in full-time education.

The optician MUST give you a prescription (or admission that you do not need glasses), even if your sight has not changed. You cannot be asked to pay for your eye test until you have been given your prescription. Further, you are under no obligation to buy your eye glasses from the same optician who gave you the test. Your prescription is valid for 2 years.

For further information, consult *NHS leaflet G.11*.

### Counselling

It is not always easy to get information about where to go for counselling locally, though it is possible to trace counselling organisations and even individual counsellors through your local library, your G.P., the *Citizens' Advice Bureau, the Council for Voluntary Service* and the local *Marriage Guidance Council* (RELATE).

Nationally, the *British Association for Counselling* can supply some information about counselling services and specialist organisations. The association also publishes a nationwide directory of counselling and psychotherapy resources.

Some useful addresses and telephone numbers:

*British Association for Counselling*, 1 Regent Place, Rugby, Warwickshire CV21 2PJ; (01788) 578328/9. They will be able to supply you with a comprehensive list of counsellors in your general area.

*RELATE (National Marriage Guidance)*, Herbert Gray College, Little Church Street, Rugby, Warwickshire CV21 3AP; (01788) 573241.

*The American Church of London*, Tottenham Court Road, W1; 0171-580-2791.

*Youth Access* (Youth Counselling for 16-25 year olds): Magazine Business Centre, 11 Newarke Street, Leicester LE1 5SS; (01533) 558763.

*CRUSE* (Bereavement), 126 Sheen Road, Richmond, Surrey, TW9 1UR; 0181-940-4818.

*Alcoholics Anonymous*, P.O. Box 1, Stonebow House, Stonebow, York YO1 2NJ; London telephone helpline: 0171-352-3001.

*Child and Family Department, Tavistock Clinic*, 120 Belsize Lane, NW3 5BA; 0171-435-71111.

*Westminster Pastoral Foundation*, 23 Kensington Square, W8 5HN; 0171-937-6956.

*The Institute for Family Therapy*, 43 New Cavendish Street, W1M 7RG; 0171-935-1651

**Family Planning**

A full range of family planning services are available through your G.P. or local clinic as well as specific family planning clinics run by the NHS. The larger clinics will offer all types of birth control for both men and women, well-women clinics, psycho-sexual counselling, termination referrals and follow up, and post-natal examinations. All services are available free of charge, on a walk-in basis. For further information contact; *The Family Planning Association*, 27-35 Mortimer Street, London W1N 7RJ; 0171-636-7866.

## REGISTRATION OF BIRTHS

### U.K. Registration

All births taking place in the U.K. must be registered. The hospital where the birth occurs will notify the local Registrar of Births with details of the birth. The parents (mother or father, if the parents are legally married) must register the child at the local office within 42 days of the birth. Either a short or long form of birth certificate is available. The long form is more detailed (and is the only one that the U.S. will accept as proof of the birth). There is a fee for the birth certificates.

### U.S. Registration

Babies born to U.S. citizens must be registered at the United States Embassy within five years of their birth. Parents should contact the U.S. Embassy on 0171-499-9000 to obtain the forms required for registration. The personal documents required are the U.K. long form birth certificate, the U.S. passports of both parents, and a certified copy of the parents' marriage certificate. Divorce decrees or death certificates of all previous marriages, if any, are also required.

Once all the appropriate documentation has been submitted, in person, to the Consul at the U.S. Embassy, the child will be issued with a *Consular Report of Birth Abroad of a Citizen of the United States of America*, and a *Certificate of Birth Abroad*. Parents may then apply for a U.S. passport and a Social Security number for the child. There is a fee, payable by cash only,

Healthcare

for all the above mentioned services.  The entire process requires two to three hours at the Embassy;  however, the baby does not need to accompany the parent.

### Obtaining British Nationality for a Child

In certain circumstances, it will also be possible to register a child born in the U.K. as a U.K. national, and to obtain a British passport for the child.. (This will in no way affect the child's U.S. citizenship).  Parents interested in this possibility should contact the *Nationality Division*, (0151) 236-4723.

### Obtaining Child Benefit

If your child is born in the U.K. you are eligible to claim for a weekly Child Benefit Allowance until your child leaves school.  Child Benefit is a tax free Social Security benefit that does not depend on how much money you earn or on how much savings you have.  For information regarding the Child Benefit Allowance call your local Social Security office.  The phone number and address are in the telephone book under Social Security or Benefits Agency.  Your local baby clinic usually has information as well.

## IMMUNISATIONS AND VACCINATIONS

In order to enter certain countries, when travelling on business or pleasure, immunisations are necessary.  Under the NHS, some immunisations and vaccinations may be carried out by your G.P. free of charge, or with a minimal charge.  The doctor may, however, charge for signing the certificate.

An alternative way to proceed is by using an immunisation clinic. Appointments can easily be made and the clinics are familiar with the necessary battery of injections needed.  Many large travel agents such as *Thomas Cook* (Berkeley Square, W1) and *Trailfinders* (Kensington High Street, W8) have immunisation clinics as well as the main international airlines.  Two particularly good services are:

*British Airways, Immunisation Clinic*, 156 Regent Street, W1;
    0171-439-9584

*The West London Designated Vaccinating Centre*, 53 Great Cumberland Place, W1H 7LH;  0171-262-6456

## EMERGENCY FACILITIES AND CASUALTY UNITS

If an emergency situation does arise, proceed immediately to a hospital with a casualty unit.  It is most important to know the nearest casualty hospital in your area.  IN A SERIOUS EMERGENCY, DIAL 999 and ask for ambulance service.  Emergency service to a residence is provided free of charge by the NHS and is available to anyone, including tourists.  It is interesting to note, however, that in the case of most road traffic accidents, the victim must pay for the ambulance service.

Each police station keeps a list of emergency doctors and chemists who are available on a 24 hour basis.

Almost all London NHS hospitals have a 24 hour casualty unit.  Listed below are some of the largest in different areas.

**London Hospitals with 24 Hour Casualty Units** (Partial List)

**SE1**

*Guy's Hospital*, St. Thomas Street, SE1 9RT;  0171-955-5000
*St. Thomas' Hospital*, Lambeth Palace Road, SE1 7EH;  0171-928-9292

**W2, W9, W10**

*St. Mary's Hospital*, Praed Street, W2 1NY;  0171-725-6666

**W1, NW1, WC1, N1**

*University College Hospital*, Gower Street, WC1E 6AU;  0171-387-9300

**SW1, SW3, SW7, SW10**

*Chelsea & Westminster Hospital*, 369 Fulham Road, SW10; 0181-746-8000

**SW6, W14, W6, W12**

*Charing Cross Hospital*, Fulham Palace Road, W6;  0181-846-1234
*Hammersmith Hospital*, Du Cane Road, W12;  0181-743-2030

**NW3, NW4, NW6, NW8, NW11**

*Royal Free Hospital*, Pond Street, NW3 2QX;  0171-794-0500

**SW13, SW15, SW19**

*Queen Mary's Hospital*, Roehampton Lane, SW15;  0181-789-6611

**Eye Emergencies Only**

*Moorfields Eye Hospital*, 162 Old Street, City Road, EC1 2PD;
    0171-253-3411

**Children's Emergencies Only**

*Chelsea & Westminster Children's Hospital*, 369 Fulham Road, SW10;
  0181-746-8000

**Dental Emergencies Only**

0181-677-8383: A central number open 24 hours daily which can refer you
to a surgery open for treatment - private or NHS.

## AMBULANCE SERVICES

*London Ambulance Service* (NHS);  999
*St. John's Ambulance Service*, NW1 (private);  0171-258-3456
*Acme Private Ambulance Service*, SW7;  0171-373-1820, 0171-370-6692

## LATE NIGHT CHEMISTS

*Bliss Chemists*, 50-56 Willesden Lane, NW6;  0171-624-8000
  (09.00 to 24.00, 365 days a year)

*Bliss Chemists*, 5 Marble Arch, W1H 7AP;  0171-723-6116
  (09.00 to 24.00, 365 days a year)

*Dajani*, 92 Old Brompton Road, SW7;  0171-581-5549 or 0171-589-8263
  (09.00 to 22.00, Monday to Friday;   09.00 to 21.00, Saturday;
  10.00 to 20.00, Sunday)

## DEATH OF AN AMERICAN IN THE U.K.

If an American dies in the U.K., the *American Citizens' Service Branch*,
Consular Section of the U.S. Embassy; 0171-499-9000, can advise on all
procedures, including the undertaker, coroner, and shipment of the body
back to the U.S. The Consular Section of the U.S. Embassy in London has
jurisdiction over England and Wales. For Scotland, contact the *Consular
Section*, 3 Regent Terrace, Edinburgh, Scotland EH7 5BW;  (0131) 556-
83158. For Northern Ireland, contact the *American Consul General*, Queen's
House, 14 Queen Street, Belfast, N. Ireland BT1 6EQ; (01232) 328-239.

# Chapter Seven:  Children

Moving overseas can be made much more daunting by the presence of babies and/or children.  The following information has been compiled by "Mums" who have successfully survived the experience.


**BEFORE YOU ARRIVE**

**Quick Glossary of Terms**

| English | American |
|---------|----------|
| Cot | Crib |
| Dummy | Pacifier |
| Nappies | Diapers |
| Teet | Nipple |
| Pushchair | Stroller |

See Glossary for an expanded list.

**Things which are available in the U.K.:**

Pampers

Huggies

Baby wipes

NUK products

Johnson & Johnson products

Vaseline

Beechnut baby food (fruits, vegetables and juices only)

Ready to Feed or Powder formula, the following brands only:
    SMA
    Cow and Gate
    Wysoy (a Soya milk formula)

Playtex Disposable Bottle components

Multi vitamins

Fluoride drops (the water is not fluoridated in the U.K.)

Breast pumps

Dimotap

**Things which are not available in the U.K.:**

Specialised formulas e.g. low iron or diarrhoea formulas
Enfimil
Similac

Beechnut prepared food containing meat products
Minimam pacifiers
Cherub pacifiers
Desitin
Tylenol
Advil
Benydryl
Triaminic

## Some Reminders

All U.S. linens, including cot linens, are slightly different sizes than their U.K. counterparts.

American or European videos will not work unless you have a multi system VCR. (Sesame Street is broadcast daily on U.K. television).

Electrical outlets are different so monitors will not work without an adaptor and transformer (Tomy and Safe'n'Sound are good U.K. brands).

## Equipment Hire/Nappy and Household Goods Delivery

*Chelsea Baby Equipment Hire*, 7 Openview, SW18;  0181-670-7304

*The Nappy Express*, 128 High Road, N11;  0181-361-4040

*Bare Necessities*, 4 Heathgate, NW11 7AR;  0181-455-0015

## MEDICAL NEEDS

### Illness

You can see a National Health Service (NHS) doctor or a private G.P. for emergency or routine medical care. (See Chapter Six for more details). Paediatricians are considered specialists and generally are seen annually or when referred by a G.P. However, you can make an appointment directly if you wish.

### Medicines

Benylin (cough medicine) is available at chemists but Benydryl (antihistamine) is not. Infant and children's products that contain 'paracetamol' (fever and pain relief) are available in liquid or tablet form as 'Junior disprol', 'Panadol', or 'Calpol'. 'Karvol' can be purchased for children and is a natural decongestant that is inhaled. The British equivalent to 'Pedialyte' is 'Dioralyte' which comes in a packet and is mixed with water.

---

Some other children's medicines and products:-

   Calpol - aspirin substitute containing paracetamol
   Gripe Water - colic and hiccups
   Infacol - colic
   Junifen - fever relief containing ibuprofen
   Phenergan - antihistamine causes drowsiness
   Sudacreme - nappy rash
   Zinc and Castor oil lotion - nappy rash
   E45 creme - dry skin

## PREGNANCY

One of the first decisions you will have to make once you become pregnant
is whether or not you plan to use private or National (NHS) health care.
Most American insurance policies cover private care. British policies such
as 'BUPA' do not consider pregnancy a medical condition and will not cover
private health care costs unless you have a scheduled C-section or other high
risk condition. Ante-natal classes (pre-natal) are available at some hospitals.
Independent of any hospital the following offer ante-natal preparatory classes
and post-natal exercise classes:

*Christine Hill Associates*, Strand End, 78 Grove Park Road,W4 3QA;
0181-994-4349

*Carol Nock*, SRN, SCM, 31 Lauderdale Mansions, Lauderdale Road, W9 1LX;
0171-286-4980

*Lolly Stirk, The Acupuncture Centre*, Ladbroke Grove, W11;
0181-964-1882

*The Kensington Women's Club* and *the NCT* (see below), also organise pregnancy support groups.

See Chapter Six for more information on Maternity Services available in the U.K.

## CHILD CARE

Once you arrive in the U.K. you may wish to take advantage of the wonderful child care that seems to be so much more readily available here than at home. Before deciding on help with the children and/or housekeeping, it would be helpful to be aware of the distinctions between the following:

*Au Pair* - A young girl who comes to live with a family in order to learn the English language. She will help with child care and light housework for up to 30 hours per week in exchange for her room and board and pocket money. She is usually a student and may not speak fluent English.

*Mother's Help* - A non-professional who will do housework and care for children either full- or part-time.

*Nanny* - A certified nursery nurse who holds a Nursery Nursing Examination Board Certificate (N.N.E.B.). She does not do housework or meal preparation for the family but takes care of all needs of the children including their laundry and meal preparation. She can live in or out.

### Agencies

When working with an agency make sure that you have a complete understanding of the fees charged. There are membership fees, engagement fees and booking fees depending on the situation and agency. These fees vary widely. *The Good Nanny Guide* is an indispensable resource book outlining the traditional duties and pay scales of all types of help and it can be found at most book stores. It is advisable to contact more than one agency. Finding a good match for your specific needs will depend on the sort of people a given agency has "on the books" at the time you call. Help can be found to suit most permanent and part-time requirements.

---

*Bliss Service*, 1 Sussex House, Raymond Road, SW19; 0181-946-8705: Au Pairs

*C.A.R.E.*, 71 Fellows Road, N3; 0171-916-0117: Au Pairs

*Childminders*, 9 Paddington Street, W1; 0171-935-2049/3000: Baby-sitters, Light Domestic Help

*Delaney International*, Godalming, Surrey; (01483) 424343: Nannies, Au Pairs, Mother's Helps, Overseas Placements

*Holland Nanny Service*, 27 Holland Park Gardens, W14; 0171-602-2953: Au Pairs, Nannies, Maternity Nursers, Mother's Helps

*Montrose Agency*, 23 Bullescoft Road, Edgware HA8; 0181-958-9209: Au Pairs

*Regency Nannies*, 50 Hans Crescent, Knightsbridge, SW1X ONA; 0172-225-1055: Nannies, Maternity Nurses, Mother's Helps

*Quick Help Agency*, 307A Finchley Road, NW3 6EH; 0171-435-7671: Nannies, Mother's Helps, Au Pairs, Cleaners, Care for Elderly

*Universal Aunts*, P.O. Box 304, SW40; 0171-738-8937: Nannies, Mother's Help, Cleaners, Butlers, Cooks

*The Nanny Service*, 9 Paddington Street, W1M 3LA; 0171-935-3515: Maternity Nurses, Nannies, Mother's Helps, Baby-sitting

*Occasional and Permanent Nannies*, 2 Cromwell Place, SW7 2JE; 0171-225-1555: Nannies, Mother's Helps, Governesses

*Kensington Nannies*, 49-53 Kensington High Street, W8 5ED; 0171-937-3299/2333: Nannies, Mother's Helps: Overseas; 0171-938-5525

Another excellent service for childminders, full or part-time is *"The Lady"* magazine, 39-40 Bedford Street, WC2E 9ER; 0171-379-4717, a weekly publication available at newsagents, listing situations vacant for all domestic help. One also receives a good response by placing ads listing personal requirements.

For recent arrivals to the U.K. or anyone with young children, *The National Childbirth Trust (NCT)* is a tremendous resource (see below).

**The National Childbirth Trust**

The National Childbirth Trust is a non-profit organisation and a registered charity full of excellent information on all matters relating to childbirth and early childhood. They have branches all over London and these can be reached via the main branch which is at: Alexandra House, Oldham Terrace, Acton, W3 6NH; 0181-992-8637. Many of the neighbourhood branches of the NCT have produced wonderful information packs on having a baby in London which can be a great help to a pregnant expatriate.

The NCT branches have also published many helpful books about children in London such as: *Clapham for Kids* and *Chiswick for Kids*. *Under Fives Welcome in and around Westminster* can be obtained from Social Services Department, Westminster City Hall, Victoria Street, SW1E 6QP.

Out of the NCT have sprung many very interesting and helpful groups including: *Parents that Work*, 77 Holloway Road, N7 8JZ; 0171-700-5771 (between 10.00-15.00). They publish the *Working Mothers' Handbook*, an excellent book on the various types of care one can expect to get for children here in London and the costs, interviewing techniques, standard of training and authoritative bodies which oversee these employees whether you want a mother's help, au pair, Norland nanny or a State Registered Nurse.

## ENTERTAINING YOUR CHILD

### Playgroups

*The Kensington and Chelsea Women's Club, The National Childbirth Trust, Hampstead Women's Club*, your local library and your local Health Centre or Clinic are excellent sources for playgroups in your neighbourhood.

### Boat Trips

*On the Thames* to Richmond, the Tower of London, Greenwich, Kew Gardens, and Hampton Court, you can go round trip or one way, returning by public transportation.

*Canal trips* on Regent's Canal and Camden Lock;

*London Water Bus Company* by Warwick Avenue Underground Station, Little Venice; 0171-482-2550.

*Guildford Boat House* (01483) 504494 one - three hour trip and three to 10 day boat hire - Easter to October.

*Jason's Trips*, opposite 60 Blomfield Road, W9 2PA; 0171-286-3428: April to October.

*Jenny Wren*, 250 Camden High Street, NW1 8QS; 0171-485-4433: Early September to late Autumn

Children
84

*Paddle boat rides* in Hyde Park, Regent's Park and Battersea Park. Some parts offer rowing and sailing also.

## Entertainers

Magicians, clowns and mimes will organise children's parties (complete with prizes and favours) or just entertain at your direction. Be sure to book these popular entertainers well in advance (three to four months prior to event) to avoid disappointment.

*Smartie Artie*, 57 Cutenhoe Road, Luton, Bedfordshire LU1 3NB; (01582) 461588.

*Rhubarb the Clown*, 72 Hillside Road, N15 6NB; 0181-800-5009.

*Albert and Friends*, 36 Windermere Court, Lonsdale Road, SW13 9AR; 0181-741-5471.

*Arda Halls*; 0181-969-0154: puppet shows.

*Bob Thingummybob*, 48 Tenby Avenue, Kenton, Harrow, Middlesex HA3 8RX; (0181-907-4606.

*Joey the Clown*; 0181-668-7228.

*Marmaduke* (Impian Productions); 01992-446211.

*Oscar's Entertainers*; 0181-958-8158.

*Party Bus*; 01753-548822.

*Peter Cass - Patchy Peter Clown*, 4 Ash Grove, Hemel Hempstead, Hertfordshire; (01442) 61767.

*Twizzle the Clown*; 0181-748-3138.

*Walligog the Wizard*, Mulin Entertainments; 0181-866-6327.

**Hobbies and Crafts**

*Chelsea Pottery*, 5 Ebury Mews, SW1; 0171-259-0164.
Offers pottery classes. Visitors welcome to studio to watch pottery being made. Ages 5-15. Offers Saturday classes.

*Brass Rubbing*, Available at several churches.
London Brass Rubbing Centre, The Crypt, St. Martin's in the Fields, Trafalgar Square WC2N 4JJ; 0171-437-6023. Westminster Abbey, Little Cloisters, Dean's Yard, SW1P 3NP; 0171-222-2085.

*Paint Pots*, Edith Grove, Chelsea SW10; 0171-702-0433.
Art and music classes for children, 18 months to 6 years.

**Lessons**

Your child's school and parents of his or her classmates are the best references for all types of private instruction but you can generally obtain a full list of tutors in any subject from your local library.

**Music**

*The Royal College of Music*, Junior Department, Prince Consort Road, SW7 2BS; 0171-589-3643: Instruction and recommended teachers.

*London Suzuki Group*, White House, Crooms Hill, SE10 8HH;
0181-858-2311: Teaches the Suzuki method for string instruments to children from the age of four and up.

*Tafelmusik*, Box 13, 47-49 Chelsea Manor Street, SW3; 0171-376-5201:
Creative movement and music classes, 6 months to 3 years.

## Dance

*Cherry Childe School of Dancing*, Hodford Hall, Hodford Road, NW11;
0181-458-6962: Ballet and tap. Boys and girls 3 plus.

*Rona Hart School of Dance and Drama*, Rosslyn Hall, Willoughby Road,
Hampstead, NW3; 0171-794-7146: Ballet and movement.

*Stella Mann School of Dance*, 343A Finchley Road, NW3;
0171-435-9317; Ages 3 and up for ballet, 5 plus for modern and tap.
Boys and girls.

*Vacani School of Dancing*, 38 Harrington Road, SW7 3ND;
0171-589-6110: 2 years plus, boys and girls.

## Gymnastics

*American School in London*, 2-8 Loudoun Road, NW8; 0171-722-0101.

*Crechendo*, Active Learning Classes for children 4 months to 7 years.
Centres across London; 0171-259-2727: Classes offer movement,
music, sight and sound experiences.

*Latchmere Leisure Centre* in Battersea, Burns Road, SW11 2DY;
0181-871-7470: Runs music and movement classes.

*London Gymnastics Federation*, 4 Victoria Road, Chingford, E4 6BZ;
0181-529-1142.

*Mini Muscles*, 11 Albert Court, SW7; 0171-235-3857:
Similar to *Crechendo* and *Tumble Tots*, child needs to be walking.

*Swiss Cottage Sports Centre*, Winchester Road, NW3;
0171-413-6490: Has a great baby gym.

*Tumble Tots*, organized work on ladders, tunnels, mats, etc., with music and
songs. Age 9 months to 2 years, and 3 years and up. Many
locations; 0181-959-4261.

## Libraries

Your local library in London is well worth an investigative trip. In addition to
excellent collections of children's books, many have record and cassette
lending programmes and organised activities for children. Many libraries
have story reading for younger children during term time or school holidays.

The library is also a prime source of information on other local happenings for children, especially during the school holidays. Children receive their own lending cards by providing proof of local residence (a letter received at your new address is sufficient). The Information Service based at the Library Association, 7 Ridgmount Street, WC1E 7AE; 0171-636-5543, has a directory of all branches in the London area and will gladly assist you in finding the branch nearest your home.

## Museums

There are countless museums in and around London of interest to children of all ages. The major museums in London have special activities, exhibits and quizzes during school holidays. Ring for information or consult weekly events magazines. See Chapter Thirteen.

## Parks

There are over 80 parks within a seven mile radius of Hyde Park Corner.

*Alexandra Park and Palace*, Wood Green, N22 4AY; 0181-365-2121.
Skating rink, boating pool, children's concerts, miniature golf, adventure playground, play park.

*Battersea Park*, Albert Bridge Road, SW11 4NJ; 0181-871-7530.
Boating lake, zoo, deer park, children's play park (adventure playground), London Peace Pagoda, show greenhouse.

*Bushey Park*, Near Hampton Court is King George recreation ground.
Good value on Sunday afternoons and model boat pond; 0181-9550-1606.

*Clissold Park*, Green Lane, N4 2EY; 0181-800-1021.
Fishing lake, bowling green, adventure playground, croquet lawn, football, tennis, putting green.

*Crystal Palace*, Penge, Thicket Road, SE19 8DT: 0181-778-7148.
Boating, fishing lakes with primaeval animal replicas, bands in summer, adventure playground.

*Greenwich Park*, SE10 8QY; 0181-858-2608.
Deer park, bird sanctuary, Royal Observatory.

*Hampstead Heath*, Parliament Hill, NW3 7HD; 0171-485-4491.
Ponds, concerts in summer, grass skiing, adventure playground, tennis.

*Hampton Court* and *Bushy Park*, Surrey, KT8 9AU; 0181-977-8441.
Famous maze, open March to October, "great vine", ponds and natural farmland. Wild deer in Bushy Park. Playground.

*Holland Park*, W8 7QU; 0171-603-2838.
Tulip and rose gardens, tennis, adventure playground.

*Hyde Park*, W2 2UH; 0171-262-5484.
Lake for fishing, boating and swimming, riding, concerts, fairs.

*Kensington Gardens*, W2 2UH; 0171-723-3509.
Peter Pan's statue, children's playgrounds, round pond for model boats.

*Regent's Park*, London Zoo, NW8 7RG; 0171-724-3363.
Boating lake, bird and rose garden.

*Richmond Park Surrey*, TW10 5HS; 0181-940-0654.
Fish ponds, deer park, golf, riding, polo, football.

*Royal Botanic Garden*, Kew, TW9 3AB; 0181-940-1171.
Lake, aquatic garden, pagoda, Kew Palace, Palm House.

*St. James's Park* and *Green Park*, SW1; 0171-262-5484.
Oldest Royal Park with lake, bridges, bird sanctuary.

*Thorpe Park*, Staines Road, Chertsey, Surrey; (01932) 562633.
Amusement park for children with attractions, shows, rides and exhibits. Open June to September, seven days a week. Other times vary.

**Pools**

Swimming pools offer lessons and regular activities for children as well as special programmes during school holidays. Many facilities have a separate shallow teaching pool for very small children, separate diving areas and wave machines. A list of all swimming pools and their facilities in Greater London may be obtained from The Greater London and South East Sports Council, P.O. Box 480, Jubilee Stand, Crystal Palace National Sports Centre, Ledrington Road, SE19; 0181-778-8600. In Central London be sure to visit:

*Kensington Sports Centre*, Walmer Road, W11 4PQ; 0171-727-9747.

*Chelsea Sports Centre*, Chelsea Manor Street, SW3; 0171-352-6985.

*Latchmere Leisure Centre*, in Battersea; 0181-871-7470.

*Swiss Cottage Sports Centre*, Winchester Road, NW3 3HB;
0171-413-6490.

*The Fulham Pools*, Normand Park, Lillie Road, SW6 4PL; 0171-385-7628.

*Crystal Palace Sports Centre*, Crystal Palace Parade, SE19 2BB;
0181-778-0131.

*Poolside Manor Ltd.* (This pool is private). Lyndhurst Gardens, Finchley,
N3 1TD; 0181-349-1945. Good swimming instruction for 5 months
and older.

*Windsor Leisure Pool*; (01753) 850004. Waterslides, wave machines.

## Riding

London has several equestrian schools. Most of the schools will expect their
students to be properly attired and equipped; check with the school. Both
lessons and hacking are offered.

*Battersea Hippic*, 14A Winders Road, Battersea Park, SW11 3HE;
0171-223-0909.

*Belmont Riding School*, Belmont Farm, The Ridgeway, NW7;
0181-906-1255.

*The British Horse Society*, British Equestrian Centre, Stoneleigh,
Warwickshire, Coventry CV8 2LR; (01203) 696697.

*Richard Briggs Riding Stables*, 63 Bathurst Mews, W2;
0171-723-2813. Ride in Hyde Park.

*Ross Nye Stables*, 8 Bathurst Mews, W2 2SB; 0171-262-3791.

## Scouts

American Boy Scouts and Girl Scouts are alive and well and living in London.
Contact the American School in London; 0171-722-0101. However, you
may choose to have your children participate in English scouting instead
since this is where it all began. Contact:

*Girl Guides Association*, Buckingham Palace Road, SW1 OFT;
0171-834-6242.

*The Scout Association*, Baden Powell House, Queensgate, SW7 5JS;
0171-584-7030.

---

## Sports

Several sport/health clubs offer excellent children's programmes. See Chapter Twelve for more information.

### Little League

*Baseball and Soccer Groups*, Contact the American School in London; 0171-722-0101.

### Skating

*Lea Valley Ice Centre*, Lea Bridge Road, E10 7QL; 0181-533-3156.

*Queen's Ice Skating Club*, 17 Queensway, W2 4QP; 0171-229-0172.

*Alexandra Palace*, Wood Green, N22; 0181-365-2121. Open skating lessons, cafe.

### Theatres for Children

Guildford's *Yvonne Arnaud Theatre* (01483-64571) and Leatherhead's *Thorndike Theatre* (01372-363729) will sometimes have special children's activities on weekends and holidays. Many of the following offer not only performances but also excellent children's workshops.

*Battersea Arts Centre*, Lavender Hill, SW11 5TS; 0171-223-8413. Films, mime shows.

*Croydon Warehouse Theatre*, 67 Dingwall Road, Croydon SW18 3AZ; 0181-680-4060. Plays and shows.

*Little Angel Marionette Theatre*, 14 Dagmar Passage, Cross Street, N1 2DN; 0171-226-1787. Puppet mime shows.

*National Theatre*, South Bank, SE1 9PX; 0171-928-2252. Pantomime and theatre periodically, particularly at holidays.

*Polka Children's Theatre*, 240 The Broadway, Wimbledon, SW19 1SB; 0181-543-4888. Mimes, tricks, sketches and regular theatre for children.

*Puppet Theatre Barge* (floating theatre on Thames barge), Camden Lock, Market Wharf, NW1 8AF; 0171-249-6876. Marionette mime shows and theatre.

*Riverside Studios*, Crisp Road, W6; 0181-748-3354. Shows.

*Screen on the Hill*, 203 Haverstock Hill, NW3 4QG; 0171-435-3366.
Films.

*Tricycle Theatre*, 269 Kilburn High Road, NW6 7JR; 0171-328-1000.
Mime theatre, workshops.

*Unicorn Theatre for Children*, 6 Great Newport Street, WC2 7JA;
0171-836-3334. Theatre, puppets.

**Zoos**

*London Zoo*, Regent's Park, NW1 4RY; 0171-722-3333.

*Chessington World of Adventure*, Chessington, Surrey; (013727) 27227.

*Whipsnade Park Zoo*, Dunstable, Bedfordshire; (01582) 872171.

*The London Butterfly House*, Syon Park, Brentford, Middlesex;
0181-560-7272. A live butterfly zoo.

*Woburn Wild Animal Kingdom*, Woburn Abbey, Woburn, Bedfordshire;
(01525) 290246.


**CHILDREN'S GUIDEBOOKS**

*Nicholson's Children's Guide*, Robert Nicholson Publications Ltd.

*Kid's Britain* by Betty Jerman, Pan Publications.

*Look Out London*, Louise Nicholson, Random House.

*The London Parents' Guide*; 0171-793-1990. Bi-annual publication with a
variety of information from education to entertainment.

**FURTHER INFORMATION**

*BUNAC* (British Universities North American Club), 16 Bowling Green Lane,
EC1; 0171-251-3472. Can arrange work programmes for American
Students visiting the U.K.

*Kidsline*; 0171-222-8070. A phone number which provides information on
current events for children.

*The London Tourist Board*; 0171-730-3488. A good starting point for any
information.

# NOTES

Plant.

CADOGAN
GARDENS

# Chapter Eight: Schools

A primary concern for any family moving to London is how to educate the children. The decision must be based on a number of considerations that might not be relevant in other situations. For example, you must consider how long you plan to reside in England, how old and how adaptable your children are, and whether a change from the American system to the English system would be disruptive or beneficial to your child.

Before you make any decision, you should talk to friends and colleagues with children of similar ages to your own children and visit as many different schools as possible. There are so many excellent alternatives that you should find the best school for your child without too much difficulty.

The first thing that one should know is that there are three systems available:

> State or voluntary aided or grant maintained schools
> Independent or private (fee-paying) schools
> American and international (fee-paying) schools

At all British schools, pupils take exams. It might be helpful to know that GCSE (General Certificate of Secondary Education) exams in numerous subjects are taken at about age 15 and 'A' (for 'advanced') level exams are taken in three subjects at age 17 and 18.

## STATE OR VOLUNTARY AIDED OR GRANT MAINTAINED SCHOOLS

Full-time education is compulsory for children between the ages of five and 16 and is provided free by the government. Children enter primary school at the beginning of the term in which the child's fifth birthday occurs, transfer into a *middle school* or *secondary school* (depending on location) at eight, nine or eleven, then complete their work in *sixth form colleges*. The system is quite confusing to a newcomer and may differ from location to location.

To obtain more detailed information, you should contact:

*The British Council*, 10 Spring Gardens, SW1A 2BN; 0171-389-4383, Education Information Service.

*The Department of Education*, Library and Information Resource Centre, Sanctuary Buildings, Great Smith Street, SW1P 3BT; 0171-925-5040

Or go to your local bookshop and purchase a book entitled *"The Education System in England and Wales"* published by Longmann.

To enrol your child in a London government-run school, you should contact your local education authority.

## INDEPENDENT OR PRIVATE SCHOOLS

Although all independent schools are required to register with the Department of Education, private schools vary in size, facilities and most important of all, philosophy towards education. Entrance into many schools is determined by examination and/or personal interview. Some require long advance notice for admission; some even claim that the child must be registered at birth. Do not be put off by this; nor should you be totally discouraged by being told that there is no place for your child in a particular school. *Gracious* determination has paid off more than once in the past.

Although a very small percentage of students in England attend independent schools, there are over 2,000 to choose from, including local day schools and boarding schools. The boarding school tradition, in fact, is far stronger here than elsewhere and it is quite common for boys to be sent away at eight and girls at eleven. To help you select a day or boarding school there are publications and consulting services, both free and fee-paying, that might be of help.

### Publications

*The Independent Schools Year Book*: Available from: A and C Black, P.O. Box 19, Huntingdon, Cambridgeshire PE19 3SF; (01480) 212666 - £19.99.

*Which School*: A comprehensive directory of independent schools with a geographical directory and advertisements. Revised yearly. Available from Gabbitas, Truman and Thring, Broughton House, 6-8 Sackville Street, Piccadilly, W1X 2BR; 0171-734-0161.

*The Good Nursery Guide*, Sue Woodford, Hutchinson.

*Good Schools Guide*: Harpers and Queen Publication, Ebury Press.

*Choosing Your Independent School*: Annual publication available from Independent Schools Information Service, ISIS National Headquarters, 56 Buckingham Gate, SW1E 6AG; 0171-630-8790 - £6.95 plus p&p.

*The Parents Guide to Independent Schools*: A comprehensive guide to nearly 1,500 schools including maps. Available from SFIA Educational Trust

Ltd., 15 Forlease Road, Maidenhead, Berkshire SL6 1JA; (01628) 34291.

See listings in "Yellow Pages" under Nursery Schools, Schools and Colleges (independent) for additional information.

**Consulting Services**

*Gabbitas, Truman and Thring Educational Trust*, Broughton House, 6-8 Sackville Street, W1X 2BR; 0171-734-0161: Offers a free advisory service on the selection of independent schools and colleges in the U.K. This includes advice on tutors, training courses and language courses. A counselling service for parents and students concerned with any aspect of education including further and higher education is also available. Further details on request.

*The Independent Schools Information Service* (ISIS). For London day schools contact London and South-east regional office, 3 Vandon Street, SW1H OAN; 0171-222-7274. ISIS also has a very helpful advisory service specifically for foreigners entering the British school system: ISIS International Consultancy, 56 Buckingham Gate, SW1E 6AG; 0171-630-8790.

We have listed below a number of private or independent schools known to Junior League of London members. The schools are divided into groups: nursery schools (children to the age of four or five); pre-prep schools (to the age of eight) and prep schools (eight to 11 or 13); and public schools (13 to 18).

Examinations for entry into private secondary schools are given at different ages for boys and girls: the Common Entrance Exam for boys at 13 and the 11 + or Common Entrance Exam for girls at 11, 12 or 13.

**Nursery Schools in London** (boys and girls under five)

In many cases, it is wise to register a child for nursery school at birth. Many nursery schools take children at age two and a half.

*The Acorn Nursery School*, 2 Lansdowne Crescent, W11 2NH; 0171-727-2122.

*Broadhurst School*, 19 Greencroft Gardens, NW6 3LP; 0171-328-4280, (2½ to 5).

*Chelsea Open Air Nursery*, 51 Glebe Place, SW3 5JE; 0171-352-8374, (3 to 5).

*Dr. Rolfe's Montessori School*, 10 Pembridge Square, W2 4ED; 0171-727-8300, (2½ to 5).

*Eaton Square Nursery and Pre-preparatory School*, 30 Eccleston Street, SW1 TLF; 0171-823-6217.

*Garden House School*, 53 Sloane Gardens, SW1W 8ED; 0171-730-1652, (boys 3 to 8, girls 3 to 11).

*Hampshire School Lower School*, 63 Ennismore Gardens, SW7 1NH; 0171-584-3297 (boys and girls 3 to 13).

*Hill House Small School*, 17 Hans Place, SW1X OEP; 0171-584-1331.

*The Knightsbridge Kindergarten 1*, St. Saviours Church Hall, Walton Street, SW3 1RJ; 0171-584-9705.

*The Knightsbridge Kindergarten 2*, St. Andrews Church, Park Walk, Chelsea, SW10 OAU; 0171-352-4856.

*Ladbroke Square Montessori School*, 43 Ladbroke Square, W11 3ND; 0171-229-0125.

*Lansdowne Nursery School*, 2 Lansdowne Crescent, W11 2NH; 0171-727-5092.

*The Maria Montessori School Hampstead*, 26 Lyndhurst Gardens, NW3 5NW; 0171-435-3646 (boys and girls 2½ to 6).

*Miss Morley's Nursery School*, Fountain Court Club Room, Ebury Square, SW1W 9FT; 0171-730-5797.

*Miss Willcock's Nursery School*, Holy Trinity Church Hall, Prince Consort Road, SW7; 0171-937-2027 or 0171-584-9253.

*Northbridge House*, 33 Fitzjohn's Avenue, NW3; 0171-435-2884 or 0171-435-9641 (boys to 13, girls to 11).

*Pooh Corner Montessori School*, Christ Church Vestry, Victoria Road, W8 5RG; 0171-937-1364.

*Rainbow Montessori School*, Pond Square, Highgate, N6 6BA; 0181-348-2434.

*St. Christina's School*, 25 St. Edmund's Terrace, NW8 7PY; 0171-722-8784 (boys to 3, girls 3 to 11).

---

*St. Nicholas Montessori School*, 23-24 Princes Gate, SW7 1PT;  0171-589-3095.

*Thomas's Kindergarten*, 14 Ranelagh Grove, SW1W 8PD;  0171-730-3596.

*Thomas's Kindergarten*, The Crypt, St. Mary's Church, Battersea Church Road, SW11 3NA;  0171-738-0400.

*Young England Kindergarten*, St. Saviour's Hall, St. George's Square, SW1;  0171-834-3171.

Further information on nursery schools from:

*Pre-school Playgroups Association*, Greater London Regional Office, 314-316 Vauxhall Bridge Road, SW1V 1AA;  0171-828-2417.

*Local Town Hall*. Will send list of schools in the borough on request.

**Co-Educational Schools**

*Cameron House*, 4 The Vale, SW3 4AH;  0171-352-4040.

*The Hampshire School*, 63 Ennismore Gardens, SW7 1NH;  0171-584-3297 (boys 4 to 13, girls 4 to 13).

*Hill House International Junior School*, 17 Hans Place, SW1X OEP;  0171-584-1331 (4 to 13).

*Norland Place School*, 162-166 Holland Park Avenue, W11 4UH;  0171-603-9103 (boys 4 to 8, girls 4 to 11).

*St. Christina's School* (see Nursery schools).

*St. Joseph's Roman Catholic Primary School*, Highgate Hill, N19 5NE;  0171-272-1270.

*Thomas's School*, 28-40 Battersea High Street, SW11 3JQ;  0171-978-4224 (boys and girls 4 to 13).

*The Vale School*, 2 Elvaston Place, SW7 5QA;  0171-584-9515 (boys to 8/9, girls to 11).

**Boys' 'Pre-Prep' and 'Prep' Schools**

*Colet Court* (St. Paul's Preparatory School), Lonsdale Road, SW13 9JT;  0181-748-3461 (8 to 13)

*Eaton House*, 3-5 Eaton Gate, SW1W 9BA;  0171-730-9343 (5 to 8).

*The Falcon*, 2 Burnaby Gardens, Chiswick, W4 3DT; 0181-747-8393 (3 to 8).

*The Hall*, 23 Crossfield Road, NW3 4NU; 0171-722-1700 (5 to 13).

*Highgate School*, North Road, N6 4AY; 0181-340-1524 (8 to 18).

*St. Philip's School*, 6 Wetherby Place, SW7 4ND; 0171-373-3944.

*Sussex House*, 68 Cadogan Square, SW1X OEA; 0171-584-1741 (8 to 13).

*Westminster Under School*, 27 Vincent Square, SW1P 2NN; 0171-821-5788 (8 to 13).

*Wetherby School*, 11 Pembridge Square, W2 4ED; 0171-727-9581 (4 to 8).

**Boys' Public Schools** (13 to 18 unless noted).

*City of London School*, Queen Victoria Street, EC4 3AL; 0171-489-0291 (from age 10).

*Dulwich College*, Dulwich, SE21 7LD; 0181-693-3601. Also has a preparatory school but quite far for a child to travel from Central London. (From 8 to 18).

*Highgate School* (see Boys' 'Pre-prep').

*St. Paul's School*, Lonsdale Road, SW13 9JT; 0181-748-8135.

*Westminster School*, 17 Dean's Yard, SW1P 3PB; 0171-963-1003.

**Boarding Schools for Boys**

*Church of England*

| | | |
|---|---|---|
| Charterhouse | Eton | Harrow |
| Marlborough | Millfield | Radley |
| Rugby | Stowe | Winchester |

*Roman Catholic*

| | | |
|---|---|---|
| Ampleforth | Downside | The Oratory |

For additional information on schools contact:

For *Church of England*: Woodard Corp., 1 The Sanctuary, SW1P 3JT; 0171-222-5381. (Ask for the Registrar).

For *Roman Catholic*: Catholic Education Council for England and Wales, 41 Cromwell Road, SW7 2DJ; 0171-584-7491.

**Girls' 'Prep' Schools**

*Channing School*, Highgate High Street, N6 5HF; 0181-340-2328.

*City of London School for Girls*, Barbican, EC2Y 8BB; 0171-628-0841 (to 18).

*Falkner House*, 19 Brechin Place, SW7 4QB; 0171-373-4501.

*Francis Holland*, 39 Graham Terrace, SW1W 8JF; 0171-730-2971 (4 to 18).

*Garden House School* (see Nursery Schools).

*Glendower Preparatory School*, 87 Queen's Gate, SW7 5JX; 0171-370-1927 (to 12).

*Kensington Preparatory School for Girls*, 17 Upper Phillimore Gardens, W8 7HF; 0171-937-0108 (5 to 11).

*Lady Eden's School*, 39-41 Victoria Road, W8 5RJ; 0171-937-0583 (3½ to 11).

*Pembridge Hall Preparatory School for Girls*, 18 Pembridge Square, W2 4EH; 0171-229-0121.

*Putney High School*, 35 Putney Hill, SW15 6BH; 0181-788-4886 (5 to 18).

*Queen's Gate School*, 131-133 Queen's Gate, SW7 5LE; 0171-589-3587 (4 to 18).

*St. Paul's Girls Preparatory School*, Bute House, Luxemburg Gardens, W6 7EA; 0171-603-7381 (5 to 11).

**Girls' Public Schools**

*City of London School for Girls* (see above).

*Francis Holland*, 31 Park Road, NW1 6XR; 0171-723-0176.

*More House School*, 22 Pont Street, SW1X OAA; 0171-235-2855.

*Putney High School* (see above).

*Queen's Gate School* (see above).

*St. Paul's Girls' School*, Brook Green, W6 7BS; 0171-603-2288.

**Boarding Schools for Girls**

*Church of England*

| | |
|---|---|
| Benenden School | Cheltenham Ladies College |
| Heathfield School | Roedean School |
| St. Mary's Calne | St. Mary's Wantage |
| Sherborne School | Wycombe Abbey |

*Roman Catholic*

| | |
|---|---|
| Marymount School | St. Mary's, Ascot |
| Woldingham School | |

For additional information on schools contact:

For *Church of England*: Woodard Corp., 1 The Sanctuary, SW1P 3JT; 0171-222-5381. (Ask for the Registrar).

For *Roman Catholic*: Catholic Education Council for England and Wales, 41 Cromwell Road, SW7 2DJ; 0171-584-7491.

**Co-educational Boarding Schools**

More and more boys' schools are taking in girls at sixth form and lower. Please consult the publications listed earlier in this chapter for up-to-date information.

---

Finally, if your child has attended English schools through 'A' level exams and wishes to attend an American university, few English schools will have prepared him/her for the required S.A.T. exams or be able to help him/her select the best university for his/her needs. A service available in London that might be of help is the *Fulbright Commission* (U.S./U.K. Educational Commission), 6 Porter Street, W1M 2HR; 0171-486-1098 (11.00-17.15). Open to the public 10.30-13.00, 14.00-16.30. First time enquirers should send s.a.e. with request for information pack. Comprehensive library of U.S. College catalogues also available.


## AMERICAN SCHOOLS

The schools listed below provide a traditional American college preparatory curriculum. A few allow students to take GCSE and 'A' level exams as well. Schools are co-educational unless otherwise indicated.

### Kindergarten - 12th Grade

*The American School in London* (known as 'ASL'), 2-8 Loudoun Road, NW8 ONP; 0171-722-0101. The oldest American School in London with a large modern campus. High percentage of American students.

*The American Community Schools* have 2 campuses: ACS Surrey, 'Heywood', Portsmouth Road, Cobham, Surrey KT11 1BL; (01932 67251) and ACS Middlesex, 'Hillingdon Court', 108 Vine Lane, Hillingdon, Uxbridge, Middlesex UB10 OBE; (01895 259771). The schools are 65 per cent American. The other 35 per cent represents more than 40 different nationalities.

*Southbank International School London*, 36-38 Kensington Park Road, W11 3BU; 0171-229-8230. Day, grades 1-13. Small progressive, 20-30 per cent American.

*The TASIS England American School*, Coldharbour Lane, Thorpe, Surrey TW20 8TE; (01932) 565252. Day and boarding. Grades pre K-12. A branch of The American School in Switzerland. Large percentage of the students are American.

*U.S. Forces Schools in West Ruislip*; (01895) 632870 (K-6th grade), and High Wycombe, Buckinghamshire, London Central High School; (01494) 463356 (7th-12th grade). Children of civilian parents are only admitted as day students if there is space available and must pay tuition.

**Upper Grades Only**

*Marymount International School*, George Road, Kingston-upon-Thames, Surrey KT2 7PE; 0181-949-0571. Girls only, day and boarding, grades 6-12. Offers International Baccalaureate in addition to American curriculum.

**American Colleges in the U.K.**

Numerous American colleges and universities have branches or campuses in the U.K. In addition to these, there are several independent colleges offering American-type university courses on a part or full-time basis. Information on these schools is available from:

*The U.S. Embassy*, Grosvenor Square, W1A 1AE; 0171-499-9000.

*The American* (newspaper), Subscription Department, 114-115 West Street, Farnham, Surrey GU9 7HL; (01252) 713366. Periodically lists up-to-date information on American educational institutions.

*The Fulbright Commission* (see above).

## INTERNATIONAL SCHOOLS

*The International School of London*, 139 Gunnersbury Avenue, W3 8LG; 0181-992-5823. Day school, ages 4 to 18. Prepares students for GCSE exams and then offers a two-year international education in preparation for the International Baccalaureate.

## NATIONAL SCHOOLS

A number of schools provide education for students of specific nationalities with classes taught in their native tongue.

**French**

*Ecole Francaise de Londres*, 59 Brook Green, W6 7BE; 0171-602-6871. Day, co-ed, ages 4 to 11.

*Lycée Francais*, 35 Cromwell Road, SW7 2DG; 0171-584-6322. Day, co-ed, ages 5 to 18/19.

**Greek**

*Hellenic College of London*, 67 Pont Street, SW1X OBD; 0171-581-5044. Day, co-ed, ages 3 to 17.

---

## German

*The German School*, Douglas House, Petersham Road, Petersham, Surrey
   TW10 7AH; 0181-948-3410. Day, co-ed, 5 to 19.

## Japanese

*Japanese School*, 87 Crayfield Road, W3 9QQ; 0181-993-7145. Day, co-
   ed, ages 7 to 12.

## Norwegian

*The Norwegian School in London*, 28 Arterberry Road, Wimbledon,
   SW20 8AH; 0181-947-6627. Co-ed, ages 3 to 16.

## Swedish

*Swedish School-Society in London Ltd.*, 82 Lonsdale Road, SW13 9JS;
   0181-741-1751. Day, co-ed, ages 4 to 16.


## REMEDIAL SCHOOLS

*Center Academy, The Development Center*, Napier Hall, Hide Place, Vincent
   Square, SW1P 4NJ; 0171-821-5760. Day school and part-time
   students, ages five and one half to 17. diagnostic and remedial
   services for children with learning disabilities. Associated with *The
   Developmental Center*, St. Petersburg, Florida.

*The Franklin Delano Roosevelt School*, Avenue Road, NW8 6HZ; 0171-722-
   4490. State maintained school for physically disabled children, ages
   two to 29.

*Fairley House*, 44 Bark Place, W2 4AT; 0171-229-0977. Treats children
   with dyslexia and other learning disabilities until they are able to return
   to conventional schools. Ages 5 to 12. Also gives full assessments
   and educational advice.

*Dyslexia Teaching Centre*, 23 Kensington Square, W8 5HN; 0171-937-
   2408. Offers one-to-one tuition for adults and children.

For additional information on other dyslexia centres:

*The British Dyslexia Association*, 98 London Road, Reading, Berkshire
   RG1 5AU; (01734) 668271.

**And finally...**

A note to you parents still trying to decide whether to keep your children in the American school system or to switch to the British system. After much debate, endless debate, we decided that the best way to convey the differences was to ask two parents to express their own, personal feelings on the subject; one whose children are in an American school and one whose children are in an English school. We hope that their views will prove helpful.

§ § §

*For those living in London, there are some fine American schools in the area. If your children have started in the American system, or if they plan to return to it, it may be preferable for them to continue in the American tradition. There are major curriculum differences between the American and English systems resulting in adjustments for the children when they come to London and again when they leave. The American schools eliminate this problem since they strictly adhere to the school programme in the United States as well as the calendar year.*

*The turnover in the American schools is about 33 per cent each year, about the same as the turnover of Americans living in London. The advantage of this is that a child entering the school for the first time does not feel 'new' as there are many others in the same situation. American schools are very aware of the adjustments the children are required to make and the social programmes provided at the schools reflect an understanding of this problem.*

*As is the case in public schools in the United States, self-expression and creativity are encouraged in American schools overseas.*

*A high school student who is planning to return to the States for college will be able to take the necessary tests and receive college guidance.*

*American schools have a high percentage of Americans attending but many nationalities are represented. Consequently, there is a deeper learning adventure through shared experiences of classmates who have lived all over the world.*

§ § §

*The English school system is a traditional one and justifiably famous for its strong discipline and emphasis on the basics of education; reading, writing and maths. Proper education begins at an early age, children are expected to read at four and French and Latin are begun well before secondary school. Rote learning is standard, which might strike some as a bit stifling, but one can rest assured that the child will be well equipped for handling more complex work later.*

*In and around London there are numerous fine English schools, some large, some small. One can choose a school that is predominantly English or one that caters to the needs of the international community. Some are emphatically academic, some offer a well-rounded curriculum with excellent programmes in sports and/or music. Some schools are co-educational, but many of the finest schools remain single sex schools. The choice is yours.*

*Most English schools require students to wear uniforms. While this may seem costly initially, the outfits are usually sturdy and practical. Uniforms also ensure that your child will be reasonably well 'turned out' and eliminate all competition to be 'best dressed'. Most mothers love uniforms.*

*Perhaps the most intangible advantage of sending your child to an English school is that he/she will have a profound English experience. He/she will fully participate in English life, probably develop exemplary manners, learn to keep a stiff upper lip in most situations and speak with an English accent, guaranteed to charm everyone 'back home'.*

# Chapter Nine:  Cooking and Food

The best way to approach cooking in a foreign country is to focus on all the marvellous new tastes and new ingredients available and not on the few products that can't easily or inexpensively be obtained. The main difference between cooking in the U.S. and the U.K. is that, while Americans measure ingredients, the British weigh them. Although you can bring a few favourite cookbooks to use you may find some brand name products difficult to obtain or expensive, so a better way to start would be to purchase one of the many excellent British cookbooks (perhaps a good housewarming present). *Delia Smith's Cookery Course* and the *Reader's Digest Cookery Year* are both comprehensive whilst Elizabeth David's books are an education in French and Mediterranean foods.

The attempt of this chapter is to familiarize the U.K. cook with the local vocabulary, the mechanics of cooking, places to buy special ingredients and items that may be helpful to pack and bring along. To begin, a calculator for the kitchen may be your most important tool. Secondly, your U.S. roasting pans, baking sheets, jelly-roll pans, and casseroles, etc. may be too large for your U.K. oven, so before you begin to cook, measure the length and depth of your new oven.

## LIQUID MEASURES

|  | oz. | ml. |
|---|---|---|
| U.S./U.K. 1 teaspoon | 1/6 oz. | 5 ml. |
| U.K. 1 dessert spoon | 1/3 oz. | 10 ml. |
| U.S./U.K. 1 tablespoon | 1/2 oz. | 15 ml. |
| U.S. 1 cup | 8 oz. | 240 ml. |
| U.K. 1 cup | 10 oz. | 300 ml. |
| U.S. 1 pint | 16 oz. | 470 ml. |
| U.K. 1 imperial pint | 20 oz. | 585 ml. |
| U.K. gill | 5 oz. | 150 ml. |

In measuring dry ingredients such as flour or sugar, when using a British recipe remember to weigh the items as the ingredients will be listed in ounces or grams. (Remember 8 ounces of two different ingredients may have distinctly different volumes).

Once you start saving British recipes from magazines and newspapers, having a set of British measuring utensils and a scale on hand will make cooking much less time consuming.

## DRY MEASURES

|  | U.S. | U.K. | Metric |
|---|---|---|---|
| Flour | 1 cup | 5 oz. | 140 gms. |
| Sugar | 2 Tbsp. | 1 oz. | 25 gms. |
|  | 1 cup | 8 oz. | 225 gms. |
| Brown Sugar | 1 cup | 6 oz. | 170 gms. |
| Breadcrumbs or Nuts | 1 cup | 4 oz. | 115 gms. |
| Butter | 2 rounded Tbsp. | 1 oz. | 25 gms. |
|  | 1 cup (2 sticks) | 8 oz. | 225 gms. |
| Yeast | 1 U.S. pkg. (2½ tsp.) | ¼ oz. | 7 gms |

Butter is sold in the U.K. in blocks weighing 250 grams. If approximately 3/8" is cut off one end of the block, the remainder will equal 2 sticks of butter in a U.S. recipe. (One stick of U.S. butter contains 8 U.S. tablespoons).

## FURTHER CONVERSIONS

(See page 255 for special "tear out" copy of this information).

| | |
|---|---|
| Ounces to grams | Multiply by 28.35 |
| Quarts to litres | Multiply quarts by 0.95 |
| Grams to ounces | Multiply grams by 0.03527 |
| Pounds to grams | Multiply pounds by 453.6 |
| Pounds to kilograms | Multiply pounds by 0.4536 |
| Kilograms to pounds | Multiply kilograms by 2.2 |
| Centigrade to Fahrenheit | Multiply C by 1.8 and add 32 |
| Fahrenheit to Centigrade | Multiply F by 5, subtract 32 and then divide by 9 |

Lastly, one 'stone' as a measure of weight, equals 14 pounds.

Cooking and Food

# COOKING TEMPERATURES

| C | F | Gas Mark | Description |
|---|---|---|---|
| 110 | 225 | ¼ | Very Slow |
| 125 | 250 | ½ | Very Slow |
| 140 | 275 | 1 | Slow |
| 150 | 300 | 2 | Slow |
| 165 | 325 | 3 | Moderate |
| 180 | 350 | 4 | Moderate |
| 190 | 375 | 5 | Moderate/Hot |
| 200 | 400 | 6 | Moderate/Hot |
| 220 | 425 | 7 | Hot |
| 230 | 450 | 8 | Hot |
| 240 | 475 | 9 | Very Hot |

You will find this oven chart useful. (See page 255 for special "tear out" copy).

# BAKING PRODUCTS

### Flour

*Plain Flour;*     a soft wheat flour used as a pastry flour and for thickening sauces and gravies. Substitute for American all-purpose flour.

*Superfine Plain Flour;*     a light white flour used in British recipes for cakes with delicate texture.

*Self-raising Flour;*     a flour with the raising agent already included, requiring no extra baking powder.

*Strong Flour;*     is a white flour of a high gluten content for breads and puff pastry.

*Malted Wheat Flour;*     is a brown flour with malted wheat grains for a distinctive texture and nutty flavour.

*Wholemeal Flour;*     wholewheat flour for baking and breads.

**Baking Powder**

Most American baking powder is double-acting so when using an American recipe use double the amount of English baking powder. Conversely, remember to use only half the amount of U.S. baking powder if brought from the States and following a British recipe.

**Yeast**

¼ ounce package of dry Fleischman's is equal to ¼ ounce or 7 gram "sachet" of dry yeast available in the U.K.

**Sugar**

English granulated sugar is more coarse than its U.S. counterpart and is widely used but not recommended for baking.

| | |
|---|---|
| *Caster Sugar;* | is a finer granulated sugar which dissolves easier and is ideal for baking or desserts. |
| *Demerara Sugar;* | is a coarse, crunchy, brown sugar. It is good in coffee or over cereals but is not a substitute for brown sugar in baking. |
| *Muscovado Sugar;* | is a soft and dark sugar used in cooking fruit cakes, baked bean casseroles, and barbeque sauces. |
| *Soft Light and Dark Brown Sugars;* | are comparable to U.S. style brown cane sugar |
| *Vanilla Sugar;* | is a white sugar flavoured with vanilla and is used in custards and puddings. *Note:* vanilla extract is not widely available in the U.K. You will see vanilla essence in the stores but this will not have quite the same flavour. |
| *Preserving Sugar;* | has slow dissolving large crystals used for jam and jelly making. |
| *Sweetex;* | is a 'Nutrasweet' substitute. |

**Gelatin**

Aspic Powder or 'gelatin' is closest to 'Knox Unflavoured Gelatin'. Gelatin in the U.K. comes powdered and in packets called sachets. The amount of gelatin in sachets varies from brand to brand. As a guideline, 1 tablespoon (15 gms) should set 16 oz. (480 ml) of liquid. The contents of 1 package of 'Knox Unflavoured Gelatin' is the equivalent of 1 tablespoon or ½ ounce.

*Note*: U.K. 'jello' is called 'jelly' because it comes in a concentrated gel and may not work as well in U.S. cake recipes and other baking.

## Chocolate

*Bitter;*  not unsweetened, but a dark bittersweet covering for candy.

*Plain;*  can be compared to the U.S. semi-sweet.

*Cake Covering*
*Chocolate;*  an icing or frosting chocolate.

*Note*: There is no equivalent to 'Bakers Unsweetened Cooking Chocolate' in the U.K. Although you can find it at Selfridges, Europa, and in the American speciality food stores it is expensive. For unsweetened chocolate, substitute 3½ tablespoons of unsweetened cocoa plus 1 tablespoon of butter or margarine to equal 1 oz. square of chocolate.

## DAIRY PRODUCTS

### Milk

Milk can be purchased in supermarkets or grocers' shops but is usually delivered to your door in returnable glass bottles (one size only: Imperial pint, 20 ounces).

All milk in the U.K. is pasteurised but not all types are homogenized. For home delivered milk, the types of milk can be distinguished by the colour of the bottle top.

*Red Top;*  pasteurised, homogenized whole milk, the one most similar to U.S. whole milk. Average fat content, 4%.

| Silver Top; | pasteurised, but not homogenized whole milk. The cream rises to the top of the bottle. Average fat content, 4%. |
| *Red and Silver Striped Top;* | semi-skimmed milk. Closest to U.S. 2% milk. Good first substitute after baby formula. |
| *Gold Top;* | also known as Channel Island milk. Average fat content, 5%. |
| *Checked Top;* | skimmed milk. Average fat content, 0.1%. |
| *UHT (Ultra Heat Treated)* or *Long Life Milk;* | keeps for several months unopened. Also comes in a powder. |

## Cream

Cream in England has a higher fat content than in the U.S.

| *Half Cream;* | used like half n'half. |
| *Single Cream;* | 18% butterfat, slightly thicker than half cream. |
| *Double Cream;* | 48% butterfat. Poured over fruits and desserts. If whipped too much, double cream quickly turns to butter. |
| *Sour Cream;* | 18% butterfat. A little thinner than U.S. (Fromage Frais is a good substitute). |
| *Spooning Cream;* | 30% butterfat. Not suitable for coffee or whipping. Spoon over fruit and desserts. |
| *Whipping Cream;* | 40% butterfat. Suitable for recipes that call for heavy or whipping cream. |
| *Clotted Cream;* | a speciality from the West of England, very thick, used on fruits and desserts and on scones in "cream teas". |

## Butter and Margarine

Butter and margarine are widely available in several different varieties. Butter is supplied by different dairy regions in the U.K., Ireland, and France and the difference in taste is a matter of personal preference. Margarine made from 100% polyunsaturated fats is sold in grocery stores along with butter/margarine blends.

## Cheese

English cheeses range from Gloucester (say Gloster) which is mild, to Blue Stilton which is blue-veined and has a strong sharp flavour. In between there is Lancashire (LANKashur) which grates easily and is good in cooking and Leicester (LESter), a mild good substitute for American cheddar. English and Irish cheddars are wonderful all-purpose cheeses that range from mild to mature. Danish Havarti can be substituted for Monterey Jack and the Danish also make a mozzarella. (Monterey Jack is available at Selfridges). Cheese speciality shops include Paxton & Whitfield on Jermyn Street as well as Harrods.

## Eggs

Most eggs are brown and are graded according to size; size 1 is the largest while size 7, the smallest. Most British cooks prefer size 2 or 3 in baking and cooking. Free range eggs are produced from hens that are allowed to graze naturally.

## FRUITS AND VEGETABLES

### Berries

Strawberries, blackberries, and blueberries are available as well as the following berries grown in the U.K.:

*Black Currants*;                    Ideal for jam and pies.

| | |
|---|---|
| *Gooseberries;* | Unavailable outside Europe and great in pies when sugar is added. |
| *Red Currants;* | Very tart but great when mixed with sweeter fruits. |

## Apples

| | |
|---|---|
| *Bramley's Seedling;* | Good baking or cooking apple. |
| *Cox's Orange Pippin;* | Small and tasty. |
| *Golden and Red Delicious;* | Same as U.S. |
| *Granny Smith;* | Crisp, tart, green apple. |
| *Early Worcester Pearmain;* | Early red dessert apple. |
| *Laxton's Superb;* | Good sweet apple. |

Supermarkets now often stock more of the old fashioned English dessert apple varieties, which are well worth trying.

## Pears

| | |
|---|---|
| *Conference;* | Long and narrow, good for cooking. |
| *Doyenne de Comice;* | Large and pale green. |
| *William;* | Most like the American Bartlett. |

## Oranges

| | |
|---|---|
| *Clementine;* | Similar to Satsuma but smaller. |
| *Jaffa;* | Large and mild. |
| *Spanish Blood Orange;* | Smaller, excellent eating orange. Has a red streaked skin and flesh. |
| *Seville;* | Bitter, often used to make marmalade. |
| *Satsumas;* | Similar to tangerine, excellent, no seeds. |
| *Mineola;* | Cross between a mandarin and an orange. |

## Tomatoes

| | |
|---|---|
| *American Beefsteak;* | Are available only at certain times of the year. |
| *Marmande;* | Tomatoes from France or Holland are a large slicing variety which can be more readily obtained. |
| *Cherry;* | Tomatoes are available year round. |
| *Ailsa Craig;* | Old-fashioned tasty salad tomato. |

Generally, English tomatoes are grown small, hard and regularly shaped.

## Lettuce

| | |
|---|---|
| *Cos;* | Similar to Romaine. |
| *Webb's Wonder;* | A little like Iceberg. |

---

| | |
|---|---|
| *Garden or Round Lettuce;* | Comparable to our Bibb. |
| *American Iceberg;* | Available in most stores. |
| *Endive or Frisee;* | Curly endive. |

## MEATS

### Beef

To begin, most beef is English but Scotch beef is available at most butchers for a higher price and is considered to be of better quality.

A roast, on or off the bone, is called a *joint*. Ground Beef is called *mince*. Minced steak is the best quality as it is the leanest. The meat will taste slightly different as most cattle are not corn fed as they are in the U.S..

Steaks for grilling are *fillets* (pronounced 'fill-it') or *entrecôte* steaks which are similar to the U.S. Sirloin. A U.S. flank steak is called a *skirt of beef* and is similar to a U.S. London Broil.

For a Pot Roast ask for *topside, silverside or brisket*. Corned Beef is known as *salt beef.*

### Lamb

British spring lamb is a real treat and unsurpassed for taste but New Zealand lamb is less expensive. Lamb is available in chops, rack, cutlets, leg roasts and shoulders.

### Pork

Pork roast as well as chops, tenderloin, and spareribs (called American or Chinese spareribs) are all cuts that are easily found in supermarkets.

*Gammon* is one of the best and most expensive of hams while York ham is also of high quality. *Bradenham and Smoked French* ham is similar to Smithfield country ham. A wide variety of bacon is available smoked or unsmoked. For the familiar breakfast slice ask for *rashers* without the rind or *streaky bacon*, streaked with fat and lean. U.K. sausages have a high cereal content, and each region has its own distinctive blend of pork, beef, and spices.

Cooking and Food

117

## Poultry

A wide variety of poultry is available including free-range chicken, corn fed chicken, French chicken, and in larger supermarkets turkey, duck and game birds may also be found. Some British chickens are raised on fish meal and smell and taste slightly different. If you prefer, ask for grain-fed or free-range chickens.

## FISH

White sea fish are divided into two types, round and flat.

*Flat fish*: plaice, skate, halibut and flounder. Lemon and Dover sole are delicate white fish with quality good after April. *Round fish*: bass, cod and haddock. Salmon, best in June, July, and August can be purchased as steaks or fillets and trout is also available at fishmongers and supermarkets.

*Note*: When buying fresh fish, look for brightness, prominent eyes and red gills. The fishmonger will scale, clean and fillet a fish if asked.

*Shellfish*: There is a large range of shellfish available from fish shops, and specialist Food Halls whilst more and more supermarkets now have their own fish and shellfish counters. Look out for crabs, mussels, scallops, lobsters and oysters in their season.

## "TO MARKET, TO MARKET"

### Supermarkets

Safeway, Sainsburys, Tesco and Waitrose all have a large choice of competitively priced supermarkets throughout Britain especially in London they offer a wide range of products from other countries. In addition, do try your local butcher, fishmonger, baker and greengrocer where you will find a more personal service and begin to feel a part of your neighbourhood.

| | |
|---|---|
| *Greengrocer & Fruiterer;* | sells fruit, vegetables and flowers. |
| *Butcher;* | sells meat, poultry, game and seasonings. |
| *Bakery;* | sells bread, rolls and pastries. |
| *Fishmonger;* | sells fresh fish |

*Note*: Along with the luxury and charm of the specialised shops, one should be aware of some of the quirks of English food shopping. "Early closing days" mean that small shops are not open on certain afternoons during the week. In addition, many small shops close between 13.00 and 14.00 everyday for lunch. Many shops and supermarkets are now open on Sundays. The Europa chain is usually open late, on Sundays and holidays and supplies American and international products.

Stores can be incredibly overcrowded and run out of items quickly the day before a holiday or the Saturday before a Bank Holiday Monday. Few shops have packers or personnel to take your groceries to your car. It will take some time to master the art of manoeuvring your grocery cart ('trolley') through the store and to your car. Most stores provide plastic carrier bags for groceries and some charge for their bags. There are no brown paper bags. To pay for your groceries by cheque you need a cheque-guarantee card (see Chapter Three). This card allows you to write a cheque for up to £50.00. Some guarantee cards are now also automatic bank debit cards and the amount of your groceries will be automatically deducted from your bank account.

### Department and Speciality Stores

Department stores also offer a large range of foods and products in their 'food halls'. An international assortment can be found at Harrods, Selfridges and Fortnum & Mason. Marks & Spencer, under the brand name 'St. Michael', is Britain's finest chain for ready prepared, high quality food. Although the food is expensive in department stores, they are an additional place to go for speciality items and American products. Additionally, Harrods and Selfridges offer home delivery.

**Farms**

For the freshest fruit, pick your own. There are several 'pick-your-own' farms within the confines of the M25. It is advisable to ring each farm for directions, opening times and available crops. Many times extra items like farm fresh eggs, bread and honey are also available. A day of picking your own fruits and vegetables is a great family outing. Listed below are some of our local favourites:

*Southwood Fruit Farm*, Burhill Road, Hersham, Surrey;
(01932) 220808

*E. Brill & Sons, Peterly Manor Farm*, Great Missenden;
(01494) 863566

*Aldborough Hall Farm*, Aldborough Road North, Aldborough Hatch, Essex;
0181-597-6540

*Blackbirds County Fair*, Kemprow, High Cross, Near Watford, Herts.;
(01923) 853771

*Garson Farm*, Wintersdown Road, West End, Esher, Surrey;
(01372) 464389

*Hewitts Farm*, Chelsfield, Orpington, Kent;
(01959) 534666

*Parkside Farm*, Hadley Road, Enfield, Middlesex;
0181-367-2035

*Netherhouse Farm*, Sewardstone Road, Chingford, London E4;
0181-524-7217

**Health Foods**

The Ministry of Agriculture, Fisheries and Food (MAFF) publish a booklet called *The Balanced Approach*, on the food additives regularly used in the U.K. A copy can be obtained by writing to the Ministry: *The Balanced Approach, Food Sense, MAFF Publications*, SE99 7TP. To find out more about publications available from the Ministry, you can also ring 0181-694-8862 and ask for 'Inquiries Section'.

*Cranks Health Foods*, Marshall Street W1; 0171-437-2915, have a wide assortment of organic food and ingredients. Cranks also operate several restaurants in the London area. Additionally, *Holland and Barrett* is a chain of health food stores with over 22 shops in the Greater London area.

## INTERNATIONAL FOODS AND SPECIALITIES

### American

If American products are what you are really after, try these stores as well. There should be one close to your new home.

*The American Dream*, 183 New King's Road; 0171-384-3025.

*W. H. Cullen*, many locations in Central London and also Cobham, Claygate, Esher, Leatherhead, Oxshott, Walton-on-Thames and East Horsley.

*Bentalls*, Wood Street, Kingston-upon-Thames; 0181-546-1001.

*Panzer's Delicatessen*, 13-19 Circus Road, NW8; 0171-722-8596.

*Partridges Of Sloane Street*, 132-134 Sloane Street, SW1; 0171-730-0651.

*The One Stop Shop*, Oxford Road (A40), Gerrards Cross; (01753) 885044.

### Chinese

*Loon Fung Supermarket*, 42/44 Gerrard Street, W1; 0171-437-7179.

*Po Sau Tau*, 24 Lisle Street, WC2; 0171-437-6029.

### French

*House of Roux*, 229 Ebury Street, SW1; 0171-730-3037.

*Randall & Aubin*, 16 Brewer Street, W1; 0171-437-3507.

*St. Quentin*, 256 Brompton Road, SW3; 0171-225-1664.

### Greek

*Athenian Grocery*, 16A Moscow Road, W2; 0171-229-6280.

### Italian

*La Picena*, 5 Walton Street, SW3; 0171-584-6573.

*Fratelli Camisa*, 1a Berwick Street, W1; 0171-734-5456.

*Lina Stores*, 18 Brewer Street, W1; 0171-437-6482.

*Luigi's*, 349 Fulham Road, London SW10; 0171-352-7739.

**Kosher**

*Grodzinsky's*, 53 Goodge Street, W1; 0171-636-0561.

Also Panzer's and Selfridges (see above).

**Gourmet**

*Finn's*, Chelsea Green, 4 Elystan Street, SW3 3NS; 0171-225-0733.

*The Pie Man Food Co.*, 16 Cale Street, SW3; 0171-225-0587: 20 Stratford
    Road, W8; 0171-937-3385 and 71 The High Street, Wimbledon
    Village, SW19; 0181-944-1200.

Also Harrods, Harvey Nichols, Fortnum & Mason and Marks & Spencer's
Food Halls.

For recommended cookbook and cookware shops see Chapter Eleven.


## LIQUOR STORES, WINE SHOPS AND PUBS

### Off-Licences

These are shops which are licensed to sell beer, wine and spirits for
consumption 'off' the premises. The best known chains are Oddbins, Peter
Dominic, Thresher and Victoria Wines. Additionally, almost every
neighbourhood has its own local off-licence. Many are incorporated within
small convenience stores that sell everything from crisps to deodorant.

*Majestic Wine Warehouse*, Albion Wharf, Hester Road, Battersea SW11;
0171-223-2983, sells beer and wine by the case, at a discount. Cases can
be mixed and they carry a large selection of French, Californian and
Australian wine. Also for sale are soft drinks, mixers and bar necessities at
a discount. There are 12 other Greater London locations. Call the main
number 0171-736-1113 for the location nearest you.

Most chain food stores have a good selection of wines and beers and some
sell spirits as well.

### Pubs

Pubs and licensed restaurants are entitled to serve drinks 'on' the premises.
Pubs actually fulfil both requirements - you can have a drink there or buy a

bottle to take out - a useful thing to know if you are travelling and picnicking. London pub hours vary with some pubs open all day but generally the hours are 11.00-15.00 and 17.30-23.00. Beware of shorter hours in the countryside and on Sundays in London.

**Wine Bars**

Wine bars serve only wine and offer a limited menu.

## FOOD GLOSSARY

| U.S. | U.K. |
|---|---|
| Almond Paste | Marzipan |
| Bacon | Streaky Bacon or Rasher |
| Baking Soda | Bicarbonate of Soda |
| Beans, Green | Haricots or Runner Beans |
| Beets | Beetroot |
| Beer, dark with bitter taste | Bitter |
| Beer, golden in colour | Lager |
| Biscuit, Baking Powder | Scone |
| Bread | Cob, Split Tin, Bloomer |
| Broil | Grill |
| Cake | Gateau |
| Candy | Sweets |
| Celery Root | Celeriac |
| Chicory | Endive |
| Chips | Crisps |
| Cheesecloth | Muslin |
| Chocolate Chips | Polka Dots |
| Confectioners Sugar | Icing Sugar |
| Cookies | Biscuits |
| Corn Starch | Cornflour |
| Cart, grocery | Trolley |
| Dessert | Puddings |
| Dishwashing Liquid | Washing-up Liquid |
| Drug Store | Chemist |
| Eggplant | Aubergines |
| English Muffins | Crumpets |
| Fish Sticks | Fish Fingers |
| Flank Steak | Skirt of Beef |
| French Bread | Bread Stick |
| (Small Loaf) | Baguette |
| French Fries | Chips |
| Frosting | Icing |
| Fruit Pie | Fruit Tart |
| Gelatin, unflavoured | Aspic Powder or Gelatin |
| Green Onions | Salad or Spring Onions |
| Ginger Snaps | Ginger Nuts |
| Ham | Gammon |
| Hamburger Meat | Mince |
| Hamburger Buns | Baps |
| Hotdogs | Frankfurters |
| Hominy Grits | Maize Meal |
| Kool-Aid | Squash (a concentrate) |
| Jello | Jelly |
| Lemonade | Lemon Squash |

| | |
|---|---|
| Liquor | Spirits |
| Liquor Store | "Off Licence" Store |
| Napkin | Serviette or Table Napkin |
| Nipple (Baby Bottle) | Teat |
| Packet | Sachet or Sleeve |
| Pie, open, single crust, fruit | Flan or Tart |
| Pie Crust | Pastry Case or Flan Case |
| Pits (Cherry, Peach) | Stones, Pips |
| Popsicle | Ice Lolly |
| Potatoes, Baked | Jacket Potatoes |
| Potato Chips | Crisps |
| Raisins, golden | Sultanas |
| Roast (Beef) | Joint |
| Sandwich (w/lettuce, tomato) | Roll (w/salad) |
| Sausages | Bangers |
| Seven-Up | Lemonade |
| Sherbet | Sorbet |
| Shrimp | Prawns |
| Shrimp, Jumbo | Crevettes |
| Snow Peas, Peapods | Mange Tout |
| Squash | Marrow |
| Turnip, Yellow | Swede |
| Vanilla Sauce | Custard |
| White Vinegar | Distilled Malt Vinegar |
| Zucchini | Courgette |

## Other Helpful Terms

### *Kitchen Items*

| | |
|---|---|
| Faucets | Taps |
| Stove Top Burners | Hobs |
| Oven | Cooker |
| Saran Wrap | Cling Film |
| Disposable Garbage Bags | Dustbin Liners |
| Wax Paper | Greaseproof Paper |

### *Foods*

| | |
|---|---|
| "Bubble and Squeak" | A patty made from cabbage and potatoes |
| "Toad in the Hole" | Sausage baked in a batter |
| "Bangers and Mash" | Sausages and mashed potatoes |
| "Clotted Cream" | Thick rich cream to top scones |
| "Branston or Ploughman's Pickle" | A vegetable chutney |
| "Children's Tea" | Children's evening meal |
| "Top and Tail" | Snipping the top and bottom off a fruit or vegetable |

# Chapter Ten:  Services

It is important for people who become residents in England, to realise that in general terms England by many standards is not a consumer orientated society.  Services are certainly available but the attitude of the "providers" can vary enormously.

There are numerous agencies which provide any number of services, but make sure that you understand the fees charged.   In some cases membership, engagement or booking fees can apply.   When employing anyone in the household service section, particularly plumbers, electricians, builders or decorators, be careful, like anywhere else, you can be easily taken advantage of so do your research very thoroughly.  To help you there are a variety of self help avenues you can pursue:

*Talking Pages* (0800 600900) and *Yellow Pages* (divided into different areas).  For household and domestic help try *Focus* (0171-937-0050) or *The Lady*, a weekly magazine.   *Jean Oddy & Co.* (0171-625-7733) is a wonderful resource for locating a wide range of reliable services free of charge.  Local newspapers, shops and libraries can also be sources of useful local information.

The list below is not intended to be inclusive, but it provides some suggestions.

**ANTIQUE AND FINE FURNITURE REPAIRERS
AND RESTORERS**

*Frank Pratt, 27 Finchley Park, North Finchley, N12 9JS;  0181-445-0611.*

*CJ Tracy*;  0181-800-4774.

**ARCHITECT**

*Mary Thum Associates, 30 Carlyle Square, SW3 6HA;  0171-376-8966.
    American architect with U.K. registration and many years practice in
    the U.K.*

**BEAUTICIANS AND FACIALS**

*Violet Adair*, 1B Kensington Church Walk, W8;  0171-584-6944.  Waxing, lash tinting, manicures, facials, etc., in a full service salon.

*Philippa Benson*, 172 Fulham Road, SW10; 0171-351-6526.

*The Green Room*, 165 Kensington High Street, W8; 0171-937-6595 and locations all over London. A full service salon using The Body Shop products.

*Knightsbridge Nail Centre*, 7 Park Close, Knightsbridge, SW1 7QT; 0171-225-3695.

## BURGLAR ALARMS AND LOCKSMITHS

*Banhams*, 233 Kensington High Street, W8 6SF; 0171-937-4311.

*Chubb Alarms*, 96-100 Clifton Street, EC2A 4TN; 0171-247-4321.

*Tara Alarms*, 33 Ebury Bridge Road, SW1W 8QX; 0171-730-0932.

## BUTCHERS

*Charles Ltd.*, Mount Barrow House, Elizabeth Street, SW1W 9PA; 0171-730-3321. Also a fishmonger.

*Curnicks*, 170 Fulham Road, SW10 9PR; 0171-370-1191.

*W. A. Lidgate*, 110 Holland Park Avenue, W11 4UA; 0171-727-8243. Deliver meats throughout London.

## CAR SERVICING

*Concorde Auto Service*, Abbey Motorist Centre, 131-177 Belsize Road, NW6; 0171-328-9549. Car tune-up and servicing.

*Fly Away Valet*, Heathrow Airport; 0181-759-1567. A unique service for the traveller who parks their car in the car park at Heathrow Airport. They collect and return your car and will also wash and service it while you are away. See Chapter Five.

*Kleencars*, 206 Ladbroke Grove, W10; 0181-968-5748 or (01223) 845645 (Mr. Michael Elkins). Car cleaner - repairs - holiday storage.

## CATERERS

*Bourne Street Brownies*; 0181-968-3301 (Sudy Schneider). Real American brownies, blondies, cookies, lemon bars, banana bread, carrot bread, and carrot cake. Wholesale.

*Fiona Dalrymple*; 0171-585-0512. Caters for brunches, lunches, hampers, afternoon teas, parties and banquets.

*Finns*, 4 Elystan Street, Chelsea Green, SW3 3NS; 0171-225-0733. Ready prepared meals made daily.

*Gorgeous Gourmets*, Unit D, Gresham Way, Wimbledon, SW19 8ED; 0181-944-7771. Catering equipment and food for banqueting or small parties.

*HSS Events Hire*, Brownlow House, Brownlow Road, W13 0SQ; 0181-567-4124. Rent out china, linen, cutlery, glassware, furniture, etc.

*Leith's Good Food*, 86 Bondway, SW8 1SF; 0171-735-6303. Any sort of catering.

*New Quebec Cuisine Ltd.*, 13 New Quebec Street, W1H 7DD; 0171-402-0476. Innovative healthy cuisine. Outside caterers.

*The Pie Man Food Co.*, 16 Cale Street, SW3; 0171-225-0587. Also 71 The High Street, Wimbledon Village SW19; 0181-944-1200 and 20 Stratford Road W8; 0171-937-3385.

*Searcy Tansley*, 124 Bolingbroke Grove, SW11 1DA; 0171-585-0505. Catering and hire.


## CHARTERED ACCOUNTANT

*Summers & Co.*, 107 Bell Street, NW1 6TL; 0171-723-7300.


## CLEANERS AND LAUNDRIES

*Jeeves of Belgravia*; 0181-809-3232. Laundry, drycleaning, shoe mending and clothing repair with multiple branches around London with collection and delivery. Definitely the place to send that special outfit.

*Just Shirts*, Unit B6, 6 Bridge Road, Middlesex UB2 4BD; 0181-843-1887. Shirts and drycleaning collected and delivered anywhere in London within 24 hours.

*Look New*, 12 Market Place, Falloden Way, NW11 6JG; 0181-455-2207. Shirts, drycleaning and carpet care with collection and delivery depending on your location.

*Shirt Stream*; 0181-743-9618. Drycleaning and shirt service done within 24 hours. Free pick up and delivery throughout Greater London.

*Smarts Drycleaning*, 104 Parkway, Regents Park, NW1 7AN; 0171-485-3839.

## COMPUTERS AND PHOTOCOPYING

For basic computer supplies check the Yellow Pages. *Computerworld* and *PC World* are possible sources or, alternatively a walk up Tottenham Court Road. If bringing a computer from home make sure it has the correct power supply; a transformer may be necessary.

For photocopying services - *Kall Kwik, Copy Centre* and *Pronta Print* have many outlets all over London.

## DELIVERIES

*Cat Litter Delivery Service*; 0181-950-1963.

*Epsteins*; 0181-450-0888/8424. Delivery of mineral water, juices, soft drinks.

*The Food Ferry*; 0171-498-0827 (Fax 0171-498-8009). A home delivery supermarket which offers same day service, including all groceries, pet foods, baby items, water, beer and will also take bottles/cans etc. for recycling.

*The Friendly Water Co.*; 0181-547-2612. London area delivery.

*Frys of Chelsea*, 14 Cale Street, SW3 3QU; 0171-589-0342. Fruit and vegetables.

---

Milk Delivery - *Express Dairy*, 213 Lower Richmond Road, Putney, SW15 1H5; 0181-788-5735.

Paper Delivery - *Renown Distributors Ltd.*, 17-23 Battersea Bridge Road, SW11 3BA; 0171-223-3199.

## ELECTRICIAN

*A. Nicholas Electrical Installations*, 1-7 Fulham High Street, SW6 3JH; 0171-731-3035.

## FLORISTS

*Jane Packer Flowers*, 56 James Street, W1M 5HS; 0171-935-2673. Unique and creative floral arrangements including floral design school at 3 Lanark Road, Maida Vale, W9 1DD and at 100 Allitsen road NW8; 0171-586-2766.

*Kensington Flowers*, 3 Launceston Place, W8 5RL; 0171-589-6654.

*Molly Blooms*, 787 Fulham Road, SW6 5HD; 0171-731-1212.

*Pot Pourri*, 255 Chiswick High Road, W4 4PU; 0181-994-2404.

*Pugh & Carr*, 26 Gloucester Road, SW7 4RB; 0171-584-7181.

*Susie Ind*; 0171-828-6430. Arrangements in your home.

*Vase*, 10 Clifton Road, W9 1SS; 0171-286-7853. Floral arrangements in your own home on a regular basis.

## GARDEN CARE

*Adair Marsh Garden and Flower Design*; (01672) 861361.

*Christopher Garden*; 0181-337-0806. Trimming and planting for window boxes, etc.

*Marion Haythe*; 0171-328-8575. Garden and patio design and window boxes.

*Mother Earth - Jan Guinness*; 0171-720-2819. Reasonable rates.

## GENERAL CONTRACTOR

*Mick Harmes*, 76 Ramuz Drive, Westcliff on Sea, Essex; (01702) 330813.

## GENERAL DOMESTIC HELP AND HOUSECLEANERS

*The Clean Team*; 0171-586-0005. A professional team of three cleaners that use their own cleaning products and equipment.

*Fait Accompli*, 32B Queensgate Mews, SW7 5QN; 0171-581-0384. A service specialising in organising party planning, decorating, building renovations and catering.

*Gareth Fitzgerald*; (017373) 54557. Window cleaner.

*Home Organisers*, Unit 3, Investment House, 28 Queen's Road, Weybridge KT13 9UT; (01932) 844321. Membership organisation - emergency help service for babysitting.

*Livelihoods Agency* (Mrs. Henderson), 54A Ebury Street, SW1W OLU; 0171-730-0329. An agency specialising in daily domestic help including housekeepers and butlers.

*Newman Cleaning Services*; 0181-670-9320. Windows and carpet cleaning service.

*Quick Help*, 307A Finchley Road, NW3 6EH; 0171-794-8666. An agency providing any type of domestic help, including daily cleaners, mother's helps, au pairs, and nannies all on relatively short notice.

## HAIRDRESSERS AND BARBERS

*Denise McAdams*, 14 Hay Hill, W1X 7LJ; 0171-499-8079. Men and women, just off Berkeley Square.

*Ellishelen*, 75 Walton Street, SW3 2HT; 0171-589-8519.

*Jean Marie*, 68 Gloucester Road SW7 4QT; 0171-584-6888. For men and ladies.

*Mr. B's*, 360 Fulham Road, SW10 9UU; 0171-352-9410.

*Stannard and Slingsby*, 211-213 High Street, Kensington W8; 0171-937-0333.

*Toni & Guy*, 49 Sloane Square, SW1W 8AX; 0171-730-8113. Several locations throughout London.

*Trotters*, 34 King's Road SW3 4UD; 0171-259-9620. Children's haircuts.

*Valentino*, 1 Thackeray Street, W8 5ET; 0171-6911. Hair and beauty.

**INTERIOR DESIGNERS**

*Capital Designs*, 25 Walton Street, SW3 2HU; 0171-581-0105.

*Fabric Shop Interiors*, 117 Old Brompton Road, SW7 3RN; 0171-244-8671.

*Fiona Campbell*, 259 New King's Road, SW6 4RB; 0171-731-3681.

*Percy Bass Ltd.*, 184-188 Walton Street, SW3 2JL; 0171-589-4853.

**KENNELS FOR QUARANTINE AND BOARDING**

*Animal Aunts*, Wydwooch, 45 Fairview Road, Headley Down, Hampshire GU35 8HQ; (01428) 712611. They care for your pets in your home or theirs, all over London, Surrey, etc.

*The Animal Inn*, Dover Road, Ringwould, Near Deal CT14 8HH; (01304) 373597 or fax (01304) 380305 (Liz and Jonathan Shaw). Cats and dogs. Five minutes from the white cliffs of Dover, this facility is considered state of the art as far as quarantines and boarding kennels go.

*Arden Grange International Quarantine Kennels*, London Road (A23), Albourne, West Sussex BN6 9BJ; (01273) 832416 or fax (01273) 83612. Dogs and cats.

*Granary Kennels*, Hawkridge Wood, Frilsham, Newbury, Berkshire RG16 9XA; (01635) 201489. Dogs - boarding and quarantine.

*Wey Farm Cattery and Kennels*, Guildford Road, Ottershaw, Surrey KT16 OQW; (0193287) 3239/3529. Dogs and cats and quarantine.

For a more complete listing contact the *Ministry of Agriculture, Fisheries and Food*, Hook Rise South, Tolworth, Surbiton, Surrey KT6 7NF; 0181-330-4411.


## LEATHER, LUGGAGE AND SHOE REPAIRS

*Elias*, 3/4 Chiswick Common Road, W4 1RR; 0181-955-2755.

*Fifth Avenue Shoe Repairs*, 230 Fortys Green Road, N10; 0181-444-4237.


## MONOGRAMMING SERVICES

*Peter Jones* will monogram towels and sheets purchased from them, or items you bring in. *Harrods* has a monogramming service in their Linen Department for items purchased at Harrods.

*Eximious Ltd.*, 10 West Halkin Street, SW1R HAL; 0171-235-7828. Personalised items for sale only.

*The Monogrammed Linen Shop*, 168 Walton Street, SW3 2JL; 0171-589-4033. Personalised items; will also embroider your own items.

*Scribes Engraving*, Unit C-10, Grays Mews Antique Market, 1-7 Davies Mews, Davies Street, W1Y 1AR; 0171-408-1880. Engravers of precious metals and glass.


## PACKAGE DELIVERY, COLLECTION AND COURIERS

*Box Business*, 30 Queensway, W2; 0171-221-1801. First total packaging store.

*DHL Worldwide Express*; 0181-890-9000.

*Federal Express International*; 0800 123800.

*The Packing Shop*, G13 The Plaza, 535 King's Road, SW10 O5Z; 0171-352-2021. They will collect, pack and ship packages worldwide.

*West One*, Bridge Wharf, 156 Caledonian Road, N1 9RD; 0171-833-4666. International couriers.

## PARTY PLANNERS

*Juliana's, Party Organising*, 4 Windmill Business Park, Riverside Road, Wimbledon, SW17 OBH; 0171-937-1555.

*Non Stop Party Shop*, Chelsea Farmer's Market, 125 Sydney Street, SW3 6NR; 0171-351-5771. A retail store that offers a balloon decoration and party accessory service. Five branches.

*Party Planners*, Lady Elizabeth Anson, 56 Ladbroke Grove, W11 2PB; 0171-229-9666. Will arrange everything for any social function.

*Party Professionals*, 33 Kensington Park Road, W11 2EU; 0171-221-3438.

## PICTURE FRAMING

*John Campbell*, 164 Walton Street, SW3 2JL; 0171-584-9268.

## RECYCLING

Clean milk bottle tops, cans and used postage stamps are collected for the charity Guide Dogs for the Blind; 0181-464-1433.

*War on Waste*; 0181-961-8221. Is a private company that collects recyclable waste in the North London and North-west London area. The company will collect metal, paper, glass, fabric and plastic from your home and charge approximately £1.50-£3.00 per week, depending on the amount to collect.

### Recycling Facilities

Check with your local town hall or public library for full list of locations and what they recycle.

*Hammersmith and Fulham*, Recycling Office; 0181-576-5295.

*Kensington and Chelsea, Borough of*, Recycling Office; 0171-373-6099, ext. 5148/5199.

*Merton Council*, (Wimbledon Area), Recycling Information; 0181-545-3142.

*Wandsworth Borough*, Recycling Office; 0181-871-6381.

## RENTAL (Hire)

Check the London (Central) Yellow Pages and Children's Classified for separate listings.

### Baby Equipment

See Children's Chapter.

### Bicycles

*Bell Street Bikes*, 73 Bell Street, NW1; 0171-724-0456.

*Mend-A-Bike*, 13 Park Walk, SW10; 0171-352-3999.

### Costumes

*Barnum's Carnival Novelties*, 67 Hammersmith Road, W14 8UZ; 0171-602-1211. As well as selling party goods, they hire out Father Christmas costumes.

*Berman's & Nathans*, 18 Irving Street, WC2H 7AX; 0171-836-5678. All sorts of costumes (no animals).

*The Carnival Store*, 95 Hammersmith Road, W14 0QH; 0171-603-7824. Specialises in animal costumes but has many others too.

### Do-It-Yourself Tools

*The Hire Shop*, 865 Fulham Road, SW6 5HP; 0171-736-1769. Hire out small tools, drills, lawn mowers, carpet cleaners, etc.

### Television and Video Equipment

See the London (Central) Yellow Pages and Shopping Chapter.

### Wedding and Formal Attire

*After Dark*, 6 Ashbourne Parade, Finchley Road, NW11 0AD; 0181-209-0195. Ladies formal attire for hire.

---

*A Chance to Dance*, 57A Latchmere Road, SW11 QDS; 0171-350-1579. Ladies formalwear for hire.

*Moss Bros.*, 88 Regent Street, W1R 5PA; 0171-494-0665. Gentlemen's formal wear.

*One Night Stand*, 44 Pimlico Road, SW1 8LP; 0171-730-8708. Ladies formal wear.

*Parker Brown's*, 34 Tavistock Street, WC2E 7PB; 0171-928-4603. Hire or buy designer dresses.

*Putting on the Glitz*, Galen Place, Pied Bull Court, Bloomsbury, WC1A 2JR; 0171-404-5067.

## SECOND HAND CARS

*Rupert Golan*, 19A Wilton Row, SW1X 7NS; 0171-235-6326.

*Rodney Turner*; (01398) 23157. Car broking.

## SELF STORAGE

*Abbey Self Storage*, Abbey Business Centre, Ingate Place, Battersea, SW8 3N5; 0800 622244. Twelve London locations.

*Metrostore Ltd.*, Camelford Walk, Clarendon Road, Notting Hill, W11 1TX; 0171-792-1087. Four London locations.

*Shepherd's Bush Self Storage*, 29 Shepherd's Bush Place, W12 8LX; 0181-743-4647.

## SPECIAL APPLIANCE REPAIRS

*Advest*; 0181-965-1150. Microwave repair.

*Andrews and Company*, 26 King's Terrace, Plender Street, NW1; 0171-388-5952. Silverplating.

*Elizabeth Hanley*, 97 Cadogan Lane, SW1; 0171-823-1752. Repairing and converting lamps and offering handmade lampshades.

*Luxury Lamps*, 60 Upper Montagu Street, W1; 0171-723-7381.

*Waldebeck Services*, Unit 18, Abenglen Industrial Estate, Betam road, Hayes, Middlesex UB3 1SS; 0181-848-7520. Repair all American major appliances.

## TAILOR

*Express Tailoring*, 3 New Burlington Place, Saville Row, W1X 1FB; 0171-437-9345. Open Saturdays for fittings.

## VETERINARY SERVICES

*Abingdon Veterinary Clinic*, 85 Earls Court Road, W8; 0171-937-8215.

*K. M. Butt*, 8 Kynance Mews, SW7; 0171-584-2019.

*Elizabeth Street Veterinary Clinic*, 55 Elizabeth Street, SW1W 9PP; 0171-730-9102. An emergency veterinary service 24-hours a day, 365 days a year. The regular day clinic is very good as well.

## WORD PROCESSING AND PRINTING

*Keytappers Office Services*, 10 Taylor Close, N17 OUB; 0181-808-9709. Comprehensive range of word processing services from C.V.s to book manuscripts. Artwork preparation/design and printing of letterheads, business cards, booklets, etc.

# NOTES

# Chapter Eleven:  Shopping

London offers an international selection of goods to the shopper.  There are centuries-old shops selling traditional goods for which Britain is famous.  There are chic boutiques offering the latest in international fashion.  There are large high street stores and quaint neighbourhood shops catering to every household need.  We offer some suggestions to help you on your way.

## DEPARTMENT STORES

The list below contains a mixture of large department stores, similar to those found in America, and smaller, speciality department stores.

*Army and Navy Stores*, 101 Victoria Street, SW1; 0171-834-1234.  Not related to the American Store.   Offers fashions including Mondi, Jaeger, Country Casuals and House of Fraser labels.  Also good for household basics such as kitchen and hardware.

*Barkers of Kensington*, 63 Kensington High Street, W8; 0171-937-5432.

*Debenhams*, 334-348 Oxford Street, W1; 0171-580-3000.  Also branches throughout London.

*Dickins & Jones*, 224 Regent Street, W1; 0171-734-7070.  Women's and children's fashions.

*D. H. Evans*, 318 Oxford Street, W1;  0171-629-8800.   Women's and children's clothing.

*Fenwick of Bond Street*, 63 New Bond Street, W1;  0171-629-9161.  Upmarket clothes and accessories.

*Fortnum and Mason*, 181 Piccadilly, W1;  0171-734-8040.  Especially famous for their formal food hall which stocks a wide variety of goods including speciality teas.

*Harrods*, 87 Brompton Road, SW1;  0171-730-1234.   London's most famous emporium.  Says it will provide you with almost anything you could possibly desire.  Great food halls.

*Harvey Nichols*, 109-125 Knightsbridge, SW1;  0171-235-5000.  Good selection of American designer fashions, linens, accessories and a good men's department.

*John Lewis*, 278-306 Oxford Street, W1; 0171-629-7711. Good fabrics and household items; also fashions. Branches throughout London.

*Liberty*, 210-220 Regent Street, W1; 0171-734-1234. Beautiful fabrics and household items; designer fashions.

*Peter Jones*, Sloane Square, SW1; 0171-730-3434. Part of the John Lewis Partnership, offers a wide variety of basic home and fashion goods.

*Selfridges*, 400 Oxford Street, W1; 0171-629-1234. Large and varied selection, good children's department. Miss Selfridge is its young department, reasonable for inexpensive, fun clothing and accessories.

*Simpson (Piccadilly) Ltd.*, 203 Piccadilly, W1; 0171-734-2002. Sportswear, leathergoods and accessories.

## CHAIN STORES

*BHS*, 252 Oxford Street, W1; 0171-629-2011.

*C&A*, 501-519 Oxford Street, W1; 0171-629-7279. Other branches throughout London.

*Littlewoods*, 203-211 Oxford Street, W1; 0171-434-4301.

*Marks & Spencer*, 458 Oxford Street, W1; 0171-935-7954. Other branches throughout London. Stocks reliable versions of more expensive clothes. Underwear and knitwear are staples of the British wardrobe. Also good food departments focusing on convenience foods.

## CLOTHES

### Designer Boutiques

The two general areas to head for when looking for the ultimate in designer clothing are South Molton Street and New Bond Street, and/or Knightsbridge, Sloane Street and Beauchamp Place. The following are some of the more well known shops.

*Belville Sasson*, 73 Pavillion Road, SW1; 0171-581-3500.

*Bruce Oldfield*, 27 Beauchamp Place, SW3; 0171-584-1363.

*Browns*, 23-27 South Molton Street, W1; 0171-491-7833. Offers designer collections including Romeo Gigli, Helmut Lang, Jil Sander, Donna Karan, Sonia Rykiel, Claude Montana, Chloe and Zoran.

*Caroline Charles*, 56-57 Beauchamp Place, SW3; 0171-589-5850.

*Chanel Boutique*, 26 Old Bond Street, W1; 0171-493-5040; Also 31 Sloane Street; 0171-235-6631.

*Chelsea Design Company*, 65 Sydney Street, SW3; 0171-352-4626. Very elegant clothes designed by Catherine Walker.

*Edina Ronay*, 141 King's Road, SW3; 0171-352-1085.

*Emporio Armani*, 191 Brompton Road, SW3; 0171-823-8818.

*Escada*, 66-67 New Bond Street, W1; 0171-629-0934.

*Ferragamo*, 24 Old Bond Street, W1; 0171-629-5007.

*Gucci*, 27 Old Bond Street, W1; 0171-629-2716.

*Hermes*, 155 New Bond Street, W1; 0171-499-8856; and 179 Sloane Street, SW1; 0171-823-1014.

*Joseph*, 16, 21, 26 Sloane Street, SW1; 0171-235-5470 and other branches.

*Karl Lagerfeld*, 173 New Bond Street, W1; 0171-493-6277.

*Philip Somerville*, 11 Blenheim Street, W1; 0171-629-4442. Good for designer hats.

*Ralph Lauren*, 143 New Bond Street, W1; 0171-491-4967.

*Lucienne Phillips*, 89 Knightsbridge, SW1; 0171-235-2134.

*Yves St. Laurent*, 113 New Bond Street, W1; 0171-493-1800.

## English Classics

Well cut raincoats and fine woollens are the trademarks of classic English clothing. Your best bet when out looking for these is Regent Street and Piccadilly.

*Alexon*, 197 New Bond Street, W1; 0171-629-9237.

---

*Austin Reed*, 103-113 Regent Street, W1; 0171-734-6789.

*Aquascutum*, 100 Regent Street, W1; 0171-734-6090.

*Burberrys*, 18-22 Haymarket, SW1; 0171-930-3343.

*Jaeger*, 200-206 Regent Street, W1; 0171-734-8211. Also other branches throughout London.

*The Scotch House*, 2 Brompton Road, SW1; 0171-581-2151; Also 84 Regent Street; 0171-734-5966.

*Viyella*, 148 Regent Street, W1; 0171-734-1728.

**Knitwear**

London is a great hunting ground for knitwear of all kinds. The best place for traditional British knitwear is Piccadilly, especially around the Burlington Arcade, Regent Street and Knightsbridge.

*Jane and Dada*, 20-21 St. Christopher's Place, W1; 0171-486-0977. Unusual machine and hand-knit sweaters.

*Joseph*, 28 Brook Street, W1; 0171-629-6077. Full collection of Joseph Tricot.

*N. Peal*, Burlington Arcade, Piccadilly, W1; 0171-493-9220. Other branches throughout London. Classic knitwear including classics from the Shetland Isles and lambswools and cashmeres from Scotland.

*Patricia Roberts*, 60 Kinnerton Street, SW1; 0171-235-4742. Wonderful range of sweaters in lambswool, cashmere, cotton, angora and chenille.

*Edina Ronay Ltd.*, 141 King's Road, SW3; 0171-352-1085. Specialise in hand-knitted sweaters in wool, cotton and silk.

**Casualwear**

For everyday wear, as well as the odd favourite, hit the High Street. King's Road, Kensington High Street, Fulham Road and Oxford Street are all great haunts for casual wear.

*Laura Ashley*, 256-258 Regent Street, W1; 0171-437-9760; Also 449-451 Oxford Street, W1; 0171-355-1363 and other branches throughout London.

---

*Benetton*, 221 Oxford Street, W1.; Also 253 Regent Street, W1; 0171-355-4881. Other branches throughout London.

*The Gap*, 315-317 Oxford Street, W1; 0171-408-2400. Other branches found on most high streets.

*Henry Cottons*, 199 Sloane Street, SW1; 0171-823-1417.

*Hobbs*, 47 South Molton Street, W1; 0171-629-0750. Other branches throughout London.

*Jigsaw*, 124 King's Road, SW3; 0171-589-5083. Other branches throughout London.

*Miss Selfridge*, 75 Brompton Road, SW3; 0171-584-7814 and other branches.

*Monsoon*, 67 South Molton Street, W1; 0171-499-3987. Other branches throughout London.

*Mulberry Company* 11-12 Gees Court, St. Christopher's Place, W1; 0171-493-2546.

*Naf Naf*, 229 King's Road, SW3; 0171-351-5611.

*Next*, 160 Regent Street, W1; 0171-434-2515. Other branches throughout London.

*Timberland*, 72 New Bond Street, W1; 0171-495-2133.

*Warehouse*, 96 King's Road, SW3; 0171-584-0069. Other branches throughout London.

*Whistles*, 27 Sloane Square, SW1; 0171-730-9819. Other branches throughout London.

**Maternity Wear**

Some major department stores offer a small selection of maternity clothes, the best probably being *Harrods*. Most major department stores offer a large and varied selection of baby equipment.

*Additions*, 52 Chiltern Street, W1; 0171-486-3065. Career women's clothes and other styles.

*Balloon*, 77 Walton Street, SW3; 0171-584-3668. Mostly French maternity clothes with a small selection for babies.

*Elegance Maternelle*, 35 Chiltern Street, W1; 0171-487-5520. Maternity clothes, also for the larger lady. Branch in the Brompton Arcade, SW3.

*Great Expectations*, 78 Fulham Road, SW3; 0171-584-2451. Designer clothes for the mother-to-be and some gifts for babies.

*La Cicogna*, 6A Sloane Street, SW1; 0171-235-3845. Quality Italian maternity clothes, baby and children's clothes, including a range of Italian baby equipment.

*Maman*, 13 Walton Street, SW3; 0171-589-8414. Good range of smart maternity wear.

*Monsoon*, 33d King's Road, SW3; 0171-730-7552. Doesn't specialise in maternity wear but can often be a Godsend if you are willing to buy larger sized clothes.

*Mothercare*, 461 Oxford Street, W1; 0171-629-6621. Many branches around London. Complete range of items for mothers-to-be and children up to size 10, including baby beds, linens and toiletries.

**Menswear**

Available at most department stores. The many shops on Jermyn Street, Sackville Street, and Saville Row offer custom made (bespoke or made-to-measure) clothing for the discerning gentlemen. There are numerous gentlemen's stores with branches throughout London such as *Cecil Gee* and *Burton*. The following is a sample of men's clothing retailers.

*Aquascutum*, 100 Regent Street, W1; 0171-734-6090.

*Austin Reed*, 103-113 Regent Street, W1; 0171-734-6789.

*Blazer*, 33A King's Road, SW3; 0171-730-0793. Many branches around London.

*Burberrys*, 18-22 Haymarket, SW1; 0171-930-3343; Also 165 Regent Street, W1; 0171-734-4060.

*Favourbrook*, 19-21 Piccadilly Arcade, Jermyn Street, SW1; 0171-491-2337. Very English style which combines traditional designs with contemporary and period fabrics.

*Gucci*, 27 Old Bond Street, W1; 0171-629-2716.

*Hackett*, 136-138 Sloane Street, SW1; 0171-730-3331. Other branches throughout London. Specialises in tailored, traditional everyday clothing, formal wear and country attire.

*Herbie Frogg Ltd.*, 21 Jermyn Street, SW1; 0171-437-6069.

*High and Mighty*, 145-147 Edgware Road, W2; 0171-723-8754. Many branches. Clothing for the taller and larger gentleman.

*Jaeger*, 200 Regent Street, W1; 0171-734-8211.

*Hilditch & Key*, Shirtmakers and ties; 0171-930-5336.

*Liberty*, 210-220 Regent Street, W1; 0171-734-1234.

*James Lock*, 6 St. James Street, SW1; 0171-930-8874. Hats for gentlemen and ladies.

*Lords*, Burlington Arcade, W1; 0171-493-5808. Shirtmakers.

*Marks & Spencer*. Carries full range of menswear. Branches throughout London.

*Moss Bros.*, 88 Regent Street, W1; 0171-494-0665. Retail and hire for special occasions, such as 'morning suits' for gentlemen and riding clothes for the entire family.

*Next for Men*, 327-329 Oxford Street, W1; 0171-409-2746. Many branches. Casual wear.

*Thomas Pink*, Shop 2 Donovan Court, Drayton Gardens, SW10; 0171-373-5795. Also, 85 Jermyn Street, SW1; 0171-930-6364. Many other branches throughout London. Large range of shirts in various patterns including stripes, checks and plain colours. Generously cut with extra long tails.

*Simpson*, 203 Piccadilly, W1; 0171-734-2002.

*Timberland*, 72 New Bond Street, W1; 0171-495-2133. Casual men's wear and shoes.

*Turnbull & Asser*, 70-71 Jermyn Street, SW1; 0171-930-0502.

## Clothing Size Charts

The tables below should be used as an approximate guide, as the actual sizes may vary according to the manufacturer, as well as the country of origin. Small sizes are generally difficult to obtain. It is advisable to try the clothing on to ensure the correct size.

### Adults

*Women's Dresses, Suits and Coats:*

| | | | | | | |
|---|---|---|---|---|---|---|
| American | 6 | 8 | 10 | 12 | 14 | 16 |
| British | 8 | 10 | 12 | 14 | 16 | 18 |
| Continental | 36/38 | 38/40 | 40/42 | 42/44 | 44/46 | 46/48 |

*Women's Sweaters and Blouses:*

| | | | | | | |
|---|---|---|---|---|---|---|
| American | 6 | 8 | 10 | 12 | 14 | 16 |
| British | 8/30 | 10/32 | 12/34 | 14/36 | 16/38 | 18/40 |
| Continental | 36/38 | 38/40 | 40/42 | 42/44 | 44/46 | 46/48 |

*Women's Shoes:*

| | | | | | | |
|---|---|---|---|---|---|---|
| American | 5½ | 6 | 6½ | 7 | 7½ | 8 |
| British | 3½ | 4 | 4½ | 5 | 5½ | 6 |
| French | 36 | 36½ | 37 | 37½ | 38 | 38½ |
| Italian | 36½ | 37 | 37½ | 38 | 38½ | 39 |

| | | | | |
|---|---|---|---|---|
| American | 8½ | 9 | 9½ | 10 |
| British | 6½ | 7 | 7½ | 8 |
| French | 39 | 39½ | 40 | 40½ |
| Italian | 39½ | 40 | 40½ | 41 |

*Men's Suits and Overcoats:*

American and British sizes are the same, although British sizes run narrower in the shoulder.

| | | | | | |
|---|---|---|---|---|---|
| American/ British | 36 | 38 | 40 | 42 | 44 |
| Continental | 46 | 48 | 50 | 52 | 54 |

*Men's Shirts or Collar Sizes:*

| | | | | | | | |
|---|---|---|---|---|---|---|---|
| American/ British | 14 | 14½ | 15 | 15½ | 16 | 16½ | 17 |
| Continental | 36 | 37 | 38 | 39 | 40 | 41 | 42 |

*Men's Shoes:*

| American | 8 | 8½ | 9 | 9½ | 10 | 10½ | 11 | 11½ |
|---|---|---|---|---|---|---|---|---|
| British | 7½ | 8 | 8½ | 9 | 9½ | 10 | 10½ | 11 |
| Continental | 41 | 42 | | 43 | | 44 | | 45 |

## Children

| American | 3 | 4 | 5 | 6 |
|---|---|---|---|---|
| British | 3-4(40") | 4-5(43") | 5-6(45") | 6-7(48") |
| Continental | 6(120cm) | 7(125cm) | 8(130cm) | 9(135cm) |

| American | 7 | 8 | 9 | 10 |
|---|---|---|---|---|
| British | 7-8(50") | 8-9(53") | 9-10(55") | 11(58") |
| Continental | 10(140cm) | 11(145cm) | 12(150cm) | 13(155cm) |

| American | 12 | 14 |
|---|---|---|
| British | 12(60") | 13(62") |
| Continental | 14(160cm) | 15(165cm) |

## SHOPPING FOR CHILDREN

### Childrenswear

The chain stores such as *Marks & Spencer*, *BHS* and *C&A* are excellent for competitively priced, unfussy clothes for boys and girls from 0-14 years of age. Most department stores have children's departments - *Harrods* and *Peter Jones* are probably the best.

*Absolute Beginners*, 129 High Road, East Finchley, N2; 0181-442-0631. Children's designer wear.

*Benetton 0-12*, 131 Kensington High Street, W8; 0171-937-3034. Carries selection of colour coordinated trousers, shirts and sweaters for boys and girls. Prices are good value.

*Chelsea Design Company*, 65 Sydney Street, SW3; 0171-352-4626.

*La Cicogna*, 6a Sloane Street, SW1; 0171-235-3739. Well-known Italian children's chain store that specialises in clothes for boys and girls from 0 to 14. Also carries maternity clothes, prams, pushchairs and highchairs.

*Confiture*, 19 Harrington Road, SW7; 0171-581-3432. Exclusive French children's wear including shoes.

*Createx*, 27 Harrington Road, SW7; 0171-589-8306. French and Italian children's wear.

*Early Clothing*, 79-85 Fortis Green Road, Muswell Hill, N20; 0181-444-9309.

*Gapkids*, 122 King's Road, SW3; 0171-581-9720. Other branches throughout London.

*Hennes*, 123 Kensington High Street, W8; 0171-937-3329. Other branches throughout London. Swedish chain with well priced contemporary children's wear.

*Anthea Moore Ede*, 16 Victoria Grove, W8; 0171-584-8826. Traditional clothing for girls (0-14 age group) and boys (0-10 age group). Also good selection of fancy dress costumes.

*Laura Ashley*, 9 Harriet Street, SW1; 0171-235-9797; Also 256 Regent Street, W1R 7AD; 0171-437-9760, and other branches.

*Mothercare*, 461 Oxford Street, W1; 0171-580-1688. Other branches throughout London. Absolutely everything can be bought from Mothercare including maternity clothes, pushchairs, nursery furniture, home and car safety equipment and children's clothing from 0-8 years.

*Oshkosh B'Gosh U.K. Ltd.*, 17 King's Road, SW3; 0171-730-1341.

*Patrizia Wigan Designs Ltd.*, 72 New King's Road, SW6; 0171-736-3336. Other branches on Walton Street, SW3 and Heath Street, NW3. Clothes for children from 0-12 in traditional and contemporary styles.

*Please Mum*, 69 New Bond Street, W1; 0171-493-5880; Also 88 Golders Green Road, NW11; 0181-458-4445 or 9233.

*POM Children's Wear Ltd.*, 47 Kensington Church Street, W8; 0171-937-8641.

*Sally Parsons*, 15a Bute Street, SW7; 0171-584-8866. Traditional English children's wear.

*Scott-Aide*, 53 Godfrey Street, SW3; 0171-352-1718. Excellent selection of traditional and quality children's wear. Particularly nice for christening and layette gifts.

*Trotters*, 34 King's Road, SW1; 0171-259-9620. Wide range of clothing and shoes.

---

*White House*, 51 New Bond Street, W1; 0171-629-3521. Very expensive, traditional English clothing. Specialise in layettes.

*Young England*, 47 Elizabeth Street, SW1; 0171-259-9003. Traditional clothes such as smocks, gowns and tweed coats.

## Toys

Most major department stores have large toy departments. Some smaller shops around London specialise in different things and *Hamley's* has everything!

*Early Learning Centre*, 225 Kensington High Street, W8; 0171-937-0419. Other branches throughout London. Specialises in educational toys for young children.

*Frog Hollow*, 15 Victoria Grove, W8; 0171-581-5493. Special selection of froggery!

*Hamley's*, 188 Regent Street, W1; 0171-734-3161. World's largest toy shop!

*J. J. Toys*, 138 St. John's Wood High Street, NW8; 0171-722-4855.

*Pollocks Toy Museum*, 1 Scala Street, W1; 0171-636-3452. Both a museum and a toy shop. Sells cardboard toy theatres complete with characters and scripts.

*Singing Tree* , 69 New King's Road, SW6; 0171-736-4527. Specialises in all types of doll houses and accessories.

*Toddler Toys*, 4 Harriet Street, SW1; 0171-245-6316.

*Toys-R-Us*, Brent Cross Shopping Centre, NW2; 0181-209-0019; Also Church Street West, Woking, Surrey GU21; 01483-726449. Other locations.

*Toys, Toys, Toys*, 10 Northways Parade, Finchley Road, NW3; 0171-722-9821.

*Tridias Toy*, 25 Bute Street, SW7; 0171-584-2330.

## Books

*Children's Book Centre Ltd.*, 229 Kensington High Street, W8; 0171-937-7497. The largest selection in London; also toys, presents and gifts.

*Puffin Bookshop*, 1 The Market, Covent Garden Piazza, WC2; 0171-379-6465. Large selection of paperbacks for children.

**Furniture and Gifts**

*Dragons of Walton Street*, 23 Walton Street, SW3; 0171-589-3795. Specialises in painted furniture.

*The Nursery Window*, 81 Walton Street, SW3; 0171-581-3358. Specialises in gifts made from their own fabrics, with decorations and curtains for the nursery, etc.

**ACCESSORIES**

**Luggage and Accessories**

Again, the large department stores all carry excellent selections. *Harrods* has probably the best selection. *Selfridges* has a range of inexpensive, value-for-money luggage with many of the best known makes, as does *Peter Jones*, *Marks & Spencer* carry a range of own-brand luggage which is durable and well-priced.

*Accessorize*, Unit 22 Covent Garden Market, WC2; 0171-240-2107. Specialises in accessories including jewellery, watches, belts, gloves, tights and scarves.

*City Bag Store*, 3 South Molton Street, W1; 0171-499-2549. Selection of inexpensive holdalls, purses and handbags.

*Gucci*, 32-33 Old Bond Street, W1; 0171-629-2716. Good range of handbags, luggage and small leather goods.

*Henrys*, 143 Fulham Road, SW3; 0171-581-1321. Renowned for fine leather goods in innovative colours and designs.

*Hermes*, 155 New Bond Street, W1; 0171-499-8856.

*James Smith & Sons*, 53 New Oxford Street, WC1; 0171-836-4731. Produces wonderful umbrellas, walking sticks, canes and riding crops.

*Loewe*, 130 New Bond Street, W1; 0171-493-3914. Wonderful quality leather accessories, luggage and gifts.

*Mulberry*, 11-12 Gees Court, W1; 0171-493-2547. Also boutiques in *Liberty, Harrods* and *Harvey Nichols*. Medium-priced range of luggage, handbags, belts and other accessories.

## Women's Shoes

London has numerous shoe stores and shoes are available in most department stores. Narrow width shoes are generally available in the more expensive shops. Listed below are some of the better known shops.

*Bally*, 260 Regent Street, W1; 0171-734-2500. Other branches throughout London. Well made classic shoes.

*Bertie*, 118 King's Road, SW3; 0171-584-9578. Other branches throughout London. Contemporary English designs.

*Church's Shoes*, 163 New Bond Street, W1; 0171-499-9449. Other branches throughout London. Renowned for their men's shoes - but also carry well made classic shoes for women.

*Manolo Blahnik*, 49 Old Church Street, SW3; 0171-352-8622. Very chic, elegant shoes.

*Emma Hope*, 33 Amwell Street, EC1; 0171-833-2367. Specialises in embroidered slippers and boots.

*Ferragamo*, 24 Old Bond Street, W1; 0171-629-5007.

*Kurt Geiger*, 95 New Bond Street, W1; 0171-499-2707.

*Gucci*, 27 Old Bond Street, W1; 0171-629-2716.

*Hobbs*, 47 South Molton Street, W1; 0171-629-0750. Other branches throughout London. Keenly priced shoes and clothing.

*Joan and David*, 150 New Bond Street, W1; 0171-499-7506. Also has a boutique in *Harvey Nichols*.

*Charles Jourdan*, 39 Brompton Road, SW3; 0171-581-3333. Noted for excellent shoes and boots, handbags and evening shoes.

*Bruno Magli*, 114 New Bond Street, W1; 0171-491-8562.

*Pied A Terre*, 19 South Moulton Street, W1; 0171-629-1362. Other branches throughout London.

*Pinet*, 47 New Bond Street, W1; 0171-629-2174.

*Rayne*, 15-16 Old Bond Street, W1; 0171-493-9077. Well made classic shoes. Will make classic court shoes in fabric of your choice.

---

*Rosetti*, 177 New Bond Street, W1; 0171-491-7066.

*Russell & Bromley*, 24 New Bond Street, W1; 0171-629-6903.

*Tube*, 41 South Molton Street, W1; 0171-491-1075.

## Men's Shoes

Both traditional and more trendy designers and manufacturers shoes can be found in the department stores - the best being *Fortnum & Mason, Harrods* and *Harvey Nichols*. Most of the trendy shoe shops in Chelsea and Knightsbridge stock both men's and women's shoes. Some of these are listed below.

*Bally*, 260 Regent Street, W1; 0171-734-2500. Other branches throughout London.

*Church's Shoes*, 163 New Bond Street, W1; 0171-499-9449. Other branches throughout London. Great for ready-made traditional brogues and Oxfords.

*Gucci*, 27 Old Bond Street, W1; 0171-629-2716.

*Joan & David*, 150 New Bond Street, W1; 0171-499-7506. Carries the U.S.-made Joan and David shoes.

*Charles Jourdan*, 39-43 Brompton Road, SW3; 0171-581-3333.

*John Lobb*, 9 St. James's Street, SW1; 0171-930-3664. Specialises in hand-made classic footwear.

*Next for Men*, 327-329 Oxford Street, W1; 0171-409-2746. Other branches throughout London. Good for casual shoes.

*Pied A Terre*, 19 South Molton Street, W1; 0171-629-1362. Many branches throughout London. Good hunting ground for less expensive, interesting designs.

*Russell & Bromley*, 24-25 New Bond Street, W1; 0171-629-6903. Several branches throughout London.

*Timberland*, 72 New Bond Street, W1; 0171-495-2133. Good rugged casual shoes.

*Wildsmith & Co.*, 15 Princes Arcade, Jermyn Street, SW1; 0171-437-4289. High quality hand-made shoes.

## Hats

*Fenwicks, Harrods* and *Harvey Nichols* have good selections. *Liberty* has what many consider the most exquisite selection in town.

*John Boyd*, 16 Beauchamp Place, SW3; 0171-589-7601. You can have your hat specially designed for you or you can select from stock.

*The Hat Shop*, 8 South Molton Street, W1; 0171-495-5727. Also, 58 Neal Street, WC2; 0171-836-6718. Huge selection of ready-to-wear hats for all ages.

*Herbert Johnson*, 30 New Bond Street, W1; 0171-408-1174. Large selection of hats for men and women. Great source for Ascot.

*David Shilling*, 5 Homer Street, W1; 0171-262-2363. A hat designer with a theatrical flair! Expensive but the quality and service are great. Call first for an appointment.

## SPECIALITY SHOPS

### Art Materials

Most major department stores offer a selection of materials.

*Cowling and Wilcox*, 26-28 Broadwick Street, W1; 0171-734-5781.

*Daler Rowney*, 12 Percy Street, W1; 0171-636-8241.

*Green and Stone Ltd.*, 259 King's Road, SW3; 0171-352-0837.

*London Graphic Centre*, 107-115 Long Acre, WC2; 0171-240-0235.

*Paperchase Products Ltd.*, 167 Fulham Road, SW1; 0171-925-2647. Other branches throughout London.

*Windsor and Newton*, 51 Rathbone Place, W1; 0171-636-4231.

*The Stencil Store*, 91 Lower Sloane Street, SW1; 0171-730-0728. Has everything you need to do your own stencilling.

### Book Shops

*Books Etc.*, 26 James Street, Covent Garden, WC2; 0171-379-6947. Many other branches. Open 7 days a week. Good general selection.

*Books for a Change*, 52 Charing Cross Road, WC2; 0171-836-2315. Offers books on green politics.

*Books for Cooks*, 4 Blenheim Crescent, W11; 0171-221-1992. Only cook books, with a little kitchen at the back where they try out recipes for the customers.

*Business Bookshop*, 72 Park Road, NW1; 0171-723-3902. As its name suggests, has wide selection of business books.

*Cinema Bookshop*, 13-14 Great Russell Street, WC1; 0171-637-0206. Offers best selection of books on the cinema.

*Claude Gill Books*, 19-23 Oxford Street, W1; 0171-434-9759. Also a branch in Piccadilly.

*Comic Showcase*, 76 Neal Street, WC2; 0171-240-3664. Specialises in adult comics and books by well-known cartoonists.

*Daunt Books for Travellers*, 83 Marylebone High Street, W1; 0171-224-2295. Aims to provide a complete picture of a country. Stocks cookery books, histories, biographies and novels as well as a range of guides and maps.

*Dillon's Bookstore*, 82 Gower Street, WC1; 0171-636-1577. Excellent and very wide choice. Also stocks academic books. Has speciality branches including Dillon's Art Bookshop on Long Acre, WC2; 0171-836-1359 and Dillon's Educational; 0171-706-3040. Also other branches throughout London.

*The Economist Bookshop*, Clare Market, Portugal Street, WC2; 0171-405-5531. Specialises in social sciences. Open during LSE term time. (Not to be confused with The Economist magazine!).

*Foyle's*, 119 Charing Cross Road, WC2; 0171-437-5660. The largest and best stocked bookstore in London. Notoriously badly organised, so be patient.

*Hatchard's*, 187 Piccadilly, W1; 0171-439-9921. Excellent selection; the oldest and one of the best bookstores in London. Has various branches throughout London.

*Murder One*, 71 Charing Cross Road, WC2; 0171-734-3485. Specialises in crime books.

*Pan Bookshop*, 158-162 Fulham Road, SW10; 0171-373-4997. Good selection, non-academic.

---

*Penguin Bookshop*, 10 The Market, Covent Garden Piazza, WC2; 0171-379-7650. Stock wide range of recent paperbacks.

*Travel Bookshop*, 13 Blenheim Crescent, W11; 0171-229-5260. Exclusively books on travel.

*Waterstone's*, 193 Kensington High Street, W8; 0171-937-8432. Excellent general selection, numerous art books. Branches throughout London.

*W. H. Smith*. Branches throughout London and at most railway stations.

*Zwemmer*, 26 Litchfield Street, WC2; 0171-379-7886. Has the finest choice of art books in London.

### Records, Tapes, CDs, Videos and Hi-Fi

Edgware Road and Tottenham Court Road are two of the major locations for equipment, records, tapes and compact discs. There are numerous chain stores throughout London, which can be found in the London (Central) Yellow Pages. Most major department stores, such as *Harrods, Peter Jones, John Lewis* and *Selfridges*, have an excellent selection of equipment.

*Comet Discount Warehouses*, 190 London Road, Hackbridge, Surrey SM6; 0181-773-9909. Warehouses throughout London, see the national press for details. Carries discounted hi-fi equipment.

*Honest Jon's Records*, 278 Portobello Road, W10; 0181-969-9822. Selection of jazz records, tapes and compact discs.

*HMV*, 150 Oxford Street (Oxford Circus), W1; 0171-631-3423. Other branches located at 363 Oxford Street, W1 and Trocadero Centre, Piccadilly Circus, W1. Oxford Circus branch is the largest record store in the World. Caters for all tastes of music.

*Music Discount Centre*, 437 The Strand, WC2; 0171-240-2157. Other branches throughout London. Sells only classical records, tapes and compact discs at discount prices.

*Our Price Records*, 33 King's Road, SW3; 0171-730-1008. Other branches throughout London.

*Ray's Jazz*, 180 Shaftesbury Avenue, WC2; 0171-240-3969.

*Thomas Heinitz*, 35 Moscow Road, W2; 0171-229-2077. Carries video and hi-fi equipment.

*Tower Records*, 1 Piccadilly Circus, W1; 0171-439-2500. Other branches located at 62-64 Kensington High Street, W8 and Whiteley's Centre, Queensway, WC2. Wide selection of records, compact discs, tapes, videos, etc. Open 09.00-24.00 Monday-Saturday. Open Sundays.

*Virgin Megastore*, 14-16 Oxford Street, W1; 0171-631-1234. Wide range of records, tapes and compact discs.

**Sportswear and Sporting Equipment**

*Alpine Sports*, 215 Kensington High Street, W8; 0171-938-1911. Other branches throughout London. Ski, tennis and outdoor equipment to rent or buy.

*C&A*, 160 Kensington High Street, W8; 0171-937-6362. Branches throughout London. Outdoor wear.

*Captain O. M. Watts*, 45 Albemarle Street, W1; 0171-493-4633. Boating equipment and leisure wear.

*Debenham's Basement*, 1 Welbeck Street, W1; 0171-580-3000. Good selection of sporting goods, reasonably priced horse-riding gear.

*Farlow's of Pall Mall*, 5 Pall Mall, SW1; 0171-839-2423. London's oldest fishing tackle shop. Has large selection of fishing tackle, shooting accessories and country clothing including *Barbour* waxed clothing.

*W & H Gidden Ltd.*, 15d Clifford Street, W1; 0171-734-2788. Wide range of traditional riding equipment including saddles, boots, whips, etc.

*Golf City*, 13 New Bridge Street, EC4; 0171-353-9872. Specialist shop for golfers which sells wide range of equipment including clubs, gloves, bags and sweaters.

*Harrods Olympic Way*, Knightsbridge, SW1; 0171-730-1234. Large selection of goods.

*Lillywhites*, 24-36 Lower Regent Street, W1; 0171-930-3181. Large department store devoted solely to sporting goods.

*Oddball Juggling*, 56 Islington Park Road, N1; 0171-354-5660. Juggling equipment and unicycles.

*Olympus Sport*, 301 Oxford Street, W1; 0171-409-2619. Branches. All types of sporting goods.

*On Your Bike Ltd.*, 52-54 Tooley Street, London Bridge, SE1; 0171-407-1309. Bicycles.

*Pindisports*, 14-18 Holborn, EC1; 0171-242-3278. Specialists in mountaineering and skiing equipment.

*Purdey*, 57 South Audley Street, W1; 0171-499-1801. Hunting and shooting shop with classic English country clothing.

*Run & Become*, 42 Palmer Street, SW1; 0171-222-1314. Running gear.

*Snow & Rock Sports Ltd.*, 188 Kensington High Street, W8; 0171-937-0872. Skiing and mountaineering equipment for the entire family.

*Swaine Adeney*, 185 Piccadilly, W1; 0171-734-4277. Very upmarket horseriding gear and English country accessories.

*Captain O. M. Watts Ltd.*, 49 Albemarle Street, W1; 0171-493-4633. Everything for yachting.

*Y.H.A. Adventure Shop*, 14 Southampton Street, Covent Garden, WC2; 0171-836-8541. Wide range of travel and adventure clothing and equipment.

## Stationery

Most major department stores and some larger chemists offer a selection of stationery. Also try the High Street "quick print" shops for a selection of inexpensive personalised paper.

*Able-Wove*, Steepleprint Ltd., Northampton NN6; (01604) 810781. Very reasonably priced personalised stationery by mail order.

*CL Data Fast Ltd.*, 24 Astell Street, SW3; 0171-352-1796.

*Italian Paper Shop*, 11 Brompton Arcade, SW3; 0171-589-1668. Has wide range of Florentine paper and stationery and marbled wrapping paper from the Netherlands.

*Lonsdale Engraving*, 28 New King's Road, SW6; 0171-736-9520.

*Paperchase*, 213 Tottenham Court Road, W1; 0171-580-8496. Has wide range of cards, pens, wrapping paper, ribbons, plus paper gifts and all kinds of party things. Also, other branches throughout London.

*Pencraft*, 91 Kingsway, WC2; 0171-405-3639. Has full range of pens by Mont Blanc, Watermans, Parker and Sheaffer.

*Ryman*, branches throughout London. Excellent for office supplies and stationery.

*W. H. Smith*, branches throughout London.

*Smythson of Bond Street*, 54 New Bond Street, W1; 0171-629-8558. The Queen's Stationer stocks the finest personal stationery as well as leather bound address books, diaries, blotters and pencil holders.

*Tessa Fantoni*, 77 Abbeville Road, SW7; 0181-673-1253. Has wonderful paper-covered boxes, photo frames and albums which are sold in specialist stationery shops, Conran's and her own shop in Clapham.

*The Walton Street Stationery Company*, 97 Walton Street, SW3; 0171-589-0777. Top quality writing paper of all types, plus inks, wrapping papers and cards.

*The Wren Press*, 26 Chelsea Wharf, 15 Lots Road, SW10; 0171-351-5887. Fine engraving and printing at affordable prices - everything from letterheads to party invitations.

**Unusual Gifts**

All major department stores have special departments for distinctive and unusual gifts. Here are a few shops and stores which have many different and fun items.

*Asprey plc*, 165 New Bond Street, W1; 0171-493-6767. Fine gifts, silver and china.

*Nina Campbell*, 9 Walton Street, SW3; 0171-225-1011. Eclectic assortment of decorative items for the home.

*Conran Shop*, Michelin House, 81 Fulham Road, SW3; 0171-589-7401. Designer household items from furniture to kitchenware.

*Crabtree and Evelyn*, 6 Kensington Church Street, W8; 0171-937-9335. Other branches throughout London.

*The Design Centre*, 28 Haymarket, SW1; 0171-839-8000. Novel gifts.

*Dragons of Walton Street*, 23 Walton Street, SW3; 0171-589-3795. Children's designer accessories.

*Alfred Dunhill*, 30 Duke Street, SW1; 0171-499-9566; Also 5 Sloane Street, SW1; 0171-235-9799. Men's accessories.

*J. Floris Ltd.*, 89 Jermyn Street, SW1; 0171-930-2885. Soaps, perfumes and bath requisites for men and women.

*General Trading Company*, 144 Sloane Street, SW1; 0171-730-0411. Upmarket items for the entire house, including furniture, china, kitchenware and eclectic accessories.

*Graham & Green*, 4-10 Elgin Crescent, W11; 0171-727-4594. Unusual collection of household accessories.

*Thomas Goode*, 12 South Audley Street, W1; 0171-499-2823. China, crystal and antiques.

*Halcyon Days*, 14 Brook Street, W1; 0171-629-8811; Also 4 Royal Exchange, EC3; 0171-626-1120. Enamel boxes, clocks and many other decorative items.

*Oggetti*, 133 Fulham Road, SW3; 0171-581-8088. Everything for the kitchen.

*Osborne & Little*, 304 King's Road, SW3; 0171-352-1456. Interior designer, household gifts.

*Penhaligons*, 41 Wellington Street, WC2; 0171-836-4973. Perfumers.

*The Reject Shop*, 245-249 Brompton Road, SW3; 0171-584-7611; Also 234 King's Road, SW3; 0171-352-2750 and other branches throughout London. General household items at reasonable prices.

*Saville-Edells*, 25 Walton Street, SW3; 0171-584-4398. Host of unusual gift items.

## SHOPPING FOR THE HOME

### China and Crystal

All major department stores offer a large selection, although many have to order required items or large numbers of items.

*Asprey & Co. Ltd.*, 165 New Bond Street, W1; 0171-493-6767.

*Bridgewater China and Glass*, 739 Fulham Road, SW6; 0171-371-9033. Emma Bridgewater's sponged china.

*China Craft*, 556 Oxford Street, W1; 0171-724-8493. Branches throughout London, including Brent Cross Shopping Centre.

*The Dining Room Shop*, 62 White Hart Lane, SW13; 0181-878-1020.

*Garrard & Co. Ltd.*, Crown Jewellers, 112 Regent Street, W1; 0171-734-7020.

*General Trading Company*, 144 Sloane Street, SW1; 0171-730-0411.

*The Irish Linen Shop*, 11 Duke Street, W1; 0171-493-8949.

*Lawley's Ltd.*, 154 Regent Street, W1; 0171-734-2621.

*Noritake Ltd.*, 105 Baker Street, W1; 0171-935-7543.

*Rosenthal*, 137 Regent Street, W1; 0171-734-3076.

*Royal Copenhagen & George Jensen Silver*, 15B New Bond Street, W1; 0171-253-0373.

*Thomas Goode & Co.*, 19 South Audley Street, W1; 0171-499-2823.

---

*Waterford Wedgwood*, 158 Regent Street, W1; 0171-734-7262.

**Discount China and Crystal**

*London*

*Reject China Shop*, 33 Beauchamp Place, SW3; 0171-581-0737. Discounts on first and second quality china and crystal.

*Outside London*

*Aynsley*, 27-29 Uttoxeter Road, Longton, Staffordshire ST3; (01782) 599499.

*Crown Staffordshire*, Minerva Works, King Street, Fenton, Stoke-on-Trent; (01782) 49174.

*C. Hartley & Sons Ltd.*, Ley Avenue (and other locations) Letchworth, Hertfordshire; (014626) 79483. Fifteen per cent off china and Waterford, first quality only. They will take phone orders and deliver in London at no extra charge.

*Minton Bone China and Royal Doulton*, London Road, Stoke-on-Trent, Staffordshire; (01782) 7447766. Located 3 miles from Crown Staffordshire.

*Portmeirion*, 523 King Street, Longton, Staffordshire; (01782) 326412.

*Reeves & Son*, 142 High Street, Rochester, Kent; (01634) 843339. First quality china 20 per cent discount, some discount on crystal as well.

*Royal Crown Derby*, P.O. Box 1, 194 Osmaston Road, Derby, Derbyshire DE3; (01332) 47051.

*Royal Worcester*, Worcester Royal Porcelain Ltd., Severn Street, WR1; (01905) 23221.

*Spode Ltd.*, Church Street, Stoke-on-Trent, Staffordshire ST4; (01782) 744011.

*Wedgwood*, Josiah Wedgwood and Sons Ltd., Barlaston, Stoke-on-Trent, Staffordshire ST12; (01782) 204141.

**Crystal Factories** (with outlet shops)

*Royal Brierley Crystal*, North Street, Brierley Hill, West Midlands DY5; (01384) 70161.

*Stuart Crystal*, Stuart & Sons Ltd., Redhouse Cone Glassworks, Camp Hill, Wordsley, Stourbridge, DY8; (01384) 71161.

*Tudor Crystal*, Stourbridge Ltd., Junction Road, Wordsley, Stourbridge, West Midlands DY8; (01384) 393325.

## Do It Yourself (DIY)

There are many local DIY stores. We have only listed the large chains which can be found throughout London. Look in your Yellow Pages for a complete listing.

*B&Q*, Western Avenue, Greenford, UB6; 0181-575-7175. Also Alexandra Road, Wimbledon SW19; 0181-879-3322, and other branches throughout London. A wide selection of DIY and garden needs. The only DIY to offer free delivery.

*Pitfield Brewery*, 8 Pitfield Street, N1; 0171-739-3701. Extensive range of home brewing and wine making equipment and ingredients. There is also a comprehensive range of beers and lagers for sale, including Pitfields own.

*Sainsbury's Homebase*, 193 Warwick Road, W14; 0171-603-6397. Also other branches throughout London. All your DIY needs, plus Laura Ashley, Vogue Carpets, Schreiber Kitchens, curtains and gardening. Open 7 days per week.

*Texas Homecare*, York Road, Battersea, SW11; 0171-228-7666, and branches throughout London.

## Electrical and Gas Appliances

Most major department stores offer a range of appliances from toasters to microwave ovens. The best known are:

*Peter Jones*, Sloane Square, SW1; 0171-730-3434.

*Harrods*, 87 Brompton Road, SW1; 0171-730-1234.

*John Lewis*, 278-306 Oxford Street, W1; 0171-629-7711.

*Selfridges*, 400 Oxford Street, W1; 0171-629-1234.

*Also available at:-*

*London Electricity Board* (LEB) listed under 'Electricity' in the telephone directory.

---

Shopping
164

*British Gas* listed under 'Gas' in the telephone directory.

*Comet*, discount warehouses throughout London selling electrical and domestic appliances.

*Currys*, discount warehouses throughout London selling electrical and domestic appliances.

*Samson's (Electrical)*, 21 Crawford Place W1; 0171-723-7851; Sells transformers and electronic goods (no appliances).

*P.M. Linpower*, 8 Micklethwaite Road, SW6; 0171-385-2349. Installation of American appliances and general household plumbing. Has partner who converts electrical goods from 110 watts to 240 watts.

*Tempo Electrical Discount Store*, 190 Kensington High Street, W8; 0171-937-5166. Discount shop for large and small electrical appliances.

## Fabrics, Wallpapers and Paints

Most major department stores carrying decorating materials will advise and do drapery, upholstery and other work. Fabric and wallpaper are sold by the metre. *Liberty* fabrics are world famous and of a consistently high quality. *John Lewis* and *Peter Jones* are also known for their excellent haberdashery and own label quality fabric departments.

Equivalents:

| | | |
|---|---|---|
| 1 inch | = | 2.5 centimetres |
| 1 foot | = | 30 centimetres |
| 1 yard | = | 0.9 metres |
| 1 centimetre | = | 0.333 inch |
| 1 metre | = | 39.37 inches |

*Laura Ashley*, 7-9 Harriet Street, SW1; 0171-235-9797. Other branches throughout London.

*Cole & Son*, 18 Mortimer Street, W1; 0171-580-1066. Specialise in hand-printed wallpapers and own range paints.

*Colefax & Fowler*, 39 Brook Street, W1; 0171-493-2231. Also branches on Fulham Road. Famous for chintz.

*Conran Shop*, Michelin House, 81 Fulham Road, SW3; 0171-589-7401.

*Designer's Guild*, Showroom 267-271 and 277 King's Road, SW6; 0171-351-5775.  Wide range of contemporary, colourful wallpapers and paints.

*Fiona Campbell*, 259 New King's Road, SW6; 0171-731-3681.

*Jane Churchill*, 151 Sloane Street, SW1; 0171-730-9847.

*Habitat*, 208 King's Road, SW3;  0171-351-1211.  Also branches on Tottenham Court Road and Finchley Road.

*Liberty*, 210-220 Regent Street, W1; 0171-734-1234.

*Mary Fox Linton Ltd.*, 249 Fulham Road, SW3; 0171-622-0920.

*Material World*, 256b Wimbledon Park Road, SW19; 0181-785-3366.  Sell discount designer fabrics.  Also branch on 49 New King's Road, SW6.

*Nina Campbell*, 9 Walton Street, SW3; 0171-225-1011.  Sells her own fabrics and wallpapers.

*John S. Oliver Ltd.*, 33 Pembridge Road, W11;  0171-221-6466.  Produce a unique range of paints that match their hand-made wallpapers.

*Osborne & Little Ltd.*, 304-308 King's Road, SW3;  0171-352-1456.

*Arthur Sanderson & Sons Ltd.*, 112-120 Brompton Road, SW3; 0171-584-3344.  London's widest choice of wallpapers and furnishing fabrics.

If you are interested in both furnishing and dress-making fabrics you may also like to visit some of the following:

*Allans of Duke Street*, 56-58 Duke Street, W1;  0171-629-3781.

*Jacob Gordon*, 75 Duke Street, W1; 0171-629-5947.  Sells wide range of fabrics at discount prices.  Has large array of pure silks.

*Jason's of Bond Street*, 53 Bond Street, W1;  0171-629-2606.

*Jean Muir*, 59-61 Farringdon Road, EC1; 0171-831-0691.  Good source for discounted fabrics.  Stocks Jean Muir's matte jersey, pure wools, tweeds and cottons throughout the year.

*Viyella*, 96-98 Brompton Road, SW3; 0171-584-7075.  Sells full range of men's and women's Viyella clothing.  Also stocks the fabric!

---

**Flowers**

Some major department stores have flower departments, including *Harrods* and *Harvey Nichols* and offer Interflora services.

*Azagury*, 50 Knightsbridge, London SW1; 0171-259-5141.

*Heal's Flower Shop*, 196 Tottenham Court Road, W1; 0171-636-1666.
　Also sells the flowers outside the Michelin Building on Fulham Road.

*Moyses Stevens*, 157-158 Sloane Street, SW1; 0171-493-8171.

*Joan Palmer*, 31 Palmer Street, SW1; 0171-222-4364. Long established and dependable florist which dispatches flowers and arrangements packed in cardboard boxes throughout Central London.

*Pulbrook & Gould*, 127 Sloane Street, SW1; 0171-730-0030. Offers Interflora service.

*Silk Landscape Contracts*, 164 Old Brompton Road, SW5; 0171-835-1500.
　Also a branch on Fulham Road.

*New Covent Garden Market*, Nine Elms Lane, SW8; 0171-720-2211. Bulk sales of fruit, vegetables and flowers to the trade. Individuals may enter by paying a parking fee (£2) and may buy flowers and produce at the vendors' discretion. Market hours: Flowers 04.00-11.00 (Saturdays 04.00-09.00 during summer); fruit and vegetables 04.00-11.00, weekdays only.

**Furniture**

Most major department stores offer furniture ranging from traditional to modern styles; some have antiques. There are also specialist furniture stores which deal in reproductions.

*Albrizzi*, 1 Sloane Square, SW1; 0171-730-6119. Italian and continental modern furniture designs.

*And So To Bed*, 638-640 King's Road, SW6; 0171-731-3593. Specialises in brass beds. Also occasional furniture including tables, chairs, etc.

*Conran Shop*, 81 Fulham Road, SW3; 0171-589-7401. Modern and contemporary furniture and accessories.

*Elizabeth Eaton*, 25a Basil Street, SW3; 0171-589-0118. Specialises in French provincial. Closed Saturday.

*General Trading Company*, 144 Sloane Street, SW1; 0171-730-0411. Antiques, ethnic artefacts, china, etc.

*Habitat*, 208 King's Road, SW3; 0171-351-1211; Tottenham Court Road, W1; 0171-631-3880. Other branches, owned by the Conran Group.

*Heal's*, 196 Tottenham Court Road, W1; 0171-636-1666. Modern international selection. Inspiring room sets. Good selection of English contemporary furniture.

*IKEA*, Brent Park, 255 North Circular Road, NW10; 0181-451-5566. Swedish budget furniture. Contemporary, inexpensive and hard wearing.

*Kingcome*, 302-304 Fulham Road, SW10; 0171-351-3998. Sofa and chair specialists.

*Liberty*, Regent Street, W1; 0171-734-1234. Interesting selection of modern furniture from some of the best designers in Europe.

*Maples*, 145 Tottenham Court Road, W1; 0171-387-7000. Reproductions of traditional pieces.

*Parsons Green Reproductions*, 151 Lower Richmond Road, SW15; 0181-788-3616.

*Purves & Purves*, 80-81 and 83 Tottenham Court Road, W1; 0171-580-8223. Good selection of fine contemporary European furniture, furnishings and accessories.

*The Reject Shop*, 234 King's Road, SW3; 0171-352-2820. Also other shops throughout London. Keenly priced modern furniture.

*Tulley's*, 28d Fulham Road, SW10; 0171-352-1078.

*Zarach*, 48 South Audley Street, W1; 0171-730-3339. Modern furniture in leather and chrome.

## Gardening, Window Boxes and Christmas Trees

From the most elaborate garden to the simplest flower box, London is in bloom most of the year. A few suggestions to put some colour into your life.

*Barralets of Ealing Ltd.*, Houseplant Centre, Pitshanger Lane, W5; 0181-997-0576. Garden and horticultural centre. Also supplies indoor plants and organises window box displays.

*British Christmas Tree Growers Association*; 0181-946-2695. Telephone for details of the nearest 'chop your own' Christmas tree.

*The Chelsea Gardener*, 125 Sydney Street, SW3; 0171-352-5656. Comprehensive garden centre selling everything from shrubs and plants to gardening furniture and books. Also has excellent selection of houseplants and a florist department.

*Clifton Nurseries*, 5A Clifton Villas, W9; 0171-289-6851. An excellent all purpose garden centre. Services also include garden designing and delivery.

*Columbia Road Market*, E2. Sundays 08.00-12.30. Outside street market selling plants, shrubs, flowers and garden accessories.

*Fulham Palace Garden Centre*, Bishop's Avenue, SW6; 0171-736-2640. Good selection of plants, pots and shrubs. Garden landscaping and delivery available.

*Garden Crafts*, 158 New King's Road, SW6; 0171-736-1615. Excellent selection of garden furniture and garden ornaments.

*Homebase*, 195 Warwick Road, W14; 0171-603-6397. Large selection of basic shrubs and plants as well as all types of garden tools and accessories. Branches throughout London.

*Rassell's Nursery*, 80 Earl's Court Road, W8; 0171-937-0481. Garden plants and shrubs, window boxes and hanging baskets made to order.

*Royal Horticultural Society*, 80 Vincent Square, SW1; 0171-834-4333. Have a comprehensive reference library available to non-members.

**Kitchen Equipment**

Most major department stores offer a large selection of kitchen equipment, particularly good are: *Conran's, Habitat, Peter Jones/John Lewis, Harrods* and *Selfridges*. Some of the better known shops are listed below.

*Anything Left-Handed*, 57 Brewer Street, W1; 0171-437-3910. Stocks left-handed kitchen equipment.

*David Mellor*, 4 Sloane Square, SW1; 0171-730-4259.

*Divertimenti*, 139-141 Fulham Road, SW3; 0171-581-8065. Also 45-47 Wigmore Street, W1; 0171-935-0689.

*Elizabeth David*, Unit 3A North Row, Covent Garden Market, WC2; 0171-836-9167.

*Fairfax Kitchen Shop*, 1 Regency Parade, NW3; 0171-722-7648.

*General Trading Company*, 144 Sloane Street, SW1; 0171-730-0411.

*Hansen's Kitchen & Bakery Equipment Ltd.*, 306 Fulham Road, SW10; 0171-351-6933.

*The Kitchen Place*, 92 Heath Street, NW3; 0171-431-0469. Fitted kitchen retailer with many appliances.

*Leon Jaeggi & Sons Ltd.*, 77 Shaftesbury Avenue, W1; 0171-580-1974. Caters to commercial trade, good for appliances.

*Oggetti*, 133 Fulham Road, SW3; 0171-581-8088. Offers British and continental accessories.

*Pages*, 121 Shaftesbury Avenue, WC2; 0171-378-6334.

**Linens**

Most department stores carry a wide selection of linens. Other stores are listed below.

*Albary Linens*, 6 Baker Street, W1; 0171-487-4105. Large selection of American size sheets and towels.

*Givans*, 207 King's Road, SW3; 0171-352-6352.

---

*Irish Linen Co.*, 35-36 Burlington Arcade, W1; 0171-493-8949.

*Linen Cupboard*, 21 Great Castle Street, W1; 0171-629-4062.

*The Monogrammed Linen Shop*, 168 Walton Street, SW3; 0171-589-4033.
    Personalised items; will also embroider your own items.

*The White House*, 51 New Bond Street, W1; 0171-629-3521.


## ART AND ANTIQUES

Antique hunting in London is a joy. You can look for hidden treasures in the small stalls of the early-morning street markets, or for magnificent *objets d'art* in the fine, established antique shops of Fulham Road, Bond Street, Knightsbridge, Kensington Church Street or King's Road. Remember that no matter how elegant or humble the establishment, gracious haggling is permitted. Perhaps the best approach is to ask sweetly, "Is this your best price?" Dealers are often prepared to come down 10 percent, which they say is a trade discount. If they do not come down, do not persist, as the price may genuinely be the best they can give.

### Antique Shops

London has so many fine antique shops, it is impossible to list them all. Instead we have given a general indication of where clusters of shops are located.

If you are looking for a specialist dealer, *The British Antique Dealers Association*, (20 Rutland Gate, SW7; 0171-589-4128) will send a list of members on request.

Choice, and expensive, antiques can be found in Bond Street, Mount Street, Brook Street, Sloane Street, Brompton Road and the South Kensington end of Fulham Road. Kensington Church Street has lots of interesting antique shops, with many specialising in china and glass. Pimlico Road is interesting for unusual and decorative pieces.

There are antique markets all over London where groups of dealers, specialising in a variety of antiques or collectables at all different price levels, display their goods. Some of them are listed below.

### Street Markets (Specialising in Antiques)

Everything from fine silver to genuine fakes can be found at the different markets in London, but be very careful!

*Bermondsey Market (New Caledonian Market)*, Long Lane and Bermondsey Street, SE1.  Open 05.00-14.00 Fridays.  Specialises in paintings, silver and jewellery.  Best before 09.00.

*Camden Passage*, Camden Passage, N1.  Open 10.00-14.00 Wednesdays and 10.00-17.00 Saturdays.  Specialises in prints, silver, 19th century magazines, jewellery and toys.

*Portobello Road Market*, Portobello Road, W10.  07.00-17.30 Saturdays (for antiques and junk).  Has over 2,000 stalls displaying jewellery, old medals, paintings, silver and *objets d'art*.

**Indoor Markets** ("Antique Supermarkets")

These markets contain numerous permanent stalls that deal in smaller items such as silver, prints, jewellery and ceramics.

*Alfie's Antique Market*, 13-25 Church Street, NW8;  0171-723-6066.  Closed Sunday and Monday.  Source of some real bargains.

*Antiquarius*, 131-141 King's Road, SW3; 0171-351-5353.  Closed Sunday.  Has over 170 dealers.  Good for browsing.

*Bond Street Antiques Centre*, 124 New Bond Street, W1; 0171-493-1854.  Closed Saturday and Sunday.

*Chelsea Antique Market*, 253 King's Road, SW3; 0171-352-1424.  Closed Sunday.

*The Chenil Galleries*, 181 King's Road; 0171-351-5353.  Wide selection of art nouveau and deco objects and fine art.

*Gray's Antique Market*, 1-7 Davies Mews, W1; 0171-629-7034.  Closed Saturday and Sunday.

*London Silver Vaults*, 53-64 Chancery Lane, WC2; 0171-242-3844.  Every imaginable kind of silver item from antique to new.  Closed Saturday afternoon and Sunday.

**Antique Fairs**

*Chelsea Antiques Fair*, Chelsea Old Town Hall, King's Road, SW3.  Autumn and spring.

*Grosvenor House Art & Antiques Fair*, Grosvenor House Hotel, W1.  June.

*Burlington House Antiques Fair*, Burlington House, Piccadilly, W1.  Autumn.

---

*The Fine Arts & Antique Fair*, Olympia, W14. February and June.

*West London Antiques Fair*, Kensington Town Hall, Hornton Street, W8. January.

For complete listings of regularly scheduled Sunday fairs in London and throughout the U.K., check the weekly newspaper *The Antiques Trade Gazette* and two monthly magazines, *The Antique Collector* and *The Antique Dealer and Collector's Guide*. All three are available at larger news-stands.

## Auctions

Auctions are the best place for antique hunting if you have the time. Items for auction are on view a few days before the sale. At the viewing, you can purchase a catalogue, usually about £15, which includes descriptions and estimates for each lot. Bidding is easy - you register, take a paddle with a number, then raise your hand when the lot you want comes up. The auctioneer will take your bid. If you are successful, he or she will note your number. It's that simple! It can be great fun and can be one of the cheapest places to buy antiques.

The main auction houses are *Christie's* and *Sotheby's*. Here the *crème de la crème* of the art world gather and rare masterpieces exchange hands. Not everything at *Christie's* and *Sotheby's* is so far out of reach, so each is definitely worth a visit just for fun. Most of the firms listed below (and others) advertise their auctions in *The Daily Telegraph, The Times* and *The Financial Times* as well as weekly events magazines such as *Time Out*.

*Bonham's Knightsbridge*, Montpelier Street, SW7; 0171-584-9161. Holds regular sales of fine furniture, paintings, objets d'art, jewellery, silver, clocks, ceramics (Oriental, European and Contemporary), tribal art antiquities, cars, musical instruments, books, guns and fountain pens.

*Bonham's Chelsea*, 65-69 Lots Road, SW10; 0171-351-7111. Holds regular sales of 19th and 20th century furniture and carpets. Picture auctions are weekly, ceramics and silver fortnightly and prints, books and jewellery, monthly.

*Christie's*, 8 King Street, SW1; 0171-839-9060. Regular sales of period furniture, Victorian, Georgian and Edwardian furniture, Art Deco, Art Nouveau, Chinese, Japanese, and Persian works of art, ceramics, jewellery, and general ephemera. Contact for special sales and viewing dates.

*Christie's South Kensington*, 85 Old Brompton Road, SW7; 0171-581-7611. Regular sales of antiques, carpets, embroidery and textiles, Art Deco and Art Nouveau, furniture, pictures, prints, and works of art from the

Victorian period, porcelain, ceramics, English and Continental watercolours on Tuesdays, Wednesdays and Thursdays. Contact for viewing dates and sale times.

*Lots Road Galleries*, 71 Lots Road, SW10; 0171-351-7771. Two sales every Monday. At 15.00 a selection of contemporary and household furnishings ranging from sofas, tables, and rugs to ceramics, prints and engravings. The main auction of period quality furniture and objects d'art begins at 18.00. Viewing Friday-Sunday, prior to the sale.

*Phillips*, 101 New Bond Street, W1; 0171-629-6602. Regular sales of antique furniture, ceramics, carpets and works of art. Monthly specialist sales of quality antique furniture, 18th and 19th century pieces, collectors items, and fine art. Contact for viewing times.

*Phillips West Two*, 10 Salem Road, W2; 0171-229-9090. Holds auctions on Thursdays which include house clearances and all types of collectors' items.

*Roseberry's Auction Rooms*, Crystal Palace Station, Crystal Palace Station Road, SE19; 0181-778-4024. Three sales per month of antique furniture, Victorian pictures, ceramics, and bric-a-brac held on Saturdays at noon. Quality antique sale held on the last Saturday of the month at noon. Contact for viewing times.

*Sotheby's*, 34-35 New Bond Street, W1; 0171-493-8080. Regular sales of antique furniture, Edwardian, Victorian, and modern 20th century furniture, rugs, and carpets, porcelain, glass, prints, works of art and general small collectables. Contact for viewing times.

## Art Galleries

London has many fine art galleries whatever your taste, be it Old Masters or young contemporary artists. The more expensive dealers are concentrated in St. James's and Mayfair, others are scattered throughout the city. A few well-known galleries are listed below.

*Thomas Agnew*, 43 Old Bond Street, W1; 0171-629-6176. Excellent source of Old Masters, watercolours, drawings, 20th century British and contemporary pictures.

*Colnaghi*, 14 Old Bond Street, W1; 0171-491-7408. Specialises in Old Master paintings and drawings.

*Fine Art Society*, 148 New Bond Street, W1; 0171-629-5116. 19th and 20th century British paintings, sculpture and decorative arts.

*Richard Green*, 44 Dover Street, W1; 0171-493-3939. Also, 4 New Bond Street, W1; 39 Dover Street, W1; and 33 New Bond Street, W1. Offers British sporting and marine paintings, French Impressionists, modern British, Victorian, European and Old Master pictures.

*Marlborough Graphics Ltd.*, 6 Albemarle Street, W1; 0171-629-5161. Source of Impressionist, Post-Impressionist and leading contemporary artists.

*Photographers' Gallery*, 5 Great Newport Street, WC2; 0171-831-1772. Offers largest collection of original photographs for sale in the country.

*Smith's Galleries*, 56 Earlham Street, WC2; 0171-836-9701. Home to the Contemporary Art Society's annual autumn market. Offers contemporary, affordable art throughout the year.

*Specialist Photographers' Company*, 21 Kensington Park Road, W11; 0171-221-3489. Well known for selling top-quality works.

*Vanessa Devereux Gallery*, 11 Blenheim Crescent, W11; 0171-221-6836. Offers vibrant contemporary work by young artists.

*Waddington Galleries Ltd.*, 5a, 11, 12 and 34 Cork Street, W1; 0171-437-8611. Large commercial art gallery specialising in 20th century paintings, sculpture, works on paper and limited edition prints from Europe and America.

## HEALTH, PERFUMES AND TOILETRIES

### Drugstores and Chemists

Your local Police Station holds a list of Chemists in your area that are available at all hours in case of an emergency.

*John Bell & Croyden*, 50-54 Wigmore Street, W1; 0171-935-5555. Open Monday-Friday, 09.00-18.30, Saturday 09.00-17.00.

*Bliss Chemist*, 50-56 Willesden Lane, NW6; 0171-624-8000. Open 09.00-24.00 seven days a week.

*Boots*, 302 Regent Street, W1R; 0171-637-9418. Toothpaste to Toddlers clothing. Open Monday-Friday, 08.00-19.00, Saturday 09.00-18.00. Branches all over London; some open Sundays.

*Dajani Pharmacy*, 92 Old Brompton Road, SW7; 0171-589-8263. Open Monday-Friday, 09.00-22.00, Saturday 09.00-21.00, Sunday 10.00-20.00, Bank Holidays 10.00-20.00.

*Dennis and Co.*, 12 Pembridge Road, W11; 0171-229-0958. Open Monday-Friday, 08.30-19.00, Saturday 09.00-18.00.

*Trident Pharmacy*, 187 Worple Road, SW20; 0181-946-6282. Open Monday-Friday, 09.00-19.00, Saturday 09.00-18.00.

*Warmen-Freed*, 45 Golders Green Road, NW11; 0181-455-4351. Open 08.30-24.00 every day (including Bank Holidays).

**Perfumes and Toiletries**

*The Body Shop*, 54 King's Road, SW3; 0171-584-0163. Wide range of skin and hair care products with natural ingredients. None of the products or ingredients are tested on animals.

*Crabtree & Evelyn*, 6 Kensington Church Street, W8; 0171-937-9335. Other branches throughout London. Sells a wide range of popular men's and women's skin and hair care products. Also carries a selection of high quality products for children and home. Will assemble gift baskets.

*Culpeper Ltd.*, 8 The Market, Covent Garden, WC2; 0171-379-6698. Employs herbal and floral remedies as bases for their natural, therapeutic toiletries. Make cosmetics, hair preparations, pot-pourri, pomanders as well as oils for aromatherapy.

*Czech & Speake*, 39c Jermyn Street, SW1; 0171-439-0216. Flower-based scents and toiletries for men and women.

*Floris*, 89 Jermyn Street, SW1; 0171-930-2885. Uses recipes that are hundreds of years old - still manufacture flower-based scents sold in the 19th century.

*Molton Brown*, 58 South Molton Street, W1; 0171-629-1872. Sells a range of natural cosmetics, body and haircare products.

*Neal's Yard Remedies*, 15 Neal's Yard, WC2; 0171-379-7222. Also outlet in Chelsea Farmer's Market. Uses traditional herbal and floral remedies as base for natural and therapeutic remedies.

*Penhaligon's*, 15-16 Burlington Arcade, W1; 0171-629-1416. British perfumery which sells traditional toilet water and other exotic scents.

---

## MARKETS

London's street markets are great fun to visit and offer some of the most competitive prices. (Also see Art and Antiques section for further listings).

*Berwick Street Market*, Berwick Street, W1. Open 09.00-18.00 Monday-Saturday. All kinds of fruit and vegetables as well as fabrics, household goods and leather handbags.

*Brick Lane Market*, Brick Lane, E1. Open daybreak-13.00 Sunday. Furniture, old books, jewellery, watches, food, bicycles, handbags - offers something for everyone!

*Brixton Market*, Electric Avenue, SW9. Open 08.30-17.50 Monday, Tuesday, Thursday-Saturday; 08.30-13.00 Wednesday. All kinds of wonderful Afro-Caribbean food from goat's meat to plantains.

*Camden Lock Market*, Buck Street, NW1. Open 09.00-17.00 Thursday and Friday; 10.00-18.00 Saturday and Sunday. Handmade crafts, new and secondhand street fashions, books, records, etc.

*East Street Market*, East Street, SE17. Open 08.00-17.00 Tuesday, Wednesday, Friday and Saturday; 08.00-14.00 Thursday and Sunday. On Sundays has over 250 stalls selling fruit, vegetables, flowers, clothes, electrical and household goods.

*Petticoat Lane Market*, Middlesex Street, E1. Open 09.00-14.00 Sunday. Leathergoods, clothes, watches, jewellery and toys.

*Shepherd's Bush Market*, Goldhawk Road, W12. Open 09.30-17.00 Monday-Wednesday, Friday and Saturday; 09.30-14.30 Thursday. West Indian food, Asian spices and cheap electrical and household goods.

# Chapter Twelve:
# Continuing Education and Leisure

The opportunities are immense. We could not possibly list the thousands of classes, programmes, lectures, tours and college courses available in London. Consequently, we have concentrated our efforts on those which are well known and frequented by Junior League of London members. Many of these programmes are fairly costly so it is always best to enquire by phone or post for an up-to-date price list and curriculum before you make definite plans.

## UNIVERSITY AND COLLEGE COURSES

There are numerous courses available: undergraduate, graduate, part-time and full-time. Check to see whether the course might be credited to any degree you are planning to complete. Tuition fees vary and, if you have resided in the U.K. long enough, you might be eligible for 'home student tuition', which is generally half the overseas student fee. Check with the school.

*U.S.-U.K. Educational Commission* (also known as the Fulbright Commission), Educational Advisory Service, Fulbright House, 62 Doughty Street, WC1N 2LS; 0171-404-6994 (Monday to Friday, 10.30-16.00). Nearest tube: Russell Square. This organization principally advises students concerning university study in the U.S. They hold an annual university day and have a comprehensive reference library of information on U.S. colleges. Additionally, they supply information concerning American colleges in the U.K.

*The Open University*, Walton Hall, Milton Keynes, MK7 6AA; (01908) 274066/653231. Offers university courses to any resident of the European Union over 18 years of age. Methods of instruction include television courses, tutorials and correspondence work.

*The University of London*, Centre for Extramural Studies, (Birkbeck College), 26 Russell Square, WC1 5DQ; 0171-631-6633. Nearest tube: Russell Square. Offers certificate, diploma, and general interest courses to anyone over 18 years of age. Classes usually meet 2 hours a week for 24 weeks.

## LOCAL ADULT EDUCATION COURSES

Contact your local borough town hall (Kensington and Chelsea and Hammersmith and Fulham, etc.) for information on hundreds of adult education classes, ranging from pottery, car mechanics and Italian to degrees in social work. The fees are usually very reasonable because they are government subsidized and classes are held at various locations within your neighbourhood.

## COURSES IN THE ARTS

Prices vary depending on the duration of the course and the institution. Many courses follow a semester or school year schedule, therefore it is advisable to call well in advance to secure a place. Additionally, many course offerings change based on current interest. For the most current curriculum content and schedule, call the school and ask for a brochure.

### Intensive Courses

*Christie's Fine Arts Courses*, 63 Old Brompton Road, SW7 3JS; 0171-581-3933. Nearest tube: South Kensington. Diploma Course A covers antiquity to Renaissance. Diploma Course B covers Renaissance to present day. Christie's aim to give students a firm and practical foundation of knowledge in the fine and decorative arts of the western world. Students undertake projects in cataloguing and the workings of the art market. Over 3 10-week terms. Students must apply for a full-time place. A part-time, non-diploma course, the London Art Course, is also available. Visits to sales rooms and galleries are included.

*Christie's Evening Courses*. These are short courses covering a variety of specialised subjects. One evening a week for 8 weeks, by application to the above address.

*The History of Art Studies*, 13 South Terrace, SW7 2TB; 0171-584-6086 and 0181-852-1842. Courses are held at the Linnean Society, Burlington House, Piccadilly W1. Nearest tube: Piccadilly. Certificate and general interest courses are available to include the following: The History of Painting and Sculpture of the Renaissance to the Present Day, Architecture from Classical Greece to the Modern Movement, as well as Decorative Arts from Classical Greece to the Modern Movement. Additionally, there are short courses on special topics, trips abroad, private views to exhibitions, and lectures held at various London museums.

*Modern Art Studies*, 484 King's Road, SW10 0LF; 0171-351-4887. Part of Christie's education curriculum. Courses are held at Birkbeck College, 43 Gordon Square WC1. Nearest tube: Russell Square. History of Modern Art from Impressionism to the Present Day, runs 3 mornings a week for 3 terms, either on a full year or per term basis. A year long, full-time certificate course is also offered. Additionally, a short course of indepth lectures on modern art is available, offered 3 times per year, taken on a year or term basis, meeting 1 afternoon a week.

*Sotheby's Educational Studies*, 30 Oxford Street, W1N 9FL; 0171-323-5775. Nearest tube: Tottenham Court Road. Sotheby's offers an extensive curriculum geared at the undergraduate and postgraduate level, as well as providing a variety of extramural studies. Their approach differs from the traditional university in that they view the study of the fine and decorative arts first as object based, then theory based, thereby preparing students for a vocation in the art field. Secondly, they include a detailed study of the decorative arts as well as the fine arts where traditional university programmes tend to emphasize only the fine arts. Acceptance to the undergraduate and graduate programme is by application and interview. Extramural courses have no prerequisites. The Undergraduate, Graduate and Extramural courses are described below:

**Undergraduate Programme**

This is a 2 year, full-time course culminating in a Diploma of Education that is validated by the University of Manchester. A one year certificate course is also available. The diploma course has 4 modules that can be taken individually or as a group. Each module runs 15 weeks and is offered twice a year.

1.  Styles of Art Course: An introduction to the developments in the fine and decorative arts in Europe from antiquity to the present day.

2.  17th and 18th Century Decorative Arts: Objects and styles of the period.

3.  19th and 20th Century Decorative Arts: Objects and styles of the period.

4.  19th and 20th Century Fine Art: Paintings only of the period.

**Graduate Programme**

The following two courses each culminate in a Masters of Art.

1.  Works of Art Course. This course aims to broaden and deepen the understanding of Western European Art and to develop the methods necessary to catalogue at a scholarly level. A wide range of media, including painting, ceramics, furniture, and silver are studied. It runs one year. Forms the basis for a postgraduate degree in the Fine and Decorative Arts.

2.  Post War and Contemporary Art Course. This is the highly specialized study of the history and the understanding of

the study of art from 1945 till the present day. Contact with galleries, curators, journalists, artists, and Sotheby's experts are essential elements and complement an integrated programme of lectures, seminars, and visits to Germany, Holland and Belgium among other countries. Runs 14 months. Diploma is validated by the University of Manchester.

**Extramural Courses**

1. Evening Courses. A variety of short courses, covering a wide range of fields, aimed at those unable to make the commitment required for the longer courses. Fields covered include furniture, jewellery, glass, silver, prints and drawings, fakes and forgeries and Japanese and Chinese Works of Art.

2. Summer School. Offers an Art Treasures of London course that covers European Arts of the 19th and 20th Century in and around London. It runs for 4 weeks in July-August.

3. SOAS/Sotheby's Asian Art Course. Certificate course in Eastern Art, run in conjunction with SOAS (School of Oriental and African Studies), University of London. It consists of 5 modules: Islamic, Chinese, Japanese and Korean, Southeast Asia and Oceania, and Indian and South Asian art. Each module runs 12 weeks and can be elected individually. Completion of all five modules leads to a postgraduate diploma.

4. The World of Textiles. A part-time course, running 1 day a week for 1 year.

5. Understanding Jewellery. A full-time course for 4 weeks, offered twice a year.

*The Study Centre for the History of the Fine and Decorative Arts*, 16 Beauchamp Place, SW3 1NQ; 0171-225-3027. Nearest tube: South Kensington. Courses are held near the Victoria and Albert Museum. Three major courses are offered. History of the Decorative Arts from 1500 to the Present; 10 week course, two times a year, 20 places, by application. The History of the Fine and Decorative Arts from 1500 to the Present; one year diploma course, 30 places, by interview. From Holbein to Hockney, a 6 week course covering the history of decorative arts from the 16th century to the present. Other short and one off courses are offered based on current interest. Telephone for specifics.

Continuing Education and Leisure

## One Day and Short Courses

*Art Study Circle*, Sara Hebblewaite; 0181-788-6910. Art history lectures given weekly in Sara's home in Putney by experts in their fields. Some tie in with current exhibitions and include visits.

*Art Tours of London*, 51A Gloucester Street, SW1V 4DY; (01734) 699967. Nearest tube: Pimlico. Offers a comprehensive introduction to the Arts of England covering the history of porcelain, silver, textiles, furniture styles, paintings, interior decoration, architecture, and garden design. Customized classes based on interest are also available.

*Terence O'Hair*, 42 Jackman House, Watts Street, E1 9UP; 0171-481-2185. Offers a History of Art from Egypt to the present day, meeting 1 day per week for 12 weeks. Lectures are at museums and galleries. Additionally, there are lectures for current London exhibitions, both at major as well as smaller galleries. Art tours abroad and English country houses visits are also available.

*Catherine Nunnelley Perspectives*, 19 Rosaville Road, SW6 7BN; 0171-381-6683. Nearest tube: Fulham Broadway. One day and short courses primarily featuring the history of art as well as general English history. Curriculum changes quarterly based on current interest. Telephone for further information.

## MUSEUM AND GALLERY LECTURES

Most museums and galleries offer regular free lectures and tours. See Chapter Thirteen for museum addresses and telephone numbers. Call for a schedule of events, and to be placed on mailing lists. Information on talks and lectures, as well as new exhibits, can be found in the weekly magazine *Time Out*.

## INTERIOR DESIGN/DECORATION COURSES

*The Inchbald School of Design*, 7 Eaton Gate, SW1W 9BA; 0171-730-5508. Nearest tube: Sloane Square. Short-term, certificate and diploma courses in art and design history, interior design and garden design. Admission by interview and application.

## COOKERY COURSES

*Le Cordon Bleu Cookery School*, 114 Marylebone Lane, W1M 6HH; 0171-935-3503. Nearest tube: Bond Street. Offers career training, short and part-time courses, practical and demonstration classes. Because this school is world famous, there is a waiting list for its diploma and certificate courses. Cookery demonstrations are open to the public. You must book for these demonstrations.

*Ken Lo's Memories of China, Chinese Cookery School*, Chelsea Harbour; 0171-352-4953. Nearest tube: Fulham Broadway. Associated with Ken Lo's restaurant. Offers cookery demonstrations in the art of Chinese cuisine. Classes in Thai on a request basis. Courses held evenings with occasional afternoon demonstrations.

*Leith's School of Food and Wine*, 21 St. Alban's Grove, W8 5BP; 0171-229-0177. Nearest tube: High Street Kensington. Associated with Leith's restaurant, the school offers diploma and certificate courses in food and wine for all levels, and a variety of short cookery courses.

*Tante Marie School of Cookery*, Woodham House, Carlton Road, Woking, Surrey GU21 4HF; (0148372) 6957. Accredited by the British Council. Offers both certificate and diploma courses as well as occasional demonstrations. A wide range of cuisines are covered.

*Constance Spry Ltd.*, Moor Park House, Moor Park Lane, Farnham, Surrey GU10 1QP; (01252) 734477. Offers a wide variety of cooking demonstrations held in conjunction with flower arranging courses (see Flower Arranging).

## WINE COURSES

*Christie's Wine Courses*, 63 Old Brompton Road, SW7 3JS; 0171-581-3933. Nearest tube: South Kensington. Offers an Introduction to Wine Tasting course (primarily focusing on French wines) that meets 1 evening a week for 5 weeks, available 6 times per year. Also runs one off master classes on fine and rare wines and occasional classes on wines of the New World.

*Sotheby's Wine Department*, 34-35 New Bond Street, W1A 2AA; 0171-493-8080. Nearest tube: Bond Street. Separate courses covering varietal and regional wines, running 1 evening a week for 5 weeks, offered 4 times per year. Seminars can be reserved for the entire series or part of the series. Wine dinners at outside venues are also available.

## FLOWER ARRANGING COURSES

*Mary Adams*, 4 Kinnerton Place South, SW1X 8EH; 0171-235-7117. Nearest tube: Knightsbridge. Teaches fresh and dried flower arranging in a natural style using country herbs, flowers and foliages. She also holds intensive certificate courses for wedding design in floristry and flower

---

arranging. Mini demonstrations and aromatherapy lectures are also held in the studio. Offers a very flexible programme, tailored for busy people, to accommodate half day, full day, or month long sessions.

*Constance Spry Ltd.* Two or three day flower arranging classes. Diploma course also available. (See Cookery Courses for address).

## GARDENING COURSES

The British take great pride in their gardens, and the following courses are very comprehensive.

*The Kew School of Garden Design*, Education and Marketing Department, Kew, Richmond, Surrey TW9 3AB; 0181-332-5623/4. Nearest tube: Kew Gardens. One day classes for beginners on a variety of topics. Short courses in plant photography and botanical illustration available.

*The English Gardening School*, The Chelsea Physics Garden, 66 Royal Hospital Road, SW3 4HS; 0171-352-4347. Nearest tube: Sloane Square. Certificate courses in design and horticulture, held 1-2 days per week over a year. One to four day classes, on a wide range of topics such as Christmas wreaths and flower arranging, are offered. Additionally, there is a correspondence course in design available.

*The Inchbald School of Design: Garden Design*, 32 Eccleston Square, SW1V 1PB; 0171-630-9011. Nearest tube: Victoria. A 1 year diploma course or 10-week single terms. Subject matter includes: basic principles of design, plant knowledge, the role of fine art in design, garden architecture and business skills. A 2 year Master Diploma and a 3 year Higher Master Diploma are also available.

## SPORTS AND FITNESS FACILITIES/PERSONAL TRAINERS

Most boroughs have a neighbourhood public sports facility that offers a variety of recreational facilities, such as pools, tennis courts, aerobics classes and parks. Call your local council for location, costs, and availability.

The following are private clubs and, many of them are fairly costly, though prices do vary. The facilities and prices shown are a guideline and represent, unless noted otherwise, the approximate fees for a single full time membership as of this printing. Many clubs have off peak memberships that cost less than a full membership and in general, allow you to use the club on weekdays from 09.00-17.00. Additionally, many have flexible payment schedules to accommodate instalments on a monthly basis.

*The Acupuncture Centre*, Ladbroke Grove, W11; 0171-286-9655. Specialize in pre and post natal yoga classes as well as baby massage classes. Call for fees.

*Alan Herdman Studios*, 17 Homer Row, W1H 1HU; 0171-723-9953. Nearest tube: Edgware Road. Practices the Pilates Technique, including body conditioning and corrective exercise. Fee: £12 per class.

*The Budokwai*, GK House, 4 Gilston Road, SW10; 0171-370-1000. Nearest tube: South Kensington or Gloucester Road. Offers a range of instruction in judo, karate and aikido for beginners through advanced level. Judo classes for children begin at age 4. Telephone for fees.

*Cannons Sports Clubs*. Two locations: Cousin Lane, EC4R 3TE; 0171-283-0101. Nearest tube: Cannon Street and Endell Street, WC2H 9SA; 0171-240-2446. Nearest tube: Covent Garden. Aerobics, fitness training, women's only gym at Cousin Lane location, pool, squash, sauna, massage, solarium, beauty facilities, cafe. Membership honoured at both locations. Fee: £175 to join plus £560 per year membership.

*Champneys The London Club*, Le Meridien Hotel, 21 Piccadilly, W1V OBH; 0171-437-8114. Nearest tube: Piccadilly. Pool, squash, gym, Cybex, sauna, solarium, library and beauty facilities. Fee: £250 to join plus £1,512 per year membership.

*Christine Hill Associates*, Strand End, 78 Grove Park Road, Chiswick, W4 3QA; 0181-994-4349. Obstetrics physiotherapists providing pre and post natal exercise classes. Call for fee schedule.

*Cottons Health and Fitness*, London Bridge City, Tooley Street, SE1 2QN; 0171-403-1171. Nearest tube: Tower Hill. Pool, squash, aerobics, fitness training, beauty facilities, physiotherapy and restaurant. Fee: £60 to join plus £700 a year membership fee.

*Danceworks*, 16 Balderton Street, W1Y 1TF; 0171-629-6183. Nearest tube: Bond Street. All sorts of dance, fitness and aerobic classes. Fee: £75 to join, plus £4 per class.

*David Lloyd Tennis Centre*, 1 Southall Lane, Hounslow, Middlesex PW5 9PE; 0181-573-9378. Located near Heathrow Airport. Tennis (12 indoor/9 outdoor courts), squash, badminton, pool, aerobics, fitness training, creche, restaurant and beauty facilities. Fee: £280 to join and £53 per month membership fee.

*English Folk Dance and Song Society*, Cecil Sharp House, 2 Regent's Park Road, NW1 7AY; 0171-485-2206. Classes and dances held throughout the year. Also has a shop and library. Fee: £18 society membership fee plus additional charge per class/dance.

Continuing Education and Leisure

*Espree Club*, 2 Royal Mint Court, EC3N 4QN; 0171-488-1222. Nearest tube: Tower Hill. Aerobics, fitness training, pool, massage, beauty facilities, lounge, and restaurant. Fee: £150 to join plus £56 per month membership fee.

*The Harbour Club*, Watermeadow Lane, SW6 4RR; 0171-371-7700. Pool with separate baby area, tennis (indoor/outdoor), a "real tennis" court, aerobics, fitness training, restaurant, beauty facilities, creche, a variety of children's activities to include gymnastics, karate, ballet, tennis and swimming. Has a waiting list to join. Fee: £2,400 (resaleable) to join and £96.50 per month membership.

*The Hogarth Health Club*, Airedale Avenue, W4 2N4; 0181-995-4600. Pool, tennis, squash, aerobics, fitness training, beauty facilities, creche and restaurant. Fee: £175 to join and £720 per year membership.

*Holmes Place Barbican*, 97 Aldersgate Street, EC2A; 0171-374-0091. Nearest tube: Barbican. Pool, indoor running track, aerobics, fitness training, separate men's and women's gyms, beauty facilities and restaurant. Telephone for membership rate information.

*Holmes Place Chelsea*, 188a Fulham Road, SW10 3PN; 0171-352-9452. Nearest tube: South Kensington or Gloucester Road. Pool, aerobics, fitness training, separate men's and women's gym, beauty facilities, restaurant and creche. Telephone for membership rate information.

*Holmes Place Ealing*, Level 5, Ealing Broadway Centre, Ealing; 0181-579-9433. Nearest tube: Ealing Broadway. Aerobics, fitness training, beauty facilities, restaurant and pool (under construction). Telephone for membership rate information.

*Holmes Place Kingston*, Third Floor, Bentall Centre, Kingston; 0181-549-7700. Stainless steel pool, aerobics, fitness training, separate cardio- circuit room, separate men's and women's gyms, beauty facilities and restaurant. Telephone for membership rate information.

*Lambton Place Health Club*, Lambton Place, Westbourne Grove, W11 2SH; 0171-299-2291. Nearest tube: Notting Hill Gate. Pool, aerobics, fitness training, sauna, jacuzzi, solarium, beauty facilities and restaurant. Fee: £175 to join plus £700 per year membership fee. £550 per year for swimming only.

*Lotte Berk Studios*. Two locations: 29 Manchester Street, W1M 5PF; 0171-935-8905. Nearest tube: Bond Street and 465 Fulham Road, SW6 1HL; 0171-385-2477. Nearest tube: Fulham Broadway. The Lotte Berk method combines modern ballet and yoga with orthopaedic movements for the back. Fee: £7 per class, £60 for 10 classes. Private tuition is also available.

*The Peak*, The Hyatt Carlton Towers, 2 Cadogan Place, SW1X 4PY; 0171-824-7008. Nearest tube: Knightsbridge. Aerobics, fitness training, massage, sauna, steam, beauty facilities, restaurant and pool (under construction). Fee: £150 to join plus £1,100 membership fee.

*The Pineapple Dance Studios*. Two locations: 6-7 Langley Street, WC2H 9JA; 0171-836-4004. Nearest tube: Covent Garden and 28 Harrington Road, SW7 3ND; 0171-581-0466. Nearest tube: South Kensington. All kinds of dance classes for beginner through professional level. Fee: Membership is £80 per year, £25 for 3 months, or £4 per day. Each class is £4-5.

*The Riverside Racquet Centre*, Duke's Meadow, Chiswick, W4 2SX; 0181-994-0101. More of a country club with indoor and outdoor tennis courts, pool, squash, aerobics, fitness training, lots of children's activities, creche, beauty facilities and restaurant. There is a waiting list. Fee: £1,650 to join plus £1,049 per year (single membership), £3,300 to join and £1,688 per year (family membership).

**Personal Trainers**

Personal fitness trainers are an increasingly popular alternative/addition to the use of health club facilities. They can provide a programme to meet your individual fitness needs within your time schedule.

*Dr. Edward Semple*, 3 Claremont Park Road, Esher, Surrey KT10 9LT; (01372) 465057. Dr. Semple has a PhD in sports medicine. He can provide a customized programme for cardiovascular fitness, resistance training, nutrition and weight control. He works with a female trainer who has experience in pre and post natal exercise. Works with individuals and small groups. The first workout is free then £25-30 per session.

*Julia Swift*, RSA; 0171-289-0494; fax 0171-928-6001. Individualized programmes for cardiovascular fitness, body sculpting, water aerobics, pre and post natal exercise, and diet and nutrition. Works with individuals or very small groups. Fee: £35 per hour, £180 for 6 hours.

# NOTES

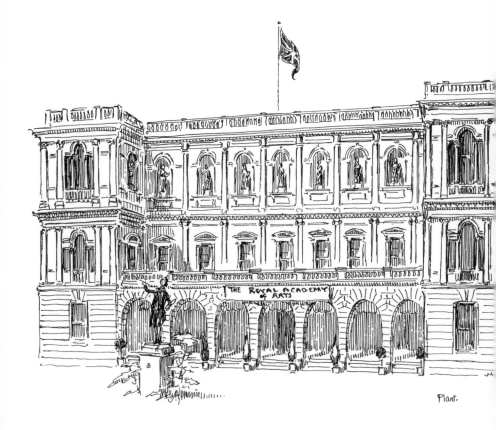

THE ROYAL ACADEMY OF ARTS

Plant.

# Chapter Thirteen: Cultural Activities

## MUSEUMS AND GALLERIES

Many major museums have 'Friends' programmes which make it easier to view major exhibitions as well as giving discounts on museum entrance and functions. Information can be obtained from each museum. A leader among the many worthwhile charities is the *National Art-Collections Fund*, 20 John Islip Street, SW1P 4LL: 0171-821-0404. This charity is dedicated to keeping Great Britain's art treasures in Great Britain by helping museums and galleries purchase works of art they could not otherwise afford. Membership provides one with reduced or free admission to most galleries and exhibitions as well as information regarding many cultural events in and around London.

♥ Indicates that the museum or gallery is particularly good for children.

*Bankside Gallery*, 48 Hopton Street, SE1 9JH; 0171-928-7521. Home of the Royal Society of Painters in Water-Colours, founded in 1804 and the Royal Society of Painter-Etchers and Engravers, founded in 1880. Contemporary and historical exhibitions from Great Britain and abroad. Charge for admission.

*Banqueting House*, Whitehall, SW1A 2ER; 0171-839-3787. Opposite the Horse Guards. Designed by Inigo Jones for James I and built as part of the old Palace of Whitehall with a magnificent ceiling painted by Reubens. Charge for admission.

*Barbican Art Gallery*, Barbican Centre for Arts and Conferences, Barbican EC2Y 8DS; 0171-638-4141. Selected pieces from the important collection belonging to the Corporation of London are sometimes on show. Major exhibitions as well. Charge for admission.

♥ *Bethnal Green Museum of Childhood*, Cambridge Heath Road, E2 9PA; 0181-980-3204. Children's dolls, doll houses, toys, etc., and an important collection of 19th century decorative arts, including continental art nouveau and Tiffany glass. Free admission, donations encouraged.

♥ *British Museum*, Great Russell Street, WC1B 3DG; 0171-636-1555. World renowned collection of antiquities, art, prints, drawings and manuscripts. Among the decorative arts on display are the Rosetta Stone, the Magna Carta, the Elgin Marbles and many other treasures. Donations encouraged.

*Cabinet War Rooms*, Clive Steps, King Charles Street, SW1 2AG; 0171-930-6961. The hidden underground rooms where Churchill and his government lived and worked during dangerous moments of World War II. Charge for admission includes sound guide.

*Carlyle's House* (National Trust), 24 Cheyne Row, SW3 5HL; 0171-352-7087. Paintings, decorative arts, personal effects, manuscripts and the library of Mr. and Mrs. Carlyle. Charge for admission.

*Chiswick House*, Burlington Lane, W4 2RP; 0181-995-0508. 18th century villa set in extensive grounds built by Lord Burlington, influenced by Palladio and Inigo Jones. Gardens by William Kent. Charge for admission.

♥ *Commonwealth Institute*, 230 Kensington High Street, W8 6NQ; 0171-603-4535. Permanent and extensive exhibitions pertaining to historical, cultural, social and commercial traditions of the Commonwealth countries. Also an art gallery with changing exhibitions and a library. Free admission.

*Courtauld Institute Galleries*, Somerset House, The Strand, WC2R ORN; 0171-873-2526. The important Courtauld collection of Impressionist and Post-Impressionist paintings as well as other notable painting and drawing collections. Charge for admission.

*The Dickens House Museum*, 48 Doughty Street, WC1N 2LF; 0171-405-2127. Period house and museum restored to the time of Dickens' occupation. Site where he wrote some of his best known works with original manuscripts on exhibit. Charge for admission.

*Dulwich Picture Gallery*, College Road, SE21 7AD; 0181-693-5254. Important collection of Old Master paintings, including works by Van Dyck, Rembrandt, Gainsborough and Poussin. Charge for admission.

*The Fan Museum*, 12 Croome Hill, SE10 8ER; 0181-858-7879. Delightful private collection of 2,000 fans from different countries displayed in an 18th century townhouse within walking distance of other Greenwich attractions. Charge for admission.

*Fenton House* (National Trust), Windmill Hill, NW3 6RT, (Hampstead Grove); 0171-435-3471. A late 17th century house with walled gardens and an outstanding collection of porcelain and early keyboard instruments. Charge for admission.

♥ *Geffrye Museum*, Kingsland Road, E2 8EA; 0171-739-9893. British period rooms especially arranged for children's enjoyment and participation. Charge for admission.

---

♥ *Geological Museum*, Exhibition Road, SW7 2DE; 0171-938-8765. Extensive geological exhibitions including a display on Mount St. Helens. Charge for admission also includes the Natural History Museum.

*Goldsmith's Hall*, Foster Lane, EC2Z 6BN; 0171-606-7010. Antique silver and gold plate collection of importance. Largest collection of modern silver and jewellery in Britain. By appointment unless a special exhibition is being held. Charge for admission.

*Guildhall*, King Street, EC2P 2EJ; 0171-606-3030. Centre of City of London's government. The gallery exhibits the permanent collection belonging to the Corporation of London and contains the Guildhall library and clock museum. Free admission.

*Gunnersbury Park Museum*, Gunnersbury Park, W3 8LQ; 0181-992-1612. Transportation collection containing coaches belonging to the Rothschild family from their former country residence. Free admission.

*Ham House* (National Trust), Ham Street, Ham, Richmond, Surrey; 0181-940-1950. Superb 17th century house along the Thames with important collection of Stuart and early Georgian furnishings. Charge for admission.

♥ *Hampton Court Palace*, Hampton Court, East Molesey, Surrey; 0181-781-9500. Royal palace from the Tudor period of Henry VIII with impressive William and Mary wing added by Christopher Wren. Houses an extensive fine and decorative arts collection. Several hundred acres of lovely gardens and parks. Charge for admission.

*Hayward Gallery*, South Bank Centre, Belvedere Road, Waterloo, SE1 8XZ; 0171-928-3144. Temporary exhibitions of historical and contemporary fine and decorative arts of major importance. Charge for admission.

*Hogarth's House*, Great West Road, Hogarth Lane, W4 2GN; 0181-994-6757. The artist's Queen Anne house and studio for the last 15 years of his life. Contains a number of his works. Free admission.

♥ *Horniman Museum*, 100 London Road, Forest Hill, SE23 3PG; 0181-699-2339. Impressive collection of musical instruments, decorative arts and natural history, and gardens. Free admission.

♥ *H.M.S. Belfast*, Morgans Lane, Tooley Street, SE1 2JH; 0171-407-6434. Reached by ferry from Tower Pier. Floating naval museum. Charge for admission.

♥ *Imperial War Museum*, Lambeth Road, SE1 6HZ; 0171-416-5000. Permanent exhibitions of all aspects of wars in which Britain has been involved since 1914. Includes weaponry, vehicles, photographs, war paintings and posters. Archival films shown on weekends and holidays. Charge for admission.

*Institute of Contemporary Arts (ICA)*, 12 Carlton House Terrace, The Mall, SW1Y 5AH; 0171-930-3647. Changing exhibitions of avant garde art. Charge for admission.

*Jewish Museum*, Woburn House, Woburn Place, WC1H 0EP; 0171-388-4525. Extensive collection of Jewish religious antiquities. Charge for admission.

*Dr. Samuel Johnson's House*, 17 Gough Square, EC4A 3DE; 0171-353-3745. Small library with relics located in furnished period house where Dr. Johnson lived and worked on England's first definitive dictionary from 1748 to 1759. Charge for admission.

*Keats' House*, Wentworth Place, Keats Grove, NW3 WRR; 0171-435-2062. Regency home of John Keats containing relics and manuscripts. Charge for admission.

*Kensington Palace*, Kensington Gardens, W8 4PX; 0171-937-9561. Royal palace and London home of the Princess of Wales, Princess Margaret and others. State rooms, designed by Christopher Wren and William Kent are open to the public and contain an interesting collection of fine and decorative arts. There is a Victorian section where Queen Victoria was born and raised which contains mementos of the period. Charge for admission.

*The Iveagh Bequest, Kenwood House*, Hampstead Lane, NW3 7JR; 081-348-1286. Robert Adam designed country house with extensive collection of furniture, Old Master paintings, also superb gardens and views over Hampstead Heath. Donations encouraged.

♥ *Kew Bridge Steam Museum*, Green Dragon Lane, Brentford, Middlesex TW8 0EN; 0181-568-4757. Giant steam engines from 1820 operating under steam at weekends. Largest of their kind in the world; working forge. Charge for admission.

*Leighton House*, 12 Holland Park Road, W14 8LZ; 0171-602-3316. Late 19th century home of the artist Lord Leighton, who designed its notable Arab Hall. Contains works by major Victorian artists. Free admission.

*Linley Sambourne House* (Victorian Society), 18 Stafford Terrace, W8 7BL; 081-994-1019. Home of the artist Linley Sambourne, cartoonist for 'Punch' magazine. The impressive contents of the house remain undisturbed from his day and reflect the taste of the 'aesthetic movement' of the late Victorian period. Charge for admission.

♥ *London Dungeon*, 28 Tooley Street, SE1 2SZ; 0171-403-0606 and 0171-403-7221. Definitely not for the squeamish or those under 10; interesting otherwise. Charge for admission.

♥ *The London Planetarium*, Marylebone Road, NW1 5LR; 0171-486-1121. Exciting astrological displays projected, to scale, on a huge dome. No children under five. Located adjacent to Madame Tussauds. Charge for admission.

♥ *London Toy and Model Museum*, 21-23 Craven Hill, Bayswater, W2 3EN; 0171-262-7905. Tintypes, toys and Europe's most complete display of model trains. Charge for admission.

♥ *London Transport Museum*, 39 Wellington Street, Covent Garden, WC2E 7BB; 0171-379-6344. Housed in the restored Old Flower Market building, this unique collection includes historic vehicles, buses, trams, trolley buses and railway cars. Charge for admission.

♥ *Museum of London*, 150 London Wall, EC2Y 5HN; 0171-600-3699. Leads the visitor through the chronological development of London's history from pre-historic times. Lord Mayor's coach exhibition here.

*Museum of Garden History*, St. Mary at Lambeth Church, Lambeth Palace Road, SE1 7JU; 0171-401-8864. The church is used for exhibitions of botanical drawings, antique garden implements, etc., and the churchyard contains an interesting collection of plants and flowers. Donations encouraged.

♥ *Museum of Mankind*, 6 Burlington Gardens, W1X 2EX; 0171-437-2224. Ethnographical branch of the British Museum. Donations encouraged.

♥ *Museum of the Moving Image*, South Bank, SE1 8XT (under Waterloo Bridge, next to Royal Festival Hall); 0171-928-3232. History of film and television from the very first images made up to latest technology. Charge for admission.

♥ *Musical Museum*, Kew Bridge, 368 High Street, Brentford, Middlesex TW8 OBD; 0181-560-8108. Unique collection of working autopianos, organs and music boxes. Charming lecturette featuring autoroll pianos and organs. Charge for admission.

♥ *National Army Museum*, Royal Hospital Road, SW3 4HT; 0171-730-0717. Extensive display of army mementos, equipment and colours from the various British and colonial regiments from 1485. Free admission.

♥ *National Gallery*, Trafalgar Square, WC2N 5DN; 0171-839-3321. World renowned collection of masterpieces from all schools and movements in art. Wonderful holiday quizzes for children. Donations encouraged.

♥ *National Maritime Museum*, Romney Road, Greenwich, SE10 9NF; 0181-858-4422. Exhibitions relating to all aspects of Britain as a maritime power. The Queen's House by Inigo Jones and the Old Observatory in Greenwich Park, by Wren, are also part of the complex. Greenwich Park stretches up the hill behind the museum. Charge for admission.

♥ *National Portrait Gallery*, 2 St. Martin's Place, WC2H OHE; 0171-306-0055. Beautifully organised galleries, arranged by period, with portraits of notable personalities from each era in British history from the Tudors to the present. Donations encouraged.

*National Postal Museum*, King Edward Street, EC1A 1LP; 0171-239-5420. Extremely interesting collection of postage stamps from all over the world. Free admission.

♥ *Natural History Museum*, Cromwell Road, SW7 5BD; 0171-938-9123. Innovative exhibitions of zoology, entomology, palaeontology, mineralogy and botany. Charge for admission.

*Osterley Park House* (National Trust), Isleworth, Middlesex; 0181-560-3918. Elizabethan Mansion transformed by Robert Adam in 1760 to 1780 with Adam decorations and furniture and 140 acres of parkland. Charge for admission.

*Percival David Foundation*, 53 Gordon Square, WC1H OPD; 0171-387-0909. Contains one of the most impressive collections of Chinese ceramics in the West, covering more than a thousand years of production. Donations encouraged.

♥ *Pollock's Toy Museum*, 1 Scala Street, W1P 1LT; 0171-636-3452. A collection of unusual children's games, dolls, doll houses and mechanical toys. Charge for admission.

*Public Records Office Museum*, Chancery Lane, WC2 1LR; 0181-876-3444. Exhibitions of British national records since the Norman Conquest, including the Domesday Book of 1066. Free admission.

*Queen's Gallery*, Buckingham Palace, Buckingham Palace Road, SW1A 1AY; 0171-930-4832, ext. 351. Changing exhibitions of objects from the Royal Collection. Charge for admission.

*Ranger's House*, Chesterfield Walk, Blackheath, SE10 8GX; 0181-853-0035. Period house with English portraits from the Elizabethan to the Georgian period and a collection of musical instruments. Donations encouraged.

*Royal Academy of Arts*, Burlington House, Piccadilly, W1V ODS; 0171-439-7438. Major changing exhibitions and the Annual Summer Exhibition of work submitted by contemporary artists, held each year without a miss since the 1700's. Charge for admission.

♥ *Royal Air Force Museum*, Grahame Park Way, Hendon, NW9 5LL; 0181-205-2266. National museum devoted to aviation and the comprehensive history of the RAF. The Battle of Britain wing houses a unique collection of memorabilia and machinery dedicated to the people involved in the 1940 battle. Charge for admission.

♥ *Royal Hospital Chelsea*, Royal Hospital Road, SW3 4SR; 0171-730-5282. Impressive Wren designed home of the famous scarlet-coated Chelsea pensioners. Paintings and maps. Visitors may also see the famous Chapel (open for services and concerts), the pensioners' dining room and walk in the park. Charge for admission.

♥ *Royal Mews*, Buckingham Palace Road, SW1A 1AA; 0171-930-4832. (Limited opening hours). Splendid collection of state coaches, carriages and the royal horses. Charge for admission.

*Royal Naval College*, King William Walk, SE10 9NN; 0181-858-2154. Housed in a late 17th century hospital on the Thames, partially designed by Christopher Wren. The chapel and Painted Hall in the main building are open to the public every afternoon except Thursday. Charge for admission.

♥ *Science Museum*, Exhibition Road, SW7 2DD; 0171-938-8008. Comprehensive displays of the history of mathematics, chemistry, physics, engineering, transportation and industry. The 'Launchpad' is a popular hands on exhibit for children. Charge for admission.

*Sir John Soane's Museum*, 13 Lincoln's Inn Fields, WC2A 3BP; 0171-405-2107. Built in the early 19th century, by the famous architect as his private residence. Contains his collection of art, furniture and antiquities. Excellent tour for limited numbers on Saturday afternoons. Donations encouraged.

*South London Art Gallery*, 65 Peckham Road, SE5 8UH; 0171-703-6120. Changing exhibitions of contemporary art. Donations encouraged.

*Syon Park*, Brentford, Middlesex TW8 8JF; 0181-560-0881. Impressive Adam interior with furnishings and important picture collection. The extensive gardens were partially designed by Capability Brown; includes a famous conservatory. Charge for admission.

*Tate Gallery*, Millbank, SW1P 4RG; 0171-821-1313. The national collection of British art (from the 16th century to the present day) and a collection of modern British and foreign art. Donations encouraged.

♥ *Theatre Museum*, 1e Tavistock Street, WC2E 7PA; 0171-836-7891. Permanent displays trace the history of the stage since the 16th century. Programmes of special activities and exhibitions, many aimed at children. Charge for admission.

♥ *Tower of London*, Tower Hill, EC3N 4AB; 0171-709-0765. Impressive Norman fortification including chapels, crown jewels and extensive armoury collection. Charge for admission.

♥ *Madame Tussaud's*, Marylebone Road, NW1 5LR; 0171-935-6861. The famous collection of wax figures of historic and contemporary celebrities. Charge for admission.

*Victoria and Albert Museum*, Cromwell Road, SW7 2RL; 0171-938-8500. One of the truly great collections of the world. Fine and decorative arts covering most periods and countries. Donations requested.

*Wallace Collection*, Hertford House, Manchester Square, W1M 6BN; 0171-935-0687. Private collection assembled during the 19th century with an emphasis on the 28th century French fine and decorative arts. Fine collection of arms and armour as well. Donations encouraged.

♥ *Wellington Museum*, Apsley House, 149 Piccadilly, Hyde Park Corner, W1V 9FA; 0171-499-5676. London home of the Duke of Wellington, containing his art collection and military memorabilia. Charge for admission. Re-opens mid-1995.

---

*Wesley's House and Chapel*, 49 City Road, EC1Y 1AU; 0171-253-2262. Home of the Methodist founder which contains a large collection of his personal possessions. Charge for admission.

*William Morris Gallery*, Water House, Lloyd Park, Forest Road, Walthamstow, E17 4PP; 0181-527-5544. Childhood home of William Morris. Collections include furniture, pictures, designs, stained glass, wallpapers and textiles designed by Morris and his contemporaries. Donations encouraged.

*Wimbledon Lawn Tennis Museum*, Church Road, SW19 5AE; 0181-946-6131. Items of interest from games pre-dating lawn tennis and displays relating to the game's development since 1870. Charge for admission.

Plant.

## THE PERFORMING ARTS

### Dance

*London Contemporary Dance Theatre*, The Place, 17 Duke's Road, WC1H 9AB; 0171-387-0324. The company performs not only in their own theatre but at the Sadler's Wells Theatre as well.

*Rambert Dance Company*, 94 Chiswick High Road, W4 1SH; 0181-995-4246. The company performs contemporary ballet in various locations.

*English National Ballet*, 39 Jay Mews, SW7 2ES; 0171-581-1245.  Box office and troupe's home is the Royal Festival Hall;  0171-928-3191 or 0171-928-8800.

*The Royal Ballet*, Royal Opera House, Covent Garden, WC2;  0171-240-1066/1911.  Their repertoire includes classical, contemporary and newly written works.

## Music

*Barbican Hall*, Barbican Centre, EC2Y 8DS;  0171-638-8891 or 0171-628-9760 for information.  Home of The London Symphony Orchestra. There are also a number of guest orchestras that perform here.

*Holland Park Theatre*, Holland Park, Kensington High Street, W8 6LU;  0171-603-1123;  0171-602-7856 (box office).  Opera, theatre and dance are presented during the summer in the only remaining wing of the 17th century Holland House.  Box office opens mid May.

*Kenwood Lakeside*, Hampstead Heath, NW3 7JR;  0171-973-3426 or 0171-413-1443 for bookings.  Concerts are performed here on summer weekends only.

*Royal Albert Hall*, Kensington Grove, SW7 2AP;  0171-589-8212.  A great variety of musical events are staged here, including Christmas Carol Concerts and 'The Proms'.

*Royal College of Music*, Prince Consort Road, SW7 2BS;  0171-589-3643.

*Royal Festival Hall or South Bank Centre* (including the Queen Elizabeth's Hall and the Purcell Room), Belvedere Road, Waterloo, South Bank, SE1 8XX;  0171-928-8800.  Home of the London Philharmonic Orchestra, and the Opera Factory among others.  A great variety of musical events are held here.  For a small subscription fee one can receive a monthly newsletter with concert information and priority booking.

*St. John's Smith Square*, SW1P 3HA;  0171-222-1061.  Non-profit organisation supported by 'The Friends of St. John's Smith Square' that holds all types of recitals and concerts in its restored Queen Anne church-cum-concert hall.

*Wigmore Hall*, 36 Wigmore Street, W1H 9DF;  0171-935-2141.  A smaller concert hall offering an excellent variety of performances which are often particularly attractive to music connoisseurs.

## Opera

*English National Opera*, London Coliseum, St. Martin's Lane, WC2N 4ES; 0171-836-3161. Home of the English National Opera who, notably, sing all their performances in English.

*Glyndebourne Festival Opera*, Glyndebourne, near Lewes, East Sussex (01273) 541111. Opera in the summer months held in the grounds of an Elizabethan House. Famous for Black-tie picnics on the lawn.

*Royal Opera*, The Royal Opera House, Covent Garden, WC2E 7GA; 0171-240-1066-1911.

*The Welsh National Opera* and *The Scottish National Opera* perform in London at various times throughout the year.

## Theatre

*Lyric Theatre*, King Street, Hammersmith, SW6 0QL; 0181-741-2311. Excellent fringe theatre and a wide variety of children's productions.

*National Theatre* (Cottesloe, Lyttleton and Olivier Theatres), Belvedere Road, Waterloo, South Bank, SE1 9PX; 0171-928-2252, information 0171-633-0880. For a small annual subscription fee you can join the mailing list and receive advance programme information, priority booking and occasional special offers. Call 0171-261-9256. Excellent inexpensive seats available at all three theatres from 10.00 on the day of the performance (two tickets per person limit). Back stage tours available.

*Open Air Theatre*, Regent's Park, NW1; 0171-486-2431. May to August.

*The Barbican Theatre/The Pit*, Barbican Centre, EC2Y 9BQ; 0171-638-8891. Home of the Royal Shakespeare Company as well as the venue for various other performances.

*Riverside Studios*, Crisp Road, Hammersmith, W6 9RL; 0181-748-3354. Excellent fringe theatre.

*West End Theatres*; Tickets to nearly all shows available from ticket agencies, major department stores, hotels, the theatre box office in person or credit card by telephone. Also at the green box office, Leicester Square, on the day of the performance where payment is by cash only.

# Chapter Fourteen: Annual Events

To assist you in planning an exciting year, we have provided a month-by-month schedule of events, along with advice on when and where to obtain tickets. For those events requiring advance planning and/or ticket purchase we have added reminders at the time of year when you must send away for tickets.

*Please Note*: The information provided here is accurate at the time of publication, however we suggest that you always verify the details before making your plans. For assistance, contact *The London Tourist Board*; 0171-730-3488 (recorded message, updated daily), or *The British Tourist Authority*; 0181-846-9000.

Here are a few other helpful hints:

1.   Dress codes are often quite stringent. Ask your host or hostess or someone who has attended the event for advice.

2.   When booking an event, always enclose an s.a.e. and enquire if it is possible or necessary to book the car park.

3.   For more popular events, such as Wimbledon, tickets must be obtained through a lottery or ballot. Entry forms, referred to as ballots, must be submitted by a certain deadline. Multiple entries increase your chances of winning.

4.   Individual castles, stately homes and numerous other venues offer their own calendar of events, telephone or write to them to request one.

## JANUARY

***NEW YEAR'S DAY***
*1 JANUARY*

Bank holiday and the official birthday for all race horses. Lord Mayor of Westminster's parade begins in early afternoon at Piccadilly and ends at Hyde Park. Entertainment continues in Hyde Park throughout the day and concludes with a fireworks display. Marching bands, colourful floats. Free.

### THE FEAST OF THE EPIPHANY
*6 JANUARY*

At 11.30, Chapel Royal, St. James's Palace, SW1. Two of the Queen's gentlemen ushers offer gifts of gold, frankincense and myrrh on her behalf, which are later distributed to the poor of the parish. A limited number of tickets are available. Write to: Chapel Royal, St. James's Palace, Marlborough Road, SW1A 1BG.

### LONDON INTERNATIONAL BOAT SHOW
*EARLY JANUARY*

At Earls Court, Warwick Road, SW5. The largest boat show in Europe, and among the most prestigious boat shows in the world, displaying the latest designs in pleasure crafts, yachts and equipment. Contact: National Boat Shows Ltd., 2 Meadlake Place, Thorpe Lea Road, Egham, Surrey TW20 8HE, or telephone (0178) 447-3377.

### JANUARY STORE SALES

Most stores have major sales around early to mid January.

### SERVICE COMMEMORATING CHARLES I
*LAST SUNDAY IN JANUARY*

At 11.30 parade begins at St. James's Palace. At 12.00 there is a service at Banqueting Hall. Event marks the beheading of Charles I on 30 January 1649. Wreaths are also placed at the statue of Charles I near Trafalgar Square. Write to: Charles I Service, 70 Hailgate, Howden, North Humberside DN14 7ST. Free.

### CHINESE NEW YEAR CELEBRATIONS
*LATE JANUARY OR EARLY FEBRUARY*

At Gerrard Street, W1. Celebrated with a festive march through London's Chinatown complete with papier-maché dragons and extravagant costumes. Noisy. Colourful. Usually on the Sunday nearest the date of the New Year. Contact: The Hong Kong Government Office on 0171-499-9821.

### MODEL ENGINEER EXHIBITION
*LATE JANUARY*

Write to: The Wembley Conference Centre, Wembley Complex, Middlesex HA9 0DW.

---

*THE CRUFT'S DOG SHOW*
*BETWEEN JANUARY AND MARCH*

At Birmingham National Exhibition Centre. Ring the Cruft's Dog Show Society, The Kennel Club, 1 Clarges Street, W1 on 0171-493-7838.

### Reminders

1 JANUARY - 28 FEBRUARY: Applications for Ballots to Trooping the Colour may be submitted. See May and June.

1 JANUARY: Bookings open for Chelsea Flower Show. See May. The Derby, Epsom. See June. Goodwood Festival. See July.

1 JANUARY: Tickets for Beating the Retreat available. See June.

31 JANUARY: Last day to send in Ballots for Wimbledon. See June.

## FEBRUARY

*ACCESSION OF H.M. THE QUEEN*
*6 FEBRUARY*

Anniversary salute of 41 guns in Hyde Park by the King's Troop of the Royal Horse Artillery and at the Tower of London a 62 gun salute by the Honourable Artillery Company. No tickets required.

*CLOWN'S SERVICE*
*FIRST SUNDAY IN FEBRUARY*

At Holy Trinity Church, Beechwood Road, E8. In memory of the famous clown Joseph Grimaldi. The service is attended by many clowns in full costume. Contact: John Willard on 0171-254-5062. No tickets required.

*GREAT SPITALFIELDS PANCAKE DAY RACE*
*LATE FEBRUARY OR EARLY MARCH*

At 47A Brushfield Street, Spitalfields, E1 6AA. Pancakes are traditionally eaten before Lent. Teams run with frying pans tossing pancakes. Telephone: 0171-375-0441.

1 FEBRUARY:  Information on the Royal Tournament available. See July.

# MARCH

### *MOTHERING SUNDAY - BRITISH MOTHER'S DAY*
*DATE VARIES*

### *BRITISH SUMMER TIME BEGINS*
*DATE VARIES*

Clocks go forward one hour.

### *HEAD OF THE RIVER RACE*
*SATURDAY BEFORE OXFORD/CAMBRIDGE BOAT RACE*

From Mortlake to Putney.  Contact:  The Amateur Rowing Association on 0181-748-3632.

### *OXFORD V. CAMBRIDGE BOAT RACE*
*MARCH OR APRIL*

Starting time varies according to the tides.  From Putney to Mortlake on the Thames.  Held annually since 1829.  The race can be viewed from many vantage points;  bridges, banks, riverside pubs.  No tickets required. Telephone:  Cambridge University Boat House on (0122) 346-7304.

### *CHELTENHAM NATIONAL HUNT MEETING*

At Cheltenham Racecourse, Prestbury Park, Cheltenham, Gloucestershire. The most important jump racing meeting in the calendar.  Apply for tickets from 30 September.  Discount scheme for early purchases.  Telephone: (0124) 251-3014.

### *CHELSEA ANTIQUES FAIR*

At Chelsea Town Hall, King's Road, SW3.  Twice yearly antiques fair.  Write to:  Penman Antiques Fair, P.O. Box 114, Haywards Heath, West Sussex RH16 2YU or telephone 0171-352-3619.

### *DAILY MAIL IDEAL HOME EXHIBITION*

At Earl's Court Exhibition Centre, Warwick Road, SW5.  Large annual consumer show for new products for the home.  Contact: DMG Angex Ltd.,

---

Times House, Station Approach, Ruislip, Middlesex HA4 8NB or telephone (0895) 677-6777.

## *BASKETBALL*

Coca Cola National Cup Finals. At London Docklands Arena, Limeharbour, E14. Telephone: (0113) 246-6044.

## *YONEX ALL ENGLAND BADMINTON CHAMPIONSHIPS*

At Wembley Arena, Middlesex HA9 ODW. Telephone: The Badminton Association on (0190) 856-8822.

### Reminders

30 MARCH: Deadline for obtaining application and sponsorship to the Royal Enclosure at Ascot. See June.

# APRIL

## *JOHN STOWE MEMORIAL SERVICE*
*5 APRIL*

At St. Andrew Undershaft Church, Great St. Helens, EC3A. Stowe published his survey of London in 1598 age 73. The service marks the anniversary of his death on 5 April and this event is held near this date. The Lord Mayor attends and places a new quill pen in the hand of the Stowe statue.

## *FOOTBALL LEAGUE CUP FINAL*
*APRIL OR MAY*

At Wembley Stadium. Climax of football season. Write to: Wembley Stadium Box Office, Wembley Stadium Ltd., Wembley, Middlesex HA9 ODW or telephone 0181-900-1234. Some tickets are available from the above number but majority of tickets go to the two teams participating.

## *THE GRAND NATIONAL STEEPLECHASE*

At the Aintree Racecourse. The greatest steeplechase in the World. Write to: Aintree Racecourse, Ormskirk Road, Aintree, Liverpool, Merseyside L9 5AS or telephone (0151) 523-2600 or 522-2900.

## MAUNDY THURSDAY
*THURSDAY BEFORE GOOD FRIDAY*

Held at Westminster Abbey every tenth year and at different cathedrals around the country during the other nine. The Queen distributes purses of specially minted coins to as many poor men and women as the years of her age. Telephone: The Buckingham Palace Information Section; 0171-930-4832.

## GOOD FRIDAY

Bank holiday.

## BUTTERWORTH CHARITY DISTRIBUTIONS OF BUNS
*GOOD FRIDAY*

At 11.30, Priory Church of St. Bartholomew the Great, West Smithfield, EC1. Tickets not required.

## HOT CROSS BUN CEREMONY
*GOOD FRIDAY*

At 13.00, Widow's Son Inn, 75 Devon Road, E3. Telephone: 0171-515-9072.

## EASTER SUNDAY SERVICE

Seating at 10.00, St. George's Chapel, Windsor Castle, SL4. The Queen and the Royal Family worship together in St. George's Chapel. Visitors can attend. If you are seated toward the front of the choir and seats are available you may be chosen to sit with the Royal Family in the Nave. The queue is long, so arrive early. Many people do not enter the chapel, so do not be discouraged by the size of the queue. Contact: The Superintendent of Windsor Castle, Windsor, Berkshire SL4 1PJ or telephone (0175) 383-1118.

## EASTER SUNDAY PARADE

At Battersea Park, SW11. Carnival parade with colourful floats and bands. Tickets not required.

## EASTER SUNDAY PARADE

At the Tower of London. Yeomen Warders in state dress parade at the Tower. Telephone: 0171-709-0765.

---

### EASTER MONDAY

Bank holiday.

### SHAKESPEARE THEATRE SEASON
*APRIL TO JANUARY*

At The Royal Shakespeare Theatre, Stratford-upon-Avon, Warwickshire. Telephone: (0178) 929-5623.

### LONDON HARNESS HORSE PARADE

At Regent's Park, NW1. Judging begins at 09.30 with fine breeds from Shires and Somersets to lighter-weight horses, ponies, carts, brewer's vans and drays parade around the inner circle at 12.00. Tickets not required. Telephone: The London Harness Horse Parade Society; (0173) 323-4451.

### THE BADMINTON HORSE TRIALS
*APRIL OR MAY*

At Badminton, Avon. International equestrian competition. Contact: The Horse Trials Office; (0145) 421-8375.

### LONDON MARATHON
*LATE APRIL*

From Blackheath/Greenwich to Westminster Bridge. World's largest road race with competitors representing a mixture of international marathon runners, serious runners, celebrities, disabled runners and just-for-fun runners. Large crowds. Telephone: 0171-620-4117.

### H.M. THE QUEEN'S BIRTHDAY
*21 APRIL*

Gun salutes at the Tower of London (see February).

### CRICKET SEASON OPENS

## MAY

### MAY DAY BANK HOLIDAY
*FIRST MONDAY IN MAY*

### SPRING BANK HOLIDAY
*LAST MONDAY IN MAY*

## POLO SEASON OPENS
*EARLY MAY TO SEPTEMBER*

15.30 at Windsor Great Park. Matches are held most Saturdays and Sundays. Contact: Prince Charles' Club, The Guards Polo Club, Smiths Lawn, Windsor Great Park, Englefield Green, Egham, Surrey SL4 1PJ; telephone (0178) 443-4212.

## GLYNDEBOURNE OPERA SEASON
*MAY TO AUGUST*

International festival of opera. Special train services from Victoria Station to Glyndebourne and return from Lewes. Formal attire. Take a picnic. Book early. Contact: Glyndebourne Festival Opera Box Office, Glyndebourne, East Sussex BN8 5UU or telephone (0127) 381-2321 or (0127) 854-1111.

## BEATING THE BOUNDS

At the Tower of London. Harkens back to the days when the majority of parishioners were illiterate, and beating on the boundary marks of the parishes taught them where the boundaries lay. The Tower holds this event tri-annually (last held 1993). Telephone: The Deputy Governor on 0171-709-0765.

## ROYAL WINDSOR HORSE SHOW

At Windsor, Berkshire. International show with jumping and driving, various displays and numerous trade exhibits. Contact: The Secretary, Royal Windsor Horse Show Club, Royal Mews, Windsor Castle, Windsor, Berkshire SL4 1PJ or telephone (0175) 386-0633.

## BATH FESTIVAL

Festival of music and arts with concerts, exhibitions, tours, lectures and film shows. Telephone: The Bath Festival Box Office, Linley House, 1 Pierrepont Place, Bath, Avon; (0122) 546-3362.

## TROOPING THE COLOUR
*LAST SATURDAY IN MAY, FIRST REHEARSAL*

From Buckingham Palace along the Mall to Horse Guards Parade, Whitehall and back again, SW1. The first of two rehearsals (the second held in June) to prepare for the actual Trooping the Colour, the second Saturday in June, in the presence of H.M. The Queen. A magnificent parade of colourful military units celebrates the Queen's official birthday. Tickets required. See June for ticket information.

### REGENT'S PARK OPEN AIR THEATRE SEASON
*MAY OR JUNE THROUGH SEPTEMBER*

At Regent's Park, NW1. A full programme of plays. Contact: New Shakespeare Company, Open Air Theatre, Regent's Park, NW1; 0171-935-5756.

### CHELSEA FLOWER SHOW
*LAST WEEK IN MAY*

At the Chelsea Royal Hospital Grounds, SW3. A four-day event displaying England's best horticultural endeavours, and often visited by the Royal Family. Tuesday, Wednesday and Thursday are reserved for RHS members with admittance to the general public on Thursday and Friday afternoons. Limited number of tickets available. Apply to RHS after 1 January. No children under 5 admitted. Contact: The Royal Horticultural Society, 80 Vincent Square, SW1P 2PE or telephone 0171-828-1744. Also watch for RHS shows approximately every 3 weeks from February to November at Vincent Square.

### ROYAL ACADEMY SUMMER EXHIBITION
*MAY OR JUNE TO AUGUST*

At the Royal Academy of Arts, Piccadilly, W1. A juried exhibition of works by contemporary artists. Telephone: 0171-439-7438.

### SAMUEL PEPYS MEMORIAL SERVICE
*MAY OR JUNE*

Held on last Wednesday in May or first in June at the Church of St. Olave, Hart Street, EC3. Telephone: 0171-488-4318.

### MALVERN FESTIVAL

Malvern Theatre, Worcestershire. Performances of the works of Sir Edward Elgar and George Bernard Shaw. Write to: Malvern Theatre Box Office, Malvern, Worcestershire WR14 3HB or telephone (0168) 489-2277.

### CHICHESTER FESTIVAL THEATRE SEASON
*MAY TO SEPTEMBER*

Write to: Chichester Festival Theatre, Oaklands Park, Chichester, West Sussex PO19 4AP or telephone (0124) 378-1312. Bookings open early April.

### FESTIVAL OF ENGLISH WINES

Leeds Castle, Maidstone, Kent. Telephone: (0162) 276-5400.

### *MEDIEVAL JOUSTING TOURNAMENTS*

Write to: Belvoir Castle, Belvoir, Leicestershire, or telephone (0147) 687-0262.

### *OPEN AIR ART EXHIBITIONS*

1. *MAY THROUGH OCTOBER*

   Saturdays - Royal Avenue, King's Road, SW3.

2. *WEEKENDS*

   Piccadilly on the Green Park Side, W1.

3. *MAY TO SEPTEMBER*

   Weekends - Heath Street, Hampstead Heath, NW3.

4. *SUNDAYS*

   Bayswater Road, North Side of Hyde Park, W2.

### *OPEN AIR CONCERTS*
*MAY TO SEPTEMBER*

At Hyde Park, St. James's Park, Regent's Park, Greenwich Park and Kensington Gardens. Contact: The London Tourist Board; 0171-730-3488.

### Reminders

AFTER 1 MAY: Apply for Steward's Enclosure at Henley Regatta. See June.

## JUNE

### *H.R.H. THE DUKE OF EDINBURGH'S BIRTHDAY*

Gun salutes. (See 6 February).

### *TROOPING THE COLOUR*

Second rehearsal is held on the first Saturday in June. Actual event is held on the second Saturday in June. Tickets are allocated by lottery. Only two tickets per successful entry. Send an s.a.e. between 1 January and 28

February to: Brigade Major, Headquarters Household Division, Horse Guards, Whitehall, SW1 9BG or telephone (0891) 505-453 for general information or 0171-930-4466 and request the Birthday Office for tickets.

### STELLA ARTOIS TENNIS TOURNAMENT
*MID JUNE*

Men's Tournament held two weeks before Wimbledon. Contact: The Queen's Club, Baron's court, W14 for general information or telephone 0171-385-3421. Tickets may be purchased 2 months prior to the event by credit card. Telephone: 0181-982-6060.

### BEATING THE RETREAT
*EARLY JUNE*

Horse Guards Parade. A military pageant held for 3 consecutive nights with bands to acknowledge retreat of setting sun. Tickets available after 1 March. Telephone: The London Tourist Board on 0171-730-3488.

### THE DERBY
*FIRST OR SECOND SATURDAY IN JUNE*

On Epsom Downs. The most famous and prestigious horse race in the world. It covers one and a half miles. Created at a noble dinner party in 1779 and named after one of the diners - Lord Derby. Bookings open 1 January at United Racecourses Ltd., Racecourse Paddock, Epsom, Surrey or telephone (0137) 272-6311.

### THE GARTER CEREMONY
*MONDAY AFTERNOON OF ASCOT WEEK*

At St. George's Chapel, Windsor Castle, SL4. A special service marks the oldest order of chivalry in England. It is attended by the Queen and is preceded by a colourful procession with the Household Cavalry and Yeomen of the Guard. 1,500 people will be admitted at the gate on a first-come first-served basis. Telephone: The Buckingham Palace Information Section; 0171-930-4832.

### BIGGIN HILL INTERNATIONAL AIR FAIR

At Biggin Hill Airport, Biggin Hill, Kent. Jet formation aerobatics, historic aircraft rally and extensive ground exhibition. Tickets are available 4 weeks in advance or at the gate. Write to: Biggin Hill Airport, Kent TN16 3BN or telephone (0195) 957-2277.

### PRINCE WILLIAM'S BIRTHDAY
*21 JUNE*

### KNOLLYS ROSE CEREMONY
*24 JUNE*

The descendants of Sir Robert Knollys continue to pay his fine of one red rose every year to the Lord Mayor for leave to build a footbridge across Seething Lane. Write to: The Clerk to the Company of Waterman and Lighterman of the River Thames at Waterman's Hall, 16 St. Mary at Hill, EC3R 8EE or telephone 0171-283-2373.

### ELECTION OF SHERIFFS OF CITY OF LONDON
*MIDSUMMER'S DAY*

Guildhall, EC2. Lord Mayor and Aldermen take part in a colourful ceremony in which posies are carried to symbolise the effort once made to ward off the Great Plague. Telephone: 0171-606-3030. Free.

### FOUNDER'S DAY

Chelsea Royal Hospital, SW3. Pensioners parade in their uniforms in honour of their founder's birthday (Charles II) for inspection, sometimes by Royalty. Telephone: 0171-730-0161.

### LORD'S TEST MATCH
*3-5 DAYS IN JUNE OR JULY*

At Lord's Cricket Ground, St. John's Wood, NW8. For general information telephone: 0171-289-1611/5. Ticket Office: 0171-289-8979. Charge.

### HENLEY ROYAL REGATTA
*LATE JUNE OR EARLY JULY*

At Henley-on-Thames, Oxfordshire. This international rowing event is also a popular social occasion. There are two enclosures at Henley. The Regatta Enclosure is for the general public. Tickets may be purchased in advance after May 1, or upon arrival. The Steward's Enclosure is for members and their guests. Dress rules are stringent and women must not wear trousers, culottes, split skirts or short skirts in the Steward's Enclosure. Write to: The Secretary, Henley Royal Regatta, Regatta Headquarters, Henley-on-Thames, Oxfordshire RG9 2LY or telephone (0149) 157-2153.

### ALL ENGLAND TENNIS CHAMPIONSHIPS
*LAST WEEK IN JUNE OR FIRST WEEK IN JULY*

Tickets are allocated by lottery. Send s.a.e. between 1 October and end of December to: All England Lawn Tennis and Croquet Club, P.O. Box 98, Church Road, Wimbledon, SW19 5AE, or telephone 0181-944-1066. Entries must be returned by 31 January. One application per household. You may also queue for tickets each day or purchase tickets from authorised ticket agents. After 17.00 each night, you may pay a small fee just to enter the grounds. It is great fun during the first week when there is so much activity on the outside courts. *Note*: Tube stop is Southfields, not Wimbledon.

### ROYAL ASCOT
*USUALLY HELD THIRD WEEK IN JUNE*

Very important week for racegoers and equally important socially. Tuesday through Friday is attended by the Royal Family. Formal attire, hats and gloves required for ladies and full morning suit for men. To obtain passes for the Royal Enclosure write for an application to: The American Ambassador, U.S. Embassy, Grosvenor Square, W1 or telephone 0171-499-9000. Applications are then passed on to a sponsor, senator or someone else who has been on the Ambassador's list. Closing date is 30 March (30 April for those who have attended in previous years). Tickets to the racecourse are purchased separately. Contact: Ascot Racecourse, Ascot, Berkshire; (0134) 422-211.

### QUEEN'S CUP INTERNATIONAL POLO TOURNAMENT

The Guards Polo Club, Great Park, Windsor. Telephone: (01784) 434-212.

### HIGHLAND GAMES BEGIN

Many held during the summer all over Scotland. Traditional Scottish games and lots of local colour. Contact: The Scottish Tourist Board, 19 Cockspur Street, SW1 by telephoning 0171-930-8661.

### NOTE:

Many manor houses hold outdoor concerts during the summer. Dates vary each year so contact the individual locations. Some of the most popular are:

Leeds Castle, Maidstone, Kent
Hever Castle, Edenbridge, Kent
Kenwood House, Hampstead, London
Audley End House, Essex
Wrest Park House, Bedfordshire
Pevensey Castle, East Sussex
Portchester Castle, Hampshire
Marble Hill Park, Twickenham

Information is also available from English Heritage on 0171-973-3427.

# JULY

**PRINCESS OF WALES' BIRTHDAY**
*1 JULY*

**DOGGETS COAT AND BADGE RACE**

Oldest race on Thames from London Bridge to Cadogan Pier, Chelsea. Began in 1715 to mark the accession of George I. Telephone: The Fishmonger's Company; 0171-626-3531.

**CUTTY SARK TALL SHIPS RACE**
*EARLY JULY*

Plymouth Harbour, Plymouth, Devon to Zeebrugge, Belgium. Contact: The English Tourist Board; 0171-730-3488.

**HAMPTON COURT FLOWER SHOW**
*EARLY JULY*

Set in 25 acres of Royal parkland, this is one of the world's largest annual gardening events. Highlights include the British Rose Festival and dozens of innovative show gardens. Visitors may select from a multitude of plants, crafts, books, paintings and horticultural equipment which are available for purchase at the show. For tickets telephone: 0171-396-4656 (all advance bookings receive a rail voucher with every ticket).

**SWAN UPPING**
*THIRD WEEK IN JULY*

The Queen, the Vintner's Company and the Dyers' Company (two City Livery Companies) own the swans on the Thames. The Royal Keeper of the swans and his crews set off from Sunbury and proceed up the river to Henley over a one day period to take a census and mark the young swans - two nicks for the Vintners, one for the Dyers and none for the Crown. Telephone: 0171-236-1863.

**VINTNERS' PROCESSION**

Following the installation of the Vintners' Company's New Master, there is a procession led by the Wine Porter, who sweeps the road clear as far as the church of St. James Garlickhithe for the annual service. Telephone: 0171-237-1863.

---

### THE ROYAL TOURNAMENT

At the Earl's Court Exhibition Centre, SW5. A genuine and spectacular military display of skills and pageantry by members of the armed forces and visiting participants. Tickets available after 1 February at the Royal Tournament Box Office, Earl's Court Exhibition Centre, Warwick Road, SW5 or telephone 0171-373-8141.

### STREET THEATRE FESTIVAL
*THROUGHOUT JULY*

At St. Martin-in-the-Fields, Trafalgar Square, WC2.

### ROYAL NATIONAL EISTEDDFORD OF WALES
*JULY OR AUGUST*

An annual competitive festival of music, drama, literature, arts and crafts. Write to: The Eisteddfod Office, Moderator Wharf, Kinsway, Newport NP9 1EX.

### HENRY WOOD PROMENADE CONCERTS BEGIN (THE PROMS)

At the Royal Albert Hall, Kensington Gore, SW7. Celebrated series of orchestral concerts promoted by the B.B.C. Telephone: 0171-589-8212 or 0171-589-9465.

### ROYAL INTERNATIONAL HORSE SHOW

Hicksted. Telephone: The British Show Jumping Association; (0120) 369-6516.

### GOODWOOD WEEK HORSE RACING
*LAST TUESDAY TO SATURDAY IN JULY*

West Sussex. Tickets to Richmond Enclosure available to annual members only. Applications can be made after 1 January. Telephone: The Goodwood Racecourse, Goodwood, West Sussex; 0124-377-4107.

### BRITISH OPEN CHAMPIONSHIP

St. Andrew's Golf Course, Scotland. Top British golfing event. Write to: The Secretary, Royal and Ancient Golf Club, St. Andrews, Fife, KY16 98T.

### LADIES BRITISH OPEN CHAMPIONSHIPS

Write to: The Tournament Secretary, Ladies' Golf Union, The Scores, St. Andrews, Fife, KY16 98T.

### BENSON AND HEDGES CUP FINAL (CRICKET)

At Lord's Cricket Ground, St. John's Wood, NW8. For general information telephone: 0171-1611/5. For tickets telephone: 0171-289-8979.

### BRITISH GRAND PRIX

Premier motor racing event with the world's top drivers in action. Write to: Silverstone, Towcester, Northampton, NN12 8TN or telephone 0132-785-7271.

### STRATFORD-UPON-AVON FESTIVAL

Stratford-upon-Avon, Warwickshire. Telephone: (0178) 929-3127.

## AUGUST

### H.M. QUEEN ELIZABETH, THE QUEEN MOTHER'S BIRTHDAY
### 4 AUGUST

Gun salutes.

### COWES WEEK
### IN JULY OR EARLY AUGUST

On the Isle of Wight. Sailing races and festival usually attended by Royalty. Contact: The Isle of Wight Tourist Board, 21 High Street, Newport, Isle of Wight by telephoning (0198) 352-4343.

### NOTTING HILL CARNIVAL
### AUGUST BANK HOLIDAY SUNDAY AND MONDAY

Largest street festival in Europe. Children's events, including a costume competition, are on Sunday. Telephone: 0181-964-0544.

### LONDON RIDING HORSE PARADE

At Rotten Row, Hyde Park. Contact: Brendan Byrne, Greater London Horseman's Association; 0181-761-5651.

### EDINBURGH INTERNATIONAL FESTIVAL

Edinburgh, Scotland. Said to be the largest festival of the arts. Write to: The Edinburgh Festival Society, 21 Market Street, Edinburgh, EH1 1QB or telephone (0131) 226-4001.

---

## EDINBURGH MILITARY TATTOO

Military pageant held on floodlit grounds of Edinburgh Castle. Tickets can be purchased in London at The Scottish Tourist Board or from Tattoo Office, 22 Market Street, Edinburgh, EH1 1QB or telephone (0142) 472-2022.

## JERSEY BATTLE OF FLOWERS

On Jersey in the Channel Islands. A three-hour parade of floats displaying thousands of flowers, bands, etc. Crowds gather along the route. Tickets required for the arena. Telephone: The Executive Secretary, Jersey Battle of Flowers, Meadowbank, St. Peter's Valley, St. Lawrence, Jersey, Channel Islands on (0154) 330178 or (0154) 378000.

## SEPTEMBER

### LIBERAL DEMOCRATS PARTY CONFERENCE

### OBSERVANCE OF AUTUMN EQUINOX
21 SEPTEMBER

Druids gather at Primrose Hill, Regent's Park, W1.

### WINDSOR FESTIVAL

Music and art. Write to: The Windsor Tourist Office, Central Station, Windsor, Berkshire SL4 1PJ or telephone (0175) 385-2010.

### NATIONAL CARRIAGE DRIVING CHAMPIONSHIPS

Windsor Castle Royal Mews. Write to: The Royal Mews, Windsor Castle, Windsor, Berkshire SL4 1PJ or telephone (0175) 386-0633.

### ELECTION OF LORD MAYOR
MICHAELMAS DAY

St. Lawrence Jewry, Gresham Street, EC2 to Guildhall, EC2. Colourful procession to celebrate election. Telephone: 0171-606-3030.

## OCTOBER

### TRAFALGAR DAY
21 OCTOBER

At Nelson's Column, Trafalgar Square, WC2. The Royal Navy organises a remembrance service for Lord Nelson. Telephone: The London Tourist Board; 0171-730-3488.

*CONSERVATIVE PARTY CONFERENCE*

*LABOUR PARTY CONFERENCE*

*BRITISH SUMMER TIME ENDS*

*Clocks are set back one hour on the Sunday following the fourth Saturday in October.*

*OPENING OF THE LAW COURTS*

At Westminster Abbey. A closed service is held at Westminster Abbey attended by Her Majesty's Judges and Queen's Counsel dressed in state robes and wigs. Afterwards, the Lord Chancellor leads the procession from the East end of the Abbey to the House of Lords. There is a reception lunch followed by a drive to the Royal Courts of Justice. The first motion of the year constitutes the official opening of the Courts. Telephone: The House of Lords Information Centre on 0171-219-3000 or The London Tourist Board on 0171-730-3488.

*COSTERMONGERS' HARVEST FESTIVAL*

At St. Martins in the Fields, Trafalgar Square, WC2. The Pearly Kings and Queens, wearing their traditional pearl-buttoned covered suits, arrive in the afternoon for their annual service bearing gifts of food. Public welcome. Telephone: 0171-930-1862.

*HORSE OF THE YEAR SHOW*
*EARLY OCTOBER*

At the Wembley Arena, Wembley, Middlesex HA9. Telephone: The Box Office; 0181-900-1234.

*NATIONAL BRASS BAND FESTIVAL*

At the Royal Albert Hall, Kensington Gore, SW7. Telephone: 0171-589-8212.

*EARL'S COURT MOTOR CYCLE SHOW*

At the Earl's Court Exhibition Centre, Warwick Road, SW5. Telephone: 0171-385-1200.

### Reminders

Send for Wimbledon Ballots. See June.

Send for Epiphany Tickets. See January.

Send for Cheltenham Hunt Meeting Tickets. See March.

## NOVEMBER

### *GUY FAWKES DAY*
*5 NOVEMBER*

Bonfires, fireworks and burning effigies of Guy Fawkes throughout London and at Leeds Castle, Kent on the nearest weekend to this date, celebrate his failure to blow up the King and Parliament in the Gun Powder Plot of 1605. Telephone: The London Tourist Board on 0171-730-3488 or Leeds Castle on (0162) 276-5400.

### *H.R.H. PRINCE OF WALES' BIRTHDAY*
*14 NOVEMBER*

### *BOUTIQUE DE NOEL*

The Junior League of London's annual Christmas Fair features items hand crafted by members as well as unique gifts from selected vendors. Funds generated by the day and evening event support the community projects of the Junior League of London. For tickets write to: The Junior League of London, 9 Fitzmaurice Place, London W1X 6JD or telephone 0171-499-8159.

### *REMEMBRANCE SUNDAY*
*ON THE SUNDAY CLOSEST TO 11 NOVEMBER*

Around the Cenotaph at Whitehall. A service is held in memory of those killed in battle since 1914. It is attended by the Queen, members of the Royal Family, the Prime Minister, members of the Cabinet and members of the Opposition. Two minutes silence are observed as Big Ben strikes 11.00. During the week which precedes this event, volunteers sell poppies in the streets to raise money for ex-servicemen. Poppy wreaths are placed at many war memorials in village high streets and grave sites. Telephone: The London Tourist Board; 0171-730-3488.

### *LONDON TO BRIGHTON VETERAN CAR RACE*
*FIRST SUNDAY*

Cars built prior to 31 December 1904 participate in the 60-mile run to Brighton. Departures from 08.00 at Hyde Park Corner. Pre-departure festivities and along the route. No tickets required. Write to: The RAC Motor Sports Association Ltd., Motor Sports House, Riverside Park, Colnbrook, Slough SL3 OHG, or telephone (0175) 368-1736.

---

### LORD MAYOR'S PROCESSION AND SHOW
*SECOND SATURDAY*

For the past 600 years, following the inauguration of the Lord Mayor, there is a great parade with elaborate floats through the City streets from Guildhall to the Royal Courts of Justice. No tickets required for viewing along the route. Telephone: The Public Relations Office; 0171-606-3030 or (0891) 505-453.

### STATE OPENING OF PARLIAMENT

English pageantry at its finest. H.M. The Queen rides in the Irish state coach from Buckingham Palace to the Houses of Parliament, where she reads a speech prepared by the party in power, outlining their intentions for the next session. Viewing along the route. Telephone: 0171-219-4272 or (0891) 505-453.

### CARAVAN CAMPING HOLIDAY SHOW

At the Earl's Court Exhibition Centre, Warwick Road, SW5. Contact: DMG Angex Ltd. and the National Caravan Council, Times House, Station Approach, Ruislip, Middlesex HA4 8NB or telephone (0895) 677-6777.

### DAILY MAIL INTERNATIONAL SKI SHOW

At the Earl's Court Exhibition Centre, Warwick Road, SW5. Contact: DMG Angex Ltd., Times House, Station Approach, Ruislip, Middlesex HA4 8NB or telephone (0895) 677-6777.

### AMERICAN THANKSGIVING SERVICE
*THIRD THURSDAY IN NOVEMBER AT HIGH NOON*

St. Paul's Cathedral, St. Paul's Churchyard, EC4M. Telephone: The American Church of London; 0171-580-2791.


# DECEMBER

### CHRISTMAS TREE LIGHTING CEREMONY
*EARLY IN THE MONTH*

At Trafalgar Square, WC2. Each year an enormous Christmas tree is donated by the people of Oslo, Norway in remembrance and thanks for British assistance during World War II. Contact: The London Tourist Bureau; 0171-730-3488.

## HANDEL'S MESSIAH

At St. Paul's Cathedral, EC4 and several other locations open to the public. Arrive early for good seats. Telephone: The Music Department at St. Paul's Cathedral; 0171-236-6883.

## CHILDREN'S PANTOMIMES

Held throughout Britain in local theatres and Town Halls. Traditional pantomimes with male/female roles reversed, audience participation, singalongs and candy thrown into the audience. Especially popular in London and the sea side resort towns (Bournemouth). Check theatre listings or local newspapers for information beginning in September.

## WINTER SOLSTICE
*21 DECEMBER*

## CHRISTMAS
*25 DECEMBER*

*Bank holiday.*

## BOXING DAY
*26 DECEMBER*

*Bank holiday.*

## NEW YEAR'S EVE
*31 DECEMBER*

Crowded celebration at Trafalgar Square. Big Ben tolls at midnight.

Plant.

# Chapter Fifteen: Organisations

**EMBASSIES**

In general, your embassy represents your government. The consular office within every embassy concerns itself with individual citizens. Most of your communication with your embassy will be through the consular office. Also, there are consular offices located in other cities where there is a high concentration of citizens of a specific nationality. In general, consular offices will help you with:

*Emergencies*

1.   Death of a citizen abroad

2.   Arrests (the embassy provides you with names of lawyers)

3.   Financial assistance

*Non-emergencies*

1.   Passports - particular help with stolen passports

2.   Registering of births and deaths

3.   Tax obligations (see Chapter Three)

4.   Voting - help with absentee balloting

5.   Notary Public

**The Embassy of the United States of America**

24-31 Grosvenor Square, W1A 1AE; 0171-499-9000 (24 hour switchboard). For visas only telephone 0891-200-290. The building was designed by Eero Saarinen and completed in 1960. Guided tours may be arranged in advance.

**Hours**

*Embassy and Consular Section*: Monday to Friday, 09.00 to 18.00.

*Reference Library*: (Ext. 2627), Monday to Friday, 09.00 to 12.00.

**Holidays**

The Embassy is closed on all official American and British holidays. If a holiday falls on a Saturday, the Embassy is closed on the preceding Friday.

If the holiday is on a Sunday, the Embassy is closed on the following Monday. Official U.S. holidays are as follows:

| | | |
|---|---|---|
| *New Year's Day* | - | 1 January |
| *Washington's Birthday* | - | third Monday of February |
| *Memorial Day* | - | last Monday of May |
| *Independence Day* | - | 4 July |
| *Labor Day* | - | first Monday of September |
| *Columbus Day* | - | second Monday of October |
| *Veterans' Day* | - | 11 November |
| *Thanksgiving Day* | - | fourth Thursday of November |
| *Christmas Day* | - | 25 December |

**Division of Agencies**

The Embassy is divided into six sections:

Administrative (Ext. 2234)

Consular (Ext. 2515)

Defense (Ext. 2745)

Economic (Ext. 2411)

Political (Ext. 2120)

Public Affairs (Ext. 2611)

Helpful Information:

*Passport and Citizenship Branch* - Ext. 2512 (Travel information and warnings are available from this office)

*Visa Branch* - Ext. 3443

*Internal Revenue Service* - Ext. 2476; Hours: Monday through Friday, 9.30-12.00 and 13.00-16.00

*Commercial Library* - Open to business professionals for research, Monday through Friday, 14.00-17.00. Telephone inquiries, 09.00-12.00.

**The Ambassador**

The Ambassador is the highest ranking American official in the United Kingdom and is the personal representative of the President of the United States of America to Her Majesty the Queen. The full title for the American Ambassador is *'Ambassador Extraordinary and Plenipotentiary to the Court of St. James, His (Her) Excellency The Honorable'*. If you should write to the Ambassador, the letter should be addressed with the full title of *'His (Her) Excellency The Ambassador of the United States of America'*.

The Deputy Chief of Mission (the 'DCM'), usually referred to as 'Minister' assists the Ambassador and is responsible for the day-to-day operation of the Embassy. He becomes Charge d'Affaires in the absence from the United Kingdom of the Ambassador and assumes all responsibilities.

## Other Embassies

*The Australian High Commission*, Australia House, Strand, WC2B 4LA; 0171-379-4334.

*The Canadian High Commission*, Macdonald House, 38 Grosvenor Square, W1X OAA; 0171-258-6600.

*The French Embassy*, 58 Knightsbridge, SW1X 7GT; 0171-201-1000.

*The Embassy of the Federal Republic of Germany*, 23 Belgravia Square, SW1X 8PZ; 0171-235-5033.

*The Embassy of Japan*, 101 Piccadilly, W1V 9FN; 0171-465-6500.

*The Embassy of the Netherlands*, 38 Hyde Park Gate, SW7 5DP; 0171-584-5040.

*The New Zealand High Commission*, 80 Haymarket, SW1Y 4TQ; 0171-930-8422.

*The Royal Embassy of Saudi Arabia*, 32 Charles Street, W1X 7PM; 0171-917-3000.

*The Embassy of Spain*, 39 Chesham Place, SW1X 8SB; 0171-235-5555.

*The Swiss Embassy*, 16 Montagu Place, W1H 2BQ; 0171-723-0701.

*Embassy of United Arab Emirates*, 30 Prince's Gate, SW7 1PT; 0171-581-1281.

## PROFESSIONAL ORGANISATIONS

*The American Banks Club*, First National Bank of Chicago, Long Acre, WC2E 9RB; 0171-240-7240.

*American Chamber of Commerce* (United Kingdom), 75 Brook Street, W1 2EB; 0171-493-0381. Independent non-profit organisation which provides assistance to member companies in the expansion of their activities on both sides of the Atlantic. Services to members include publications, luncheons, lectures, and seminars relating to Anglo-American affairs and business.

*British-American Chamber of Commerce*, 8 Staple Inn, WC1V 7QH; 0171-404-6400.

## CHARITABLE, SOCIAL AND SERVICE ORGANISATIONS

*The American Society in London*, The Secretary, Hill House, 1 Little New Street, EC4A 3TR; 0171-732-5225. Organisation for American expatriates which sponsors numerous social events and outings, celebrating American holidays and traditions including a July 4th picnic at the Ambassador's Residence and a Thanksgiving Dinner Dance.

*American Women's Club of London*, Connaught Room, Great Queen Street, WC2B 5DA; 0171-831-6660. Social, recreational and charitable club with facilities for American women living in London.

*The American Women of Surrey*, P.O. Box 170, Cobham, Surrey KT11 2YJ; 01372-4511037. A social club and support group for American women living in Surrey.

*The American Women of Berkshire/Surrey*, Membership Chairman, Hill Hampton Lodge, Sunning Avenue, Sunningdale, Berkshire SL5 9QE. A social club and support group for North American women in the Berkshire-Surrey area. Monthly meetings plus a wide variety of social, educational and charitable activities.

*British-American Arts Association*, 116 Commercial Street, E1 6NF; 0171-247-5385. Charitable organisation for professional artists. The Association is geared to strengthening links and increasing opportunities in the arts and arts administration between the United States and the United Kingdom.

*The Canadian Women's Club*, Alberta House, 1 Mount Street, W1Y 5AA; 0171-408-2459. Aims to provide opportunities for Canadian women to meet one another and to work for the benefit of Canadians living in the U.K. who may be in need, and other projects of interest to its members.

*Chilterns American Women's Club*, Contact: President Donna Belt; 01494-670650. Operates in the Gerrards Cross and Beaconsfield area. A friendly mix of women from all areas of the U.S. and Canada. Monthly meetings plus a great variety of activities and charitable fundraising.

*Cyclists Touring Club*, Cotterell House, 69 Meadrow, Godalming, Surrey GU7 3HS; 01483-417217. Britain's national cycling organisation. All ages welcome, though under 14's should be accompanied by an adult.

*Democrats Abroad* (U.K.), Chair: Michael Cox, 4 Halford Road, Ickenham, Uxbridge, Middlesex UB10 8PX. Political interest group supporting the U.S. Democratic Party with the power to organise and elect delegates to the National Convention.

*English Heritage*, Fortress House, 23 Savile Row, W1X 1RB; 0171-943-3000. Offers exhibitions, museums, guided tours as well as historical re-enactments, displays, concerts and other special events. Funds from the membership help protect and preserve England's historical legacy.

*English Speaking Union*, Dartmouth House, 37 Charles Street, W1X 8AB; 0171-493-3328. A world-wide registered charity with facilities supported by membership and donations whose aim is to promote international understanding through a variety of social and educational activities including scholarships, lectures, outings, receptions.

*Focus*, St. Mary Abbots Hall, Vicarage Gate, Kensington, W8; 0171-937-0050. (Monday to Friday, 10.00 to 14.00). Non-profit organisation which functions as a clearing-house of information concerning community services, schools, child care, organisations, etc. Offers telephone information line, career and educational services, and seminars and workshops for the international community in the United Kingdom.

*The Georgian Group*, 37 Spital Square, E1 6PY; 0171-377-1722. Special interest group concerned with the preservation of and education about Georgian England through trips, seminars and lectures.

*Hampstead Women's Club*, Margaret Rodgers, 9 Hampstead Hill Mansions, Downshire Hill, NW3; 0171-435-8460. Social club for women living in the Hampstead area.

*Ikebana International*, London Chapter; 0171-289-1651 or 0171-231-4171. Monthly meetings provide a regular forum for members to study, exhibit and participate in ikebana demonstrations. Luncheons, special tours and lectures on related arts are typical monthly activities.

*The Junior League of London*, 9 Fitzmaurice Place, W1X 6JD; 0171-499-8159. An international organisation of women committed to promoting voluntary service and improving the community through the effective action and leadership of trained volunteers. A registered charity active in the areas of social welfare, the education and welfare of children and the arts and culture.

*The Kensington Chelsea Women's Club.* Active group founded in 1983 with a current membership of over 1,200. Meet monthly to promote social contact and cultural experiences among expatriates of all nationalities, as well as British nationals. For information telephone Shirley Griffin; 0181-747-3140 or Lori Underwood; 0171-736-2547.

*Lansdowne Club*, 9 Fitzmaurice Place, W1X 6JD. A private club which offers a swimming pool, squash courts and a fencing salle as well as a ballroom, restaurant and regular activities such as Scottish country dancing, chess and bridge. Contact Mr. Jonathan Gill; 0171-629-7200, Ext. 265.

*National Trust for Places of Historic Interest or National Beauty* (known as the National Trust), 36 Queen Anne's Gate, SW1H 9AS; 0171-222-9251. A non-profit organisation and special interest group which purchases or is bequeathed historic properties or places of great natural beauty that are preserved for the nation. Membership by subscription entitles anyone to free entry to properties, various publications, etc. There are also local branches which sponsor activities and trips.

*The Bankers Club*, 7 Lothbury, EC2R 7HH; 0171-606-5883. Contact: M. J. Reaveley. Private club for senior managers of banks involved in international banking. Currently has over 1,300 members and an active luncheon club.

*Petroleum Wives Club*, 13 Logan Place, W8 6QN. A social club for oil industry wives. Monthly meetings are held at the Forum Hotel.

*The Pilgrims of Great Britain*, The Savoy Hotel, The Strand, WC2R OEU; 0171-836-4057. Anglo-American dining club which meets at the Savoy and was founded in 1902 to improve Anglo-American relations. Membership by election.

*Republicans Abroad*, Chairman: Thomas T. Berger, Suite 5, 2 Old Brompton Road, SW7 3DQ; 0171-280-2706. Political interest group supporting the U.S. Republican Party.

*Rotary Club of London*, 6 York Gate, NW1 RQG; 0171-487-5429.

*St. John's Wood Women's Club.* Social club for women living in the St. John's Wood area. For information telephone Jean Oddy; 0171-625-7733.

*Thames Valley American Women's Club*, President: Cyndi Uhlenhoff, 8 Hart Dyke Close, Wokingham, Berkshire RG11 3HQ. Social and recreational club for American women living in the Thames valley.

---

Organisations
230

*United Oxford and Cambridge University Club*, 71 Pall Mall; 0171-930-5151. Worldwide reciprocal agreements. Telephone for information on club facilities and extensive activities.

*United Kingdom Panhellenic Association*, Correspondence Secretary: Erin Brau; 0171-731-0434.

*University Women's Club*, 2 Audley Square, W1Y 6DB; 0171-499-2268. Social club with facilities for women university graduates or women who are not graduates but professionally qualified.

*Victoria and Albert - Art of Living Club*, Decorative Art Exhibitions and Lecture Programmes, 11 Kensington Park Mews, W11 2EY; 0171-727-6542.

*Victorian Society*, 1 Priory Gardens, W4 1TT; 0181-994-1019. Special interest group concerned with the preservation of and education about Victorian England through trips, seminars and lectures.

*W&G Foyle Literary Lunches*, 113 Charing Cross Road, WC2H 0EB; 0171-437-6846. Afternoon events with lectures by newsmakers and world leaders.

*Westminster Volunteer Bureau*, 8 Spring Street, W2; 0171-402-8076. Links people who are interested in voluntary, social caring and leisure work with organisations needing help in Westminster.

*Woolnoth Society*. Contact: Holly Schade, 13 Camden Grove, W8 4JG; 0171-937-0627. Charity organisation with members from London banking and financial institutions, it supports worthy causes primarily in the East End. There is also an active women's group.

# Recommended Reading

The number of books and publications available regarding information on Britain must number thousands. The listings here form a good basis for research. As you settle in and find your neighbourhood bookstore be sure to explore the wealth of information available to you. The books on Britain's villages, historical homes and heritage make wonderful keepsakes as they are often beautifully printed as well as informative.


## BACKGROUND

### Social and Political History of Great Britain: Both Past and Contemporary

*Britain: An Official Handbook*, HMSO Publications Centre (revised yearly).
*British Politics Today*, by Bill Jones, Dennis Kavanagh.
*The Changing Anatomy of Britain*, by Anthony Sampson.
*Contemporary British Politics, An Introduction*, by Bill Coxall, Lynton Robins.
*A Dictionary of British History*, edited by J. P. Kenyon.
*Introduction to British Politics*, by John Dearlove, Peter Saunders.
*John Major*, by Bruce Anderson.
*The Lives of the Kings and Queens of England*, edited by Antonia Fraser.
*The Oxford History of Britain*, edited by Kenneth O. Morgan.
*Royal Family: Years of Transition*, by Theo Aronson.
*A Social History of England*, by Asa Brigg.
*The Story of England*, by Christopher Hibbert.
*A Vision of Britain*, by Prince Charles.

### Insights into being a Foreigner in a Foreign Land

*ASA Citizens Abroad; A Handbook*, Written by American Citizens Abroad, Gannett News Media Services, Available from U.S.A. Today Books: P.O. Box 450, Washington DC, 20044, U.S.A.: 703-276-5978.
*Brit-think - Ameri-think*, by Jane Walmsley.
*Debrett's Etiquette and Modern Manners*, edited by Elsie Burch Donald.
*Dictionary of Britain; An A to Z of The British Way of Life*, by Adrian Room.
*The English Companion; An Idiosyncratic Guide to England and Englishness*, by Godfrey Smith. (Available in the U.S. only).
*The English Season*, by Godfrey Smith.
*New to the U.K.*, by Genevieve Munzier; published by Routledge and Kegan Paul Ltd.

## 'HOW TO...' GET BY

*AA Citypack: London*, by Louise Nicholson, part of a new series providing essential information in a clear format.

*An American's Guide to Living Abroad*, published by Living Abroad Publishing Inc.

*The British Puzzle*, Beaconsfield/Chiltern Women's Club.

*The Companion Guide to London*, by David Piper.

*Fodor's Budget Travel - London.*

*Going International: How to Make Friends and Deal Effectively in the Global Marketplace*, by Lennie Copeland, Lewis Griggs. (Available in the U.S.).

*How to Survive in Style*, by Caroline A. Gelderman.

*Living and Working in Britain, A Survival Handbook*, by David Hamshire.

*Moving and Living Abroad*, by Sandra Albright, Alice Chu, Lori Austen. (Available in the U.S.).

*The New Penguin Guide to London*, F. R. Banks.

*U.S.A. Citizens Abroad*, U.S.A. Today Books, Code CAI, P.O. Box 450, Washington DC, 20044.


## HOUSING

*London Commuter Guide*, by Caroline McGhie.

*Where to Live in London*, edited by Liz Veroce (revised yearly).


## CHILDREN AND MOTHERS

*And Baby Comes Too*, Egon Ronay Heinz Guide.

*Children's Book of Britain*, by Jan Williamson, Susan Meredith.

*The Good Nanny Guide*, by Charlotte Breese, Hilaire Gomer.

*The Good Schools Guide*, by Amanda Atha, Sarah Drummond.

*How to Survive as a Working Mother*, by Judith M. Steiner.

*Kid's Britain*, by Betty Jerman.

*Look Out, London*, by Louise Nicholson, an illustrated guide to London for children to use.

*Nicholson's Children's Guide*, Robert Nicholson Publications Ltd.

## MEDICAL SERVICES

*The Good Doctor Guide*, by Martin Page

---

Recommended Reading

## SERVICES

*A Time Out Guide: Services in London*, Time Out Publications Ltd.

## CULTURAL

*Fodor's London Companion*, by Louise Nicholson, winner of the London Tourist award.
*London's Best Kept Secrets*, by Mike Michaelson.
*The London Encyclopedia*, edited by Ben Weinreb, Christopher Hibbert.
*London Museums and Collections*, edited by G. M. S. Scimone, M. F. Levey.
*The Pocket Guide to London Theatre*, Kimball Publishing.
*The Time Out Guide*, Penguin Books.

## SPORTS AND FITNESS

*Where to Ride*, British Horse Society.

## ACCOMMODATION AND RESTAURANTS

*Egon Ronay's Cellnet Guide to Hotels and Restaurants*, published by Pan Macmillan Publishers Ltd. Revised annually.
*The Good Bed and Breakfast Guide*, by Elsie Dillard, Susan Causin.
*The Good Food Guide*, edited by Drew Smith.
*The Good Weekend Guide*, edited by Alisdair Aird.
*The Holiday Which? Guide to Weekend Breaks*, edited by Ingrid Morgan.
*Johansens Recommended Hotels in Great Britain and Ireland*, edited by Adrian Bridgewater. Revised yearly.
*Johansens Recommended Inns and Restaurants in Great Britain*, edited by Adrian Bridgewater. Revised yearly.
*Signpost Hotel Guide*, published by Signpost Ltd. Revised annually.
*Time Out Guide: Eating and Drinking in London*, Timeout Publishing Ltd. Revised annually.

## SHOPPING

*Sheila Chichester's London Woman, Her Shopping and Fashion Guide*, by Sheila Chichester.
*A Time Out Guide: Shopping in London*, Time Out Publications.

---

# Glossary

| | |
|---|---|
| clothes pin | clothes peg |
| cocktail party | drinks party |
| college | university |
| comforter | eiderdown/duvet |
| contractor | builder |
| coveralls (workmen's) | boiler suit |
| cookie | biscuit |
| costume | fancy dress |
| cosy/homey | homely (pleasant) |
| cotton balls | cotton wool |
| crib/baby bed | cot |
| cuffs (pants) | turn-ups (trousers) |
| curb (sidewalk) | kerb (pavement) |
| curling iron | curling tongs |

## D

| | |
|---|---|
| daycare center | creche |
| delivery truck | delivery lorry/van |
| denatured alcohol | methylated spirits |
| dessert | pudding/sweet |
| detour | diversion |
| diaper | nappy |
| dime store/five and ten | Woolworths |
| directory assistance | directory enquiries |
| dishes, do the | washing up |
| dishwashing liquid (hand) | washing up liquid |
| divided highway | dual carriageway |
| Do-It-Yourself | DIY |
| doctor's/dentist's office | surgery |
| drapes/draperies | curtains |
| drugstore/pharmacist | chemist |
| drygoods store | (materials) draper |
| dump (garbage) | tip (rubbish) |
| duplex/triplex | maisonette |
| dust ruffle | valance |

## E

| | |
|---|---|
| electric cord/wire | flex/lead |
| elevator | lift |
| eraser | rubber/india rubber |
| Europe | Continental Europe |
| extension cord | flex |

# F

| | |
|---|---|
| faucet | tap |
| fender (car) | bumper |
| first floor | ground floor |
| flashlight | torch |
| freeway/super highway | motorway |
| F.T.D. (florist) | Interflora |
| furnace/hot water heater | boiler |
| French fried potatoes | chips |

# G

| | |
|---|---|
| garbage (trash) | rubbish |
| garbage/trash can | dustbin/bin |
| garden hose | hose pipe |
| garter belt | suspenders |
| gas | petrol |
| gear shift (car) | gear lever |
| glasses (eyes) | spectacles |
| grade (school) | class/form |
| grocery cart | trolley |
| ground wire | earth wire/earth |

# H

| | |
|---|---|
| half-bath | cloakroom |
| hamburger/ground beef | mince |
| hardware store | ironmonger |
| hat check girl | cloakroom attendant |
| homework | prep |
| hood (car) | bonnet |
| housewares | hardware |

# I

| | |
|---|---|
| incorporated | limited |
| information (phone) | enquiry |
| installment payment plan | hire purchase |
| intermission | interval |

# J

| | |
|---|---|
| janitor | porter |
| jello | jelly |
| jelly | jam |
| jump rope | skipping rope |
| jumper | pinafore dress |

# K

| | |
|---|---|
| kerosene | paraffin |

# L

| | |
|---|---|
| ladder | steps |
| lawyer/attorney | solicitor |
| lawyer (trial) | barrister |
| leash (dog) | lead |
| legal holiday | bank holiday |
| licence plate | number/registration plate |
| line (stand in) | queue |
| linen closet | airing cupboard |
| liquor | spirits |
| liquor store | wine merchant/off licence |
| living room | sitting/reception room/lounge |
| lost and found | lost property |
| lounge suit | business suit |

# M

| | |
|---|---|
| maid | daily/cleaner |
| mail/mailman | post/postman |
| mailbox | pillar box/post box |
| main street | high street |
| make reservations | book |
| martini | gin or vodka martini/cocktail |
| mezzanine | dress circle |
| milk truck | milk float |
| money order | postal order |
| monkey wrench | spanner |
| motorcycle | motorbike |
| motor vehicle inspection test | M.O.T. |
| movie | film |
| movie house/theatre | cinema |
| moving van | removal van/pantechnicon |
| moving company | removal company |
| muffler (car) | silencer |

# N

| | |
|---|---|
| napkins | serviettes/table napkins |
| newsdealer/newsstand | newsagent |
| nipple (baby bottle) | teat |
| notions | haberdashery |
| number used twice (55) | double number (double 5) |

# O

| | |
|---|---|
| one way ticket | single ticket |
| orchestra seats (theatre) | stalls |
| outlet/socket (electrical) | point/power point |
| oven | cooker |
| overpass (highway) | flyover |

# P

| | |
|---|---|
| pacifier (for baby) | dummy/soother/comforter |
| package | parcel |
| paint (interior house) | emulsion |
| painter | decorator |
| panty hose | tights |
| pantry | larder |
| pants | trousers |
| paper towels | kitchen roll |
| parka | anorak |
| parking lot | car park |
| pass (vehicle) | overtake |
| pavement | road |
| pay telephone | call box |
| period (punctuation) | full stop |
| person-to-person | personal call |
| ping pong paddle | table tennis bat |
| pit (fruit) | stone |
| pitcher | jug |
| porch (enclosed) | conservatory |
| pot holder/gloves | oven gloves/mitt |
| potato chips | crisps |
| precinct | district |
| principal (school) | headmaster/mistress |
| private school | public/fee paying school |
| public school | state school |
| pull-off (driving) | lay-by |
| pump (shoe) | court shoe |
| purse/pocketbook | handbag |

# R

| | |
|---|---|
| raincheck | postponement |
| raincoat | mackintosh (mac) |
| range | cooker |
| real estate agent | estate agent |
| rear view mirror (outside) | wing mirror |
| recess (school) | break, holiday |
| rent (goods) | hire |

| | |
|---|---|
| rent (real estate) | let |
| repairman | engineer |
| restroom/toilet | cloakroom/.W.C./loo/toilet |
| roast (meat) | joint |
| roomer/boarder | lodger |
| round trip ticket | return ticket |
| rubber bands | elastic bands |
| rubber cement | cow gum/studio gum |
| rubbing alcohol | surgical spirit |
| run (for public office) | stand |
| run (in nylons) | ladder (in tights) |

## S

| | |
|---|---|
| sack lunch | packed lunch |
| sales clerk | shop assistant |
| Santa Claus | Father Christmas |
| Saran Wrap | cling film |
| schedule | time-table |
| scotch tape | cellotape |
| scratch pad | scribbling pad/book |
| second floor | first floor |
| sedan (car) | saloon |
| semester (school) | term (three yearly) |
| Seven-Up/Sprite | lemonade |
| sewer pipe/soil pipe | drain |
| shade (window) | blind/roller blind |
| sheers (under drapes) | net curtains |
| shopping bag | carrier bag |
| shorts (underwear) | pants |
| shot/injection | jab |
| sideburns | sideboards |
| sidewalk | pavement/footpath |
| sink | basin |
| slash (/) | stroke/oblique |
| snaps (sewing) | press studs/poppers |
| sneakers/tennis shoes | trainers/plimsolls |
| soccer | football |
| sod (new grass) | turf |
| soft shoulder (road) | verge/hard shoulder |
| spool (thread) | cotton reel |
| sports clothes/equipment | kit |
| stamped addressed envelope | S.A.E. |
| stand in line | queue |
| station wagon | estate car |
| sterling (silver) | hallmarked/solid |
| stove/cooktop | hob |
| straight (cocktail) | neat |

| | |
|---|---|
| stroller | pushchair/buggy |
| subway | tube/underground |
| supper | tea/supper |
| surgery (medical) | theatre/operating theatre |
| suspenders | braces |
| sweater/pullover | jumper/jersey |
| swimming pool | baths |
| swindler (home repair) | cowboy |

**T**

| | |
|---|---|
| tag | label |
| tea | afternoon tea |
| tea cart | tea trolley |
| tennis warm-up | knock-up |
| thread | cotton |
| thumb tack | drawing pin |
| tic-tac-toe | noughts and crosses |
| time payment | hire-purchase |
| toilet/bathroom/john | lavatory/toilet/loo |
| tour bus | coach |
| traffic circle | roundabout |
| trailer/camper/mobile home | caravan |
| training wheels | stabilizers |
| truck | lorry |
| truck (semi) | juggernaut |
| trunk (car) | boot |
| T.V. | telly |
| two weeks | fortnight |

**U**

| | |
|---|---|
| umbrella | brollie |
| underground/pedestrian passage | subway |
| underpants/panties | knickers/pants |
| undershirt | vest |

**V**

| | |
|---|---|
| vacation | holiday |
| vacuum (cleaner) | Hoover |
| valance (drapes) | pelmet |
| vest | waistcoat |

# W

| | |
|---|---|
| wade | paddle |
| wall-to-wall carpet | fitted carpet |
| wallet | purse |
| wash cloth | face flannel |
| wash up | wash your hands |
| water heater (electric) | immersion heater |
| water heater (gas) | geyser |
| wax paper | grease proof paper |
| wharf/pier | quay (pron. 'key') |
| whining | whinging |
| windbreaker | windcheater/kagoul |
| windshield | windscreen |
| wire/telegram | telemessage |
| with or without? (milk or cream in coffee) | white or black? |

# Y

| | |
|---|---|
| yard | garden |

# Z

| | |
|---|---|
| Z | 'zed' (pron.) |
| zero | nil/nought |
| zip code | post code |

*NOTE:*

There are additional glossaries in Chapter Two (Housing) and Chapter Nine (Cooking and Food).

# Index

Index

Index

Index

# NOTES

# The Junior League of London

The Junior League of London is an international organisation of women committed to promoting voluntary service and improving the community through the effective action and leadership of trained volunteers. The members offer their services to the London community in the areas of social welfare of children, and the arts and culture. As a registered charity, The League's activities are exclusively educational and charitable.

If you would like to receive more information about The League, or be invited to an Informational Session (held twice a year), please complete the following:-

Name: _____

Address: _____

_____

_____

Post Code: _____

Telephone No.: _____

and return to:-

The Junior League of London
9 Fitzmaurice Place
London W1X 6JD
Tel: 0171-499-8159

# Living in London

## Sixth Edition

## Reader's Questionnaire

Dear Reader,

To help us to continue to improve and update *Living in London*, we would appreciate you taking a few moments to complete the following and mail to: The Junior League of London, 9 Fitzmaurice Place, London W1X 6JD.

1. Are you currently living in or moving to London?

2. If you live in London, how long have you lived here?

3. Where did you get your copy of *Living in London*?

4. Which sections/chapters were most helpful to you?

5. Is there any topic you would like to see covered in greater depth?

6. Are there any other topics or services you would like us to consider including in the next edition of *Living in London*?

Thank you!

---

# LIVING IN LONDON: GUIDELINES

**The Junior League of London, 9 Fitzmaurice Place, London W1X 6JD, England, 071–499–8159**

*STERLING CHEQUE MADE PAYABLE TO LIL: G*
We regret that on individual orders we are unable to process US$ cheques.

| | Price | Quantity | Total payment |
|---|---|---|---|

*Shipments within the UK – quoted price includes £1 postage and handling   £10.95 × _____ = _____ Total (£)

*Shipments outside the UK – quoted price includes £3.05 postage and handling   £13.00 × _____ = _____ Total (£)

*PAYMENT BY CREDIT CARD – ACCESS, VISA, MASTER CARD (Circle one)*
Non-sterling credit cards are accepted with pleasure; the credit card company will automatically convert our sterling charge to your foreign currency.

*Shipments within the UK – quoted price includes £1 postage and handling   £10.95 × _____ = _____ Total (£)

*Shipments outside the UK – quoted price includes £3.05 postage and handling   £13.00 × _____ = _____ Total (£)

Account Number _____

Signature _____

Expiry Date _____

Print name as it appears on card _____

There is a quantity discount available for purchases of over 50 books. Please contact our offices to arrange for this type of billing.

*Shipping Address:*

Name _____

Street _____

City/Country _____    Postal Code _____

Proceeds from the sale of this book enable the Junior League of London to develop, fund and staff its community projects. Registered UK Charity Number 288427. JLL Enterprises VAT No. 461582341. Prices subject to change.